LIBERALISM FOR A NEW CENTURY

✍ **W9-BSA-357**

Liberalism for a New Century

EDITED BY

Neil Jumonville
and Kevin Mattson

WITH A FOREWORD BY

E. J. Dionne Jr.

UNIVERSITY OF CALIFORNIA PRESS   Berkeley   Los Angeles   London

University of California Press, one of the most distinguished university presses in the United States, enriches
lives around the world by advancing scholarship in the
humanities, social sciences, and natural sciences. Its activities are supported by the UC Press Foundation and
by philanthropic contributions from individuals and institutions. For more information, visit
www.ucpress.edu.

University of California Press
Berkeley and Los Angeles, California

University of California Press, Ltd.
London, England

Library of Congress Cataloging-in-Publication Data

Liberalism for a new century / edited by Neil
Jumonville and Kevin Mattson ; with a foreword
by E. J. Dionne Jr.
    p.   cm.
    Includes bibliographical references and index.
    ISBN: 978-0-520-24919-6 (cloth : alk. paper)
    ISBN: 978-0-520-25071-0 (pbk : alk. paper)
    1. Liberalism—United States.   2. United States—
Politics and government—2001–   . I. Jumonville,
Neil.   II. Mattson, Kevin, 1966–

JC574.2.U6L535   2007
320.51'30973—dc22   2006100940

Manufactured in the United States of America

15   14   13   12   11   10   09   08   07
11   10   9   8   7   6   5   4   3   2   1

This book is printed on New Leaf EcoBook 50, a
100% recycled fiber of which 50% is de-inked postcon-
sumer waste, processed chlorine free. EcoBook 50 is
acid free and meets the minimum requirements of
ANSI/ASTM D5634–01 (Permanence of Paper).

Contents

Foreword

In the fall of 1960, John F. Kennedy spoke before the New York State Liberal Party and offered one of the most robust defenses of political liberalism heard in the second half of the twentieth century. His remarks were intriguing for many reasons, not the least of which was that many liberals did not regard Kennedy as one of their own, despite the best efforts of Arthur Schlesinger Jr. and John Kenneth Galbraith to persuade them otherwise. The Liberal Party itself reflected both liberalism's heyday—it grew out of the New Deal and the labor movement—and the sectarian divisions that seem always to have bedeviled the Left. The liberals were a breakaway from another uniquely New York assemblage, the American Labor Party, which anticommunist liberals saw as having come too heavily under Communist Party influence.

But even at this moment when liberalism seemed near its high tide, Kennedy felt a political need to separate himself from those aspects of liberalism—or, more precisely, from those aspects of the popular parody of liberalism—that neither he nor anyone else would identify with.

"What do our opponents mean when they apply to us the label 'liberal'?" Kennedy asked. "If by 'liberal' they mean, as they want people to believe, someone who is soft in his policies abroad, who is against local government, and who is unconcerned with the taxpayer's dollar, then the record of this party and its members demonstrate that we are not that kind of 'liberal.'"

"But," Kennedy went on, "if by a 'liberal' they mean someone who looks ahead and not behind, someone who welcomes new ideas without rigid reactions, someone who cares about the welfare of the people—their health, their housing, their schools, their jobs, their civil rights, and their civil liberties—someone who believes that we can break through the stalemate and suspicions that grip us in our policies abroad, if that is what they mean by a 'liberal,' then I'm proud to say that I'm a 'liberal.'"

It has been a long time since a candidate for president of the United States has dared to declare, "I'm proud to say that I'm a liberal." Indeed, many liberals not running for president or any other public office have come to question the value of declaring loyalty to liberalism. They have sought other words (the most popular these days is "progressive") to describe their political orientation. Liberals often seem to accept their conservative adversaries' definitions of their creed, which hold that liberals are elitist, out of touch, the enemies of community, believe only in abstractions, and are soft and self-satisfied. Many on the political left use liberalism as a negative word to describe an orientation that rejects populism and the values and interests of the working class—a term, by the way, that many liberals are reluctant to use, lest they be accused of "class warfare."

Yet it is time, as the editors and authors here suggest with daring and intelligence, to rescue liberalism as an idea, as a tradition in which American progressives can take pride and, yes, as a word. There are tactical reasons for this and substantive reasons, too.

As a matter of tactics, no political movement that dares not speak its own name can ever expect to prosper. By failing to defend liberalism, liberals have allowed the negative stereotypes that Kennedy noted in his speech to define liberalism for a majority of Americans. It is no accident that the exit polls on Election Day in 2004 found that although 34 percent of the voters were willing to call themselves conservative, only 21 percent dared to call themselves liberal. Why should anyone want to use a term rejected even by those to whom it fairly applies? How can liberals expect to look tough, consistent, and clearheaded if they spend so much time and energy retreating from a mere label thrown at them by their political enemies? I have disagreed with Irving Kristol on many things, but I have always admired his attitude toward the word *neoconservative,* which began as a term of opprobrium by that American hero (he is certainly one of mine) the late Michael Harrington. There was no point in fighting a name, Kristol insisted: "The sensible course, therefore, is to take your label, claim it as your own, and run with it." Liberals should be willing to pick up their fallen flag.

But tactical considerations are not sufficient grounds for reviving a concept and defending a tradition. After all, if the same ideas would be more palatable under a different banner, why fight over pennants or emblems? The ideas matter most, which is precisely why the vindication of the liberal tradition proposed in these pages is important.

The liberalism that emerged in American politics during the Progressive, New Deal, and civil rights eras was not simply a set of nice thoughts and good intentions. It was the essential concept in creating the America that conservatives, no less than liberals, now embrace as their own. Put another way, absent the achievements of liberalism, I doubt that conservatives would love this country as deeply as they do today.

American liberalism saved capitalism because it did not see capitalism as perfect and insisted on reform. American liberalism vindicated the fundamental ideas of social democracy because it understood the importance of active government in fostering social justice without rejecting the benefits of economic markets. American liberalism protected a nation of ambitious strivers because it understood that striving untempered by the demands of community and charity created a society empty at its core. American liberalism protected upward mobility by opening the realm of educational, professional, and business achievement to people of color, to immigrants, and to women. American liberalism insisted on environmental stewardship, social decency toward the elderly, workplace protections for those who labor, the capacity of working people to organize themselves in their own interest, and adequate care for the sick, the suffering, and the dying. And, yes, American liberalism protected the nation against aggression and preserved liberty against the onslaughts of the Nazis, the Fascists, and the Communists.

The problem with liberalism, I suspect, may be that some liberals are embarrassed by that litany. Liberals are not accustomed to claiming their past. Indeed, liberals are often uneasy with the very idea of embracing tradition, even if it is their own. I like to recount the story of a conservative friend who asked whether liberals ever wear neckties honoring ideological heroes the way conservatives do to pay homage to Adam Smith, Friedrich von Hayek, or even Calvin Coolidge. Putting aside the question of how much liberals like to wear neckties at all, it's striking that liberals are—on principle, it seems—reluctant to put too much emphasis on old heroes or past achievements. Although liberals' foes depict them as woolly-headed intellectuals, liberals are in fact uneasy with too much theorizing. They are criticized by the Right as insufferably moralistic *and* as indifferent to moral values. (Consistency is rarely demanded of those on the political attack.) Yet American liberalism is, at its core, a set of moral commitments rooted in practical reason. Liberals are resolutely, and admirably, pragmatic about means. But the ends of liberalism are defined by ethical—and, yes, *moral*—commitments: to justice and liberty, to equality and community. Yes, these goals compete with each other and require juggling. But no good society has ever been built on devotion to a single virtue.

Of course, conservatives commonly say that liberals are primarily backward looking, that they are most interested in protecting "old" programs. Many conservatives love to use the term *reactionary liberalism*. This description, too, makes liberals uneasy about claiming their past. Liberals hate the idea of being backward looking.

But there are two large problems. The first is that conservatives who attack past liberal achievements are not forward looking, as they claim to be. Their aim is to roll history back to the time before liberalism's great achievements. They want to dismantle liberal achievements born of collective provision and to undo the mechanisms through which government advances the rights of individuals—as consumers, as employees, as members of minority groups. The second is that conservatives claim that they believe in individualism. But the individual needs protection from the powerful, including (and here libertarians and liberals can fight on common ground) protection from the overreaching of government. But liberalism also calls for (and here libertarians and liberals will disagree) protecting individuals from powerful private interests. Government can oppress. But the liberal achievement has been to show that government can also liberate.

So liberals who defend their past achievements should not be seen as "reactionary." On the contrary, they are trying to preserve yesterday's gains to make tomorrow's gains possible. Liberals should certainly not be wedded to every specific of every policy that every group of liberals has advanced. Liberals are in no way required to pretend that today's economy is the same as yesterday's or that the needs of the early twenty-first century are the same as those of the mid-twentieth century. But the broadly communitarian and egalitarian impulses that animated yesterday's liberals are not only defensible but are also highly relevant now.

Moreover, conservatives have been quite brilliant in disguising the extent to which their own program is backward looking. They have done so by arguing, with considerable success, that those poor, tired liberals were bereft of big thoughts and wallowing in a swamp of old commitments, old ideas, and old promises. In 1989, a headline in the Outlook section of the *Washington Post* confidently rendered this diagnosis of the liberals: "Tired and Defensive, They're Out of Ideas." In 1997, Charles Bray, who was then president of the Johnson Foundation, argued in the *Chronicle of Higher Education* that liberal anemia had created the opening for a conservative jolt. "The entry of new ways of thinking into the American intellectual bloodstream after two generations of liberals' monopolizing the public-policy debate has been good for the country," Bray declared.

Let's accept—for the sake of argument, but also because the critique contained some truth—that at some point during the 1970s, liberalism became tiresome, arrogant, unreflective, and hidebound. Let's further stipulate that this image gave conservatives their opening to seem fresh, creative, exciting, and otherwise attractive in all those ways that marketers love to claim for their products.

The fact is that each of those disapproving words about liberalism now applies to conservatism. Conservatives have been peddling the same worn, haggard argument for the three decades since that energetic guru of supply-side economics, Jude Wanniski, published his first articles on the subject and issued his exciting 1978 manifesto, *The Way the World Works*. In fact, and some conservatives such as Wanniski were honest enough to admit this, their ideas really went back to Calvin Coolidge, a president whom many on the right continue to admire.

Supply-siders asserted that cutting taxes on the wealthy—and especially on savings and investment—would help everyone, including the poor, by promoting economic growth. Tax cuts would produce so much growth that they would pay for themselves. Because government programs were flawed, private investment would always be more productive than government spending. And deficits, if they did come, need not worry us very much.

For many of us, this argument was always a highfalutin rationalization for giving the rich what they wanted, and often more. Bill Clinton's economic policies should have definitively destroyed supply-side claims: Clinton raised taxes on the wealthy and cut the deficit, and an exceptional period of economic growth followed.

Not until around 2005 did the lesson sink in again: the conservatives' help-the-wealthy, damn-the-deficits approach doesn't hold together, either as policy or politics. A majority of Americans simply don't buy the idea that cutting taxes on dividends and capital gains has higher priority than providing health coverage and child care for struggling Americans. Tax cuts, it turns out, don't pay for themselves. And given how much Republicans want to spend on defense, farm subsidies, homeland security, roads, bridges, subsidies for energy companies, a flawed drug program for seniors, and lots of other stuff, they could never cut enough from programs for the poor to offset the costs of their tax giveaways.

Conservatism and the Republican Party began to fracture. Moderate Republicans knew that cutting programs for the poor was unsustainable. Very conservative Republicans wanted to cut spending far more than the rest of the party—or its voters—would allow. Republican leaders tilted this way and that, juggling this tax cut with that spending cut. In the process, they alienated just about everybody. The old faith was strained. If Republicans and conservatives keep trying to sell their long-playing supply-side records in the age of the iPod, they'll confine their audience to antiquarians and ideological hobbyists. Such is the way the world works. Today's graying of conservatism invites liberals to a new era of innovation, which is why the essays in this volume are both exciting and timely.

~

But liberalism is by nature a doubting creed. St. Thomas the Apostle, Doubting Thomas, might well be liberalism's patron saint. As Alan Brinkley writes in his powerful essay in these pages, "Many disappointed liberals are themselves highly critical of the present state of their own politics. These critics are not simply the countless disheartened liberals who are frustrated most of all by liberalism's political failures and who blame them on the craven timidity of Democratic politicians. Liberal philosophers and intellectuals have also offered damning critiques of the basic premises of liberal thought."

But as Brinkley knows well, liberal self-doubt did not begin in the Bush era. Consider Arnold S. Kaufman's influential book *The Radical Liberal*. First published in 1968, the book grew out of critiques of liberalism that made Kaufman a hero to parts of the New Left and to the New Politics Democrats who rallied against the Vietnam War. A few sentences from a volume published nearly four decades ago give a sense of how familiar the new critiques are to the old. "Liberals [Kaufman wrote] have been too preoccupied with their internal conflict, too shocked by its intensity, to have spent much time trying to articulate the bases of disagreement as clearly and comprehensively as the task deserves. The critics of American liberalism have, by contrast, been actively analyzing and attacking. Both Right and Left accuse liberals of being self-deluded, weak-willed and pusillanimous." Anticipating the attacks on "the old left and the new right" of the Third Way progressives so many years later, Kaufman argued that too many liberals "respond to their critics by splitting the difference. . . . They balance the 'extremist radicalism' of the Right against the 'extremist radicalism' of the Left," he wrote, "and congratulate themselves for displaying intelligence and moral acumen." Kaufman called on liberals and their leftist critics to understand "the radicalism of liberalism's very old aims and principles."

Roughly two decades earlier, Arthur Schlesinger Jr. had also called upon liberals to understand the radical nature of their creed. But the radicalism Schlesinger described in *The Vital Center,* published in 1949, embraced a moderate center that explicitly rejected extremism of the left and extremism of the right. "The new radicalism," Schlesinger wrote, "derives its power from an acceptance of conflict—an acceptance combined with a determination to create a social framework where conflict issues, not in excessive anxiety, but in creativity." In words that still define a style of liberalism today, Schlesinger declared (the italics are my own): "*The center is vital. The center must hold.* The object of the new radicalism is to restore the center, to reunite individual and community in fruitful union. The spirit of the new radicalism is the spirit of the center—the spirit of human decency opposing the extremes of tyranny."

Today's liberals might take some solace from the arguments of both Kaufman and Schlesinger. It seems in the nature of liberals to yearn for both moderation and radicalism, to want to speak for both a governing center and a vigorous opposition to the flabby status quo. When liberals were most successful, as Michael Kazin argues in these pages, they managed to create a fruitful alliance between their radical and governing wings. When this coalition worked, the radicals could create space for new departures and pressure liberals to live up to their creed. When liberals fell into difficulty, the radicals could defend liberalism against their common conservative enemies.

Of course, this alliance was never perfect. For one thing, the Communist Party, which gave critical support to the New Deal and the labor movement in the 1930s, owed its ultimate allegiance to a foreign dictatorship and was thus not, in most of the ways that matter, "liberal." And radicals regularly fell in and out of love with liberalism. By turn, radicals embraced liberal ideals and scorned the messy compromises made by liberals in power. "The real threat to the left is not the right wing, but a strengthened liberal center," Richard Flacks, one of the New Left's most influential thinkers, said in the 1960s. "We used to talk about how, if the Kennedys fulfilled their program, it would be the end of democracy, because the whole thrust was toward technocratic, top-down control. And that was really what we were against" (quoted in James Miller's *Democracy Is in the Streets*, 172–73).

In some sense, of course, the Right was against this strategy, too. It's striking in retrospect that the Right opposed *the liberal establishment* while the New Left opposed *establishment liberalism*. The Right disliked the establishment because it was liberal; the Left disliked liberals because they were the establishment.

History has a way of clarifying matters, sometimes painfully, and it is highly unlikely that Flacks or anyone else on the left now sees "a strengthened liberal center" as more of a threat than "the right wing." Indeed, most of the Left would now agree with William Connolly, one of the most thoughtful political theorists to come out of the New Left. In a July 1981 article in *democracy,* Connolly argued that "protest politics flourishes best when it faces a healthy liberal establishment that believes that justice and the good life can be fostered by the welfare state" (17). Connolly lamented that neither the Left nor liberals fully appreciated their "cozy relationship of mutuality and interdependence."

One can imagine and hope that they do now. But this contradiction is only one of many that liberals must confront. This volume is useful for many reasons, one of which is that it puts on the table some of liberalism's unresolved dilemmas.

A clear tension exists between liberalism's interest in populism and its obligation to defend the rights of unpopular minorities. Liberals stand proudly for the interests of the many, not those of the privileged few. But liberals also stand with the few when their rights are threatened by the many. Each commitment is honorable. But liberals have to find ways to be at once creative and honest in defending these commitments persuasively. Nobody should pretend that this task is easy. Liberals, rightly, stand for democracy. They also, rightly, stand for liberty. Usually, these two commitments reinforce each other, especially when democracy is properly understood. Democracy can't operate without liberty. But the tension between the two cannot be dealt with well unless it is acknowledged.

We should not pretend that if liberals talk economic populism at election time, the challenges of ethnic, racial, and cultural politics will dis-

appear. Some cultural questions (the time crunch facing working families, for example, and the resulting difficulties parents have in raising
their kids the way they'd like) can be discussed in economic terms. So can
the matter of loyalty between employer and employee and the need to
temper the instabilities in individual and family lives that a competitive
economy can create. The Right should be challenged whenever it tries to
reduce all cultural discontents to wedge issues like abortion or gay rights.
The task of politics, as liberals would insist, is to heal our discontents,
not to exploit them.

But as many of these essays make clear, liberals will not be persuasive
if they dismiss issues of culture or religion as sideshows. Liberalism is always more powerful when it is in a comfortable relationship with people
of faith and when liberals who count themselves in the ranks of the faith-
ful are unembarrassed about saying so. Liberals would do well to remember that liberalism's essential commitments to community, justice,
equality, and liberty are well understood by most Americans who count
themselves as religious.

Liberals, as Michael Tomasky makes clear, have an honorable and
heroic history of defending the nation's interests and standing up for a
practical and visionary internationalism. But liberals have often been divided about foreign policy. Liberal ranks have always included pacifists
and those who supported just wars, internationalists and noninterven-
tionists, Wilsonian democratic idealists and realists. Because George W.
Bush was president when the attacks of September 11, 2001, happened,
the Right was able to shape the nation's response, and liberals were
forced to react to the administration's initiatives. And the liberals divided
sharply, as Tomasky documents. Those divisions could keep liberals out
of power for a long time, as Karl Rove devoutly hopes.

But there is another possibility. The failure of the Bush administration's highly ideological foreign policy, whose execution has been based
on exceptionally unrealistic assumptions, opens the way for liberals to
argue for a different approach. American power in the world is not advanced when the United States needlessly alienates allies. Idealistic goals,
including the spread of democratic values around the world, are not advanced when policy makers think that bold strokes obviate the need for
the hard and patient work of building civil societies that can nurture
democracies. America's armed forces are not well served when a limited
force is asked to carry out a mission that requires a much larger commitment. When our leaders are not willing to admit that achieving their
goals requires more resources than they are willing to commit or to ask

the American people to provide, the result is national disappointment that undermines the nation's power in the long run. Wishing a better world does not create it. Taking a holiday from complexity does not make it go away.

Liberals desperately need to think creatively about their approach to national security, both for their own sake and the country's.

~

There are many brands of liberalism and many tensions within it. Some people are drawn to liberalism because of its commitment to individual rights; others, because of its devotion to economic justice. Some liberals are communitarian. Others mistrust communitarianism. Some liberals define their cause as a defense of the well-being of "working families." Others see any mention of families as hopelessly homophobic and sexist. Some liberals are trade unionists. Others are investment bankers. Some liberals favor free trade and see globalization as inevitable. Others devoutly mistrust free trade and want to put the brakes on globalization. Can these people ever get along?

Well, yes. As this volume makes clear, the tensions are neither new nor insurmountable. There is a faith at the heart of liberalism. As Alan Brinkley argues, liberals are animated by a belief in economic justice and popular democracy, by confidence that government can be used productively, and by a vision of American security that is "fused with a commitment to a democratic world." Liberals do not accept that today's inequalities are inevitable or that collective action is always doomed to failure. Liberals believe in standing up for outcasts who face economic deprivation or cultural discrimination. Because they believe government can be effective, they also insist that it be competent. Because they believe individuals are best served by a commitment to the common good, they insist that the environment be protected and that health care be a matter of public concern.

As liberals face the future, they should remember that their conservative adversaries face divisions of their own. The priorities of the religious conservatives are vastly different from those of the corporate conservatives. Traditionalists face off against libertarians. Foreign policy idealists disagree devoutly with realists. Some conservatives believe that deficits can, sometimes, be combated by tax increases. Other conservatives reject tax increases under all circumstances. Conservatives include devotees to the ideas of Adam Smith, Milton Friedman, and Friedrich von

Hayek; of Michael Oakshott, Robert Nisbet, and Leo Strauss; of Pat Robertson and Ayn Rand; of William F. Buckley Jr., Pat Buchanan, George Will, William Safire, Bill O'Reilly, and Rush Limbaugh. Theirs is certainly a contentious family.

Conservatives have struggled since the 1950s to create order out of their own political and intellectual chaos. They succeeded because they had confidence in their own claims to power, faith in their moral purpose, and respect, even reverence, for the tradition from which they sprang. Conservatives learned from the long period in which they were deprived of power and influence that a healthy political movement cannot afford to luxuriate in sectarianism.

Liberals reached the high tide of their power in 1965 and have, in the four decades since, struggled with division and decline. During this period, liberals have sometimes lost faith in their moral claims and in their own political competence. But just as liberal arrogance brought forth a vibrant conservatism, so now does the arrogance of the political right demand a liberal resurgence. Americans have relied on a healthy liberalism to offer both pragmatic moderation and a reforming energy. At this moment in history, the country desperately needs both. Liberals should not shrink from their responsibility. They should welcome it.

E. J. Dionne Jr.

Liberalism, Past and Future Tense

NEIL JUMONVILLE AND KEVIN MATTSON

iberalism. Use the word in common conversation and people might look at you askance. The word, if it has any popular meaning today, has a largely negative one. *Liberalism* is still the "L word," as it became known in the 1988 presidential election when George H. W. Bush towered over Michael Dukakis at the podium and in voting returns. During that election, the word seemed to describe, in the words of one writer, "a minority creed of rapist-coddlers and flag burners and pornography purveyors and other elitists who were out of touch with 'mainstream American values.'"[1] This book argues that liberalism is actually in the mainstream of American history and that it is a defensible and utterly necessary creed. We'd like to explain, if only briefly, why we think so.

The background of liberalism, well before the idea was born or imagined, was the breakup of European feudal societies, which were organic, centralized systems run by powerful lords and kings with strict provisions about caste and class. Into this framework, in the fifteenth and sixteenth centuries, crept the birth of the individual, prompted by changes in the technology of printing, a new cosmology, and the age of discovery, which showed, among other things, that there were different ways to organize societies. As Richard Tawney, Max Weber, and others have shown, this early and still very weak stage of individualism took the name of Protestantism in religion, capitalism in economics, and liberalism in politics.[2]

The term *liberal* derives from the Latin *liber*, meaning free, in the sense that the liberal arts (*artes liberales*) are skills that free the human mind, as opposed to the *artes illiberales*, which are skills that are necessary for production and economic survival. Liberalism, from its origins, wedded itself to the project of "enlightenment." In 1784, Immanuel Kant famously defined "enlightenment" as "man's emergence from his self-incurred immaturity" into a state of "courage" to use "reason." This interpretation didn't call for either overextending the power of reason (as John Patrick Diggins reminds us in his essay) or demolishing religious faith. But it did give priority to the "autonomy" of "rational individuals" (again, Kant's words) and separation of church and state.[3]

Thus, in the late seventeenth-century world of John Locke and the eighteenth-century world of Thomas Jefferson, liberalism, as part of the political vocabulary of the free individual, was articulated in terms of small government; a secular state (in which the church did not rule); the rationality of individuals, which would allow them to understand their own best interest; the democratic dictate of individuals rather than classes; and the rights of individuals, which took the form of civil liberties. Because North America had no feudal or aristocratic past, this ancient form of liberalism, usually called classical liberalism, became the origin of both conservatism and liberalism in the United States. Because of this history, today's American conservatives, instead of appealing to the organic power of lords and kings and ancestral lands, appeal to the rights of individuals, civil liberties, markets, and a circumscribed government.

Because the freedom of the individual was a value that united its subscribers, liberalism desired to build a small, or at least divided, form of government, given that government was the largest and most powerful entity that could threaten individual freedom. But with the culmination of the Industrial Revolution in the United States in the 1890s, many liberals turned to the government, their former antagonist, to protect them from a force they considered a far more dangerous threat to individual liberty: the massive corporations that now dotted the economic and political landscape. They started to take so-called Hamiltonian means—the faith in a strong government that has dominated the American past—much more seriously. In this watershed transformation can be found the reorientation of liberalism that helps inform our understanding of this term. After this point, the part of the political community that remained committed to the classical liberalism of small government and the laissez-faire economic market was called conservative or libertarian, although today we also have many other kinds of conservatives (corporate conservatives, social conservatives, populist conservatives). A century ago, those who believed that the power and freedom of the individual needed government protection from the larger forces of economic centralization continued to be called liberals, and they are the ancestors of the liberalism we recognize today.

Though liberalism has some negative connotations today, its history offers a source of pride and accomplishment. It stands for representative constitutional democracy, which has marked American history since the country threw off the yoke of British colonial rule; the right to free religious expression and a secular state; a free market that balances equality of opportunity with the ability of government to correct for the market's injustices; and a balance between free individuality and a commitment to a common good. No matter what a citizen's attitude toward the Iraq War might be (and there's room for disagreement here), the system that America hopes to promote in that country—a constitutional representative democracy and a respect for individual rights—is a logical extension of the liberal tradition.

This liberal link makes the current situation puzzling at best. The president, who is promoting elements of the liberal tradition abroad, attacked that tradition during his presidential campaign at home. Though American liberals might think their philosophy has won credence across the globe, they find themselves under attack in their own country from both the Left and the Right. The "L word" implies unelectability and marginality. The situation has become so bad that some in America are seeking a new name for liberalism: "progressivism." But this move is mistaken. The term *liberalism* should be championed today and reinvigorated as a source of pride and a reminder of Americans' connection to basic values that stretch back centuries. To avoid the moniker is to run from the past, and liberals have no reason to do so. Only by explaining the true meaning of liberalism, by honoring the most important parts of the idea's past, can we win support for liberal values today. Liberals, as once was true, need to love what they stand for, and they need to have conviction about who they are and why they are liberals. They must rearticulate the "fighting faith" that Arthur Schlesinger Jr. described fifty years ago.

One reason that liberalism is in dire straits is its perceived cultural baggage. Liberals have been losing the "culture wars" because they are seen as devoid of moral values, or so numerous political journalists argue. If liberals now stand for anything, as Neil Jumonville points out in his essay in this volume, they stand for an empty and limitless toler-ance—a philosophy that prompts most Americans to wonder what val-ues liberals actually believe in. Because liberals are seen as out of line with the cultural conservatism of America's lesser-educated and working-class citizens—on issues such as abortion, the death penalty, and religious faith—some on the left suggest that liberals should focus on economic issues and thrust aside the debate about cultural values. The culture wars are unwinnable, according to critics such as Thomas Frank, so we should replace them with an emphasis on class and economics. But we disagree, because liberalism *does* stand for cultural and political val-ues, and liberals will be better off if they explain those values rather than duck the conflicts that might arise as a result.

To present a set of liberal values, we have assembled a group of his-torians and writers who understand the history of the political tradition. Some might suggest that the desire to explain the historical significance of liberalism is a sign of the times: that describing liberalism in the past tense says it all. But history can help us. Though we begin this book with the premise that liberalism has a past worth examining today, we also suggest that history is not just a description of the past but is also a tool in the present for rethinking our current and future political situations. As the essays by Mona Harrington, Amy Sullivan, and Michael Tomasky make clear, liberalism continues to be relevant in the present, offering compelling suggestions about problems in religion, the American family, and the war in Iraq.

This book begins on a historical note because we recognize a time when many Americans seemed to understand the liberal tradition better and to endorse it more enthusiastically than they do today—a time when everything seemed the reverse of what it is today. During the first years of the cold war (1945–60), liberalism defined America's national iden-tity and posture, and the doctrine towered above those of its opponents. For example, the liberal literary critic Lionel Trilling wrote in 1950, "In the United States at this time, liberalism is not only the dominant but even the sole intellectual tradition." And liberal economist John Kenneth Galbraith said the following about the welfare legislation that New Deal liberalism helped push along: "Social welfare legislation is almost en-tirely noncontroversial." The writings of midcentury liberals often reveal this sort of assuredness. There was an idea that no one sensible could be anything but a liberal. The welfare state, labor unions, civil rights for all citizens, a commitment to building a liberal internationalism through multilateral institutions in the world—what sensible person could oppose such things? This common outlook provided political comfort for the generation recovering from the upheaval of the Great Depression and World War II, but the bond of common assumptions at the time suppressed criticism and debate in the 1960s, which have since erupted into a welcome and necessary exchange of ideas.[4]

The assumptions of postwar liberals found a historical mooring. When midcentury historians looked to the past, they were stunned to find that U.S. commentators and scholars consistently failed to question the liberal tradition. When the political scientist Louis Hartz looked at the past in his classic book *The Liberal Tradition in America* (1955), he reported that no feudalism had been present during America's founding, and because America was born "liberal" and free, liberalism became "the master assumption of American political thought" with no other ideas to contest it (certainly not socialism, which never took root in America). Liberalism was therefore never questioned and, for the most part, was blindly accepted.[5]

Today we know Hartz's picture of the past was distorted: alternatives to liberalism informed the American political tradition from the beginning and continue today. During the American Revolution, for instance, in addition to the liberalism of John Locke (the liberalism Hartz emphasized) was a civic republican tradition that believed in a common good beyond individual self-interest—one that justified the sacrifice the Revolutionary War required. In turn, the Southern tradition that was the basis of nineteenth-century slavery embodied faith in racial domination, hierarchy, and "organic" social arrangements. The "Southern mind" became the basis for certain strains in modern conservatism today, as the scholar Eugene Genovese points out. A strong element of evangelical religion has also consistently found itself in contestation with secular liberalism. Some vocal conservative intellectuals—including William Buckley, Whittaker Chambers, and James Burnham—even wrote at the time that Trilling believed liberalism was the "sole intellectual tradition" (Trilling, at the same time, was criticizing liberalism for its limiting orthodoxies). Today, as observers insist, American society is heavily polarized. Americans seem divided on values—"red" versus "blue," "heartland" versus "coast." To speak of consensus, as midcentury liberals did, makes no sense for either the past or the present.

Recognizing that liberalism is one of many political and intellectual doctrines coursing through U.S. history, we must define our central term more precisely before proceeding. But we must do so while recognizing that liberalism itself is a polyglot tradition, made up of different (some would say conflicting) ideas. Though we believe that a "philosophy" of liberalism exists, this philosophy is not necessarily without internal conflicts. As Peter Berkowitz shows in this book's opening essay, which is grounded in a liberal individualism slightly more conservative than the outlook of other contributors, one can draw from different sources of liberal thought today. And some of our essayists disagree about what aspects of the tradition should be emphasized (which we take as a sign of healthy debate).

Though Berkowitz's proximity to classical liberalism—especially its faith in civil liberties and the power of individual freedom—is still present in the tradition we hope to restore, our primary aim is to remind our readers of midcentury liberalism. This version of liberalism is grounded in the Enlightenment and constitutionalism and worked during the cold war to define a "vital center," before falling to critics, first from the left during the 1960s and more recently from the right. We revive this tradition while realizing that liberals can have different ideas and can debate their variegated tradition in a healthy and vigorous way.

The midcentury liberalism we recover here draws upon the accomplishments of the New Deal; though it believes in free markets, it does not believe free markets are the sole guarantors of freedom. Indeed, midcentury liberalism articulated the need for a strong federal government to protect civil liberties and civil rights, especially those of minority citizens. In America's consolidated and centralized society of big business, democratically elected government also needed to act as a referee and "countervailing power" (to use John Kenneth Galbraith's evocative term) to ensure fairness. Midcentury liberalism also believed that government should ensure the welfare of the most disadvantaged of its citizens. Liberals debated how extensive these provisions should become (as even our own authors inevitably would), but they had a bedrock faith in the obligation of the national community to all its citizens, including its poorest members. By imagining a national community, midcentury liberalism balanced obligation—in the form of taxation and public service—with individual rights—especially in the form of civil liberties and equal opportunity through education. Midcentury liberalism, therefore, tipped its hat to the constitutionalist thought of America's original founders, both to their thinking about human limits and to their original vision to build a national community committed to greatness.

Liberalism has consistently defined itself against other doctrines on both its left and its right. During the 1930s and 1940s, liberalism battled fascism and then communism (many of our essays touch on this theme). As liberalism moved from the cold war into the tumultuous 1960s, its proponents found they had to argue against an increasingly militant student Left. Battles raged about university governance and the nature of the war in Vietnam. When protesting students took over campus buildings, liberals found themselves arguing that the idea of "participatory democracy" could be taken too far. Liberals also argued that Vietnam was a mistaken venture but not an "imperialist" war, as some on the New Left portrayed it. Liberals did this, as Michael Kazin points out, while learning from their critics, not just arguing with them.

After the 1960s, many who were influenced by the New Left traveled into the universities. There, the rise of an academic cultural Left (ACL) posed new challenges for liberals. The ACL adopted some tenets of poststructuralist thought (a decentered world without clear meaning or reliable understanding about itself), privileged the "other" (typically referring to ascriptive minority groups bound by race, gender, or sexual orientation), endorsed a relativism hostile to a clearly articulated idea of a public good, and emphasized cultural politics that were more suitable to academe than to public debate or electoral politics. In this world of the ACL, liberals who insisted on realistic political reform in the world outside of academe were considered old-fashioned and sometimes even indistinguishable from conservatives.

Many members of the ACL carried grievances that bordered on anti-Americanism, as a quick examination of American Studies Association conference programs in the past twenty years makes clear (or as the famously stupid claims of Ward Churchill about "little Eichmanns" in the World Trade Center made even clearer). The ACL embraced the worst excesses of "political correctness," affirmative action, and identity politics. Unfortunately, most Americans knew little about the differences between liberals and the cultural Left, assuming that the two groups were the same. In this volume, the writings of John Patrick Diggins, Neil Jumonville, and Alan Wolfe make clear that liberals see more of a gulf between their philosophy and the academic Left than conservatives suggest and than the greater American population might perceive.

Indeed, one of the reasons this collection of essays looks back to the values of the midcentury generation is that the ACL, although it produced some victories for diversity and multiculturalism, derailed many important liberal commitments of a half century ago and increased the American population's animosity toward liberalism. We should note that it also convinced some of the writers in this book that the time has come for liberalism to reassert itself against the ACL's claims, while never ignoring the dangers of the conservative ideas and political power that have grown (not coincidentally) along with the ACL. We are not saying that liberalism has to become more conservative. In fact, our vision of liberalism is consistent with that of the Old Left of Irving Howe's *Dissent.*

~

Fifty years ago, Arthur Schlesinger Jr. wrote one of the defining texts for the brand of liberalism that we revive here. The title of his book, *The Vital Center,* tells a great deal about the political thinking within its covers. Schlesinger believed that liberals, while defining themselves in the realms of domestic and foreign policy, should inhabit a pragmatic "center" that evaded the excesses of the communist hard Left and the free-market hard Right. He recommended that liberals make clear their differences from "progressives" (then organized in Henry Wallace's Progressive Citizens of America party) who cozied up to the forces of totalitarianism by making excuses for the Soviet Union's foreign policy of expansionism. Schlesinger argued with thinkers to his political left while never ignoring the "failure of the right."[6] Schlesinger's challenge to liberals in *The Vital Center* in 1949 is the challenge facing liberals in 2006. Of course, liberals today do not face exactly the same situation that Schlesinger did. But the *type* of thinking he did is the kind of thinking we need more of today. In this volume, for example, Michael Tomasky discusses U.S. foreign policy in the context of the Iraq War and, like Schlesinger, illustrates an intelligent liberal position between the confusion on his left and his right.

In fact, as Jennifer Burns shows in her essay, during the 1950s, an important debate ensued between conservative and liberal intellectuals, after which the United States saw a gradual ascendance of conservative politicians and conservative ideas. To see their visibility grow in a similar way, liberals need to articulate what they stand for, defining themselves in part against the increasingly vocal Right. This volume's exploration of liberal history and suggestions for future changes aim to start this project.

Conservative policies and ideas are not as popular as some might think. Of course, liberals have been concerned about the gutting of programs like the estate tax. But consider how quickly the disaster of Hurricane Katrina and the increasing cost of the war in Iraq have reduced the attractiveness of calling for future conservative tax cuts for the wealthy. (This new reticence won't necessarily prevent future tax cuts.) Consider the failure of George W. Bush to privatize Social Security. Consider the conservative crack-up over the Iraq War, the near evaporation of neoconservative foreign policy ideas, and the remaining popularity among Americans of multilateralism in foreign policy matters. Consider the divisions between conservative principles like libertarianism and legislation based on Christian (largely evangelical) values. We have no reason to believe that a conservative consensus is taking shape to replace the purported liberal consensus of yore.

However, one element is missing: a liberal alternative. We hear little from the Democrats other than their opposition—that is, little about what they stand for. Our book of essays seeks to explicate ideas and values, and we do not seek to dodge the culture wars but to fight them by explaining what liberals believe. In this collection, we and our fellow contributors are less interested in explicating policy than in illuminating core liberal principles of the past and in exploring how they can become more relevant today. Here you'll find essays about national greatness and liberal patriotism, theories of human nature, arguments about the role of science in American culture, questions about the relation between democracy and constitutionalism, and debates about America's role in the world. We believe that liberal values and commitments still have something important to offer the American public today and that the country's past holds important ethical and political commitments that it can use successfully in the future. This conviction is the reason for this book.

PART ONE

THE PHILOSOPHY
OF LIBERALISM

1

The Liberal Spirit in America
and Its Paradoxes

PETER BERKOWITZ

Notwithstanding the challenges of the post–September 11 world,
never has a people enjoyed a greater range of individual rights, or
been more jealous of its freedoms, or been more convinced that the
liberty it prizes is good not only for itself but for other peoples than do
we in the United States today. This nation, in most respects the freest one
the world has ever seen, has produced the world's most diverse society;
the world's best army; the world's most organized, industrious, and productive economy; and a political order that to a remarkable degree contains the factions and divisions that have prevented so many other countries from innovating and solving collective problems. This achievement
represents the triumph in America of liberalism, a tradition of thought
and politics stretching back at least to seventeenth-century England,
whose fundamental moral premise is the natural freedom and equality
of all and whose governing aim is to secure equal freedom in political life.

Yet cause for anxiety comes from many quarters. Freedom in America has produced or permitted massive income inequalities. It has given
rise to a popular culture that frequently and increasingly descends into
the cheap and salacious. It maintains a public school system that fails to
teach many students the basics of reading and writing and arithmetic;
and at higher levels of education, it breeds an academic culture that

preaches the relativity of values and that cannot reach agreement on what students ought to have learned by graduation to qualify as well-educated citizens. This freedom has contributed to the erosion of the old rules, written and unwritten, that governed, and once stabilized, dating, sex, love, marriage, and family. It has fostered among opinion makers and intellectual elites a distrust of religious belief that borders on contempt. And it has fortified among the highly educated an uncritical faith in the coincidence of progress in the arts and sciences and moral progress.

To clarify the challenge of conserving liberalism's achievements and pressing forward with its promises, it is first necessary to correct an unfortunate confusion of terms. In the United States, *liberal* commonly denotes the left wing of the Democratic Party. To be sure, as a result of bruising post-1960s political battles, many on the Left have disavowed the term *liberal,* choosing instead the label *progressive,* which is in fact a more apt designation of their outlook. Nevertheless, the term *liberal* retains a distinctive meaning, indeed a progressive one, in our political lexicon.

It was not foreordained that *liberal* would become synonymous with progressive politics as it has in the United States. In Europe, for example, the term has come to designate something much closer to libertarianism. Yet neither is the equation of liberalism with progressivism an accident, for the liberal tradition has a powerful progressive thrust. When the idea arose in the seventeenth century, before it acquired its name, liberalism, particularly John Locke's version, sought to limit the claims of religious authorities in politics and the claims of political authorities in religious matters. As these ideas took root, as religion receded from the center of politics (and as science and industry developed and markets spread), individual freedom acquired more space, more individuals began to enjoy its blessings, and power shifted to those who had long been denied it. When liberalism came into its own in the nineteenth century, it, particularly that of Mill, sought to limit the role in politics of status, wealth, and sex by making the state responsible for assuring formal equality or equality before the law. The result was to accelerate the pace at which power shifted to the people and to spread the blessings of freedom more equally. And when, in the United States in the last third of the twentieth century, liberalism became synonymous with the left wing of the Democratic Party, it aggressively sought to limit the role in politics, and in society, of poverty, race, sex, old age, illness, and disability by guaranteeing all individuals a minimum level of material goods and moral standing. As this outlook merged in the United States with the conventional wisdom, the press for freedom became indistinguishable in many minds from the improvement of social life through greater equality in all realms and in all ways.

Yet the defense of freedom requires more than progress in equality, as John Stuart Mill pointed out in *On Liberty* (1859) and in *Considerations on Representative Government* (1861). Because moving ahead requires holding some things still, because freedoms won must be preserved, and because both the improvement and preservation of a free society depend upon citizens with particular skills, knowledge, and qualities of mind and character, liberal democracy always requires a party of order as well as a party of progress. Hence, conservatives, who take a special interest in freedom's limits and its material and moral preconditions, are properly seen as belonging to the liberal tradition and in fact play an essential role in maintaining the liberal state. In American politics today, the Right generally differs from the Left not in the primacy it assigns to personal freedom but in the primacy it assigns to competing policies—in particular, the care for which goods, those related to order or those related to progress, freedom most urgently requires.

And the differences about competing policies stem from a more fundamental disagreement between the Left and the Right about which factors pose the greatest threat to freedom. Progressive liberals see inequality as the chief menace to freedom and government as an essential part of the solution. For libertarian liberals, who, like progressives, think that freedom yields progress and who, like conservatives, stress the order on which freedom depends, government is the chief menace to freedom, and the restraint of government is freedom's essential safeguard. And for conservative liberals, of both the traditional and neoconservative varieties, the excess of freedom and equality poses the biggest threat to freedom, and government is both a friend and a foe in the battle to limit freedom and equality on behalf of freedom and equality.

To maintain that liberalism constitutes our dominant moral and political tradition is not to deny the presence in America of competing traditions. Biblical faith, for example, remains a powerful force in the lives of many Americans. And even for the larger numbers who no longer organize their lives around sacred scripture and worship, biblical faith, through the impact it has had over the centuries on our moral concepts and categories, influences the scope and direction of our imagination and informs practical judgments, often in ways that rein in freedom's most ambitious and reckless claims. Moreover, anger, pride, envy, ambition, honor, love, and a host of other passions that dwell within us are inflected by, but resist reduction to, our love of freedom.

Nor does the suggestion that many of today's progressives and conservatives are equally members of the liberal tradition and pillars of the liberal state mean that if everybody were to sit down together, talk things over civilly, and sort through the issues reasonably, we would discover universal agreement on all the important questions. This is a popular conceit among professors, who can't bear the thought that the problems of politics are not amenable to conclusive resolution through rigorous reasoning (by them) and rational discourse (under their direction). Yet examination of the liberalism that we share suggests that the professors who dream of disinterested deliberations (grounded in self-evident premises and governed by objective and necessary rules) that yield unassailable public-policy choices may have drawn exactly the wrong conclusion.

To be sure, agreement on basic liberal political institutions is as broad as is agreement on liberalism's fundamental moral premise: the natural freedom and equality of all. Who opposes representative institutions, separated powers, an independent judiciary, a free press, and legal guarantees of freedom of speech, belief, and association? However, the very scope of partisans' agreement about the lineaments of self-government brings home the permanence of disagreement in the politics of a free people. Theory teaches both that a balance must be struck between the claims of order and the claims of progress and that theory itself cannot specify the proper balance that we Americans, in our peculiar circumstances, ought to strike. For one thing, theory does not determine the weight to be given to the competing goods that the party of order and the party of balance promote. That job falls to flesh-and-blood individuals, who are given to self-seeking and ambition. Nor can theory, once the balance has been struck, replace the need for these imperfect individuals to cooperate in maintaining it.

The liberal spirit supports free institutions. Such a spirit is tolerant of opposing opinions and choices, which means that it is prepared to respect the rights of individuals with whom it disagrees and of whose conduct it disapproves. It is generous, both in seeking to understand what is true in other people's beliefs and in looking for the shared humanity in people's diverse and divergent strivings. It is reasonable, which means that it is both proud of thinking for itself and humble in the face of reason's limits. And it is capable of restraining immediate desire in the interest of satisfying higher or more comprehensive desires. The exercise of these virtues enables citizens to ease the friction, take advantage of the opportunities, and handle the responsibilities that arise, amid frenetic motion, in a free society.

Where do the virtues that compose such a spirit come from? Will free societies always have a sufficient supply of this spirit? Thinkers on the left, particularly those influenced by Kant, such as John Rawls and Judith Shklar, have argued that free societies are, to a significant extent, self-sustaining: The experience of living under free institutions fosters in citizens a liberal character. Thinkers on the right, especially those who take their bearings from Tocqueville and Aristotle, such as Gertrude Himmelfarb and Harvey Mansfield, warn that free societies contain the seeds of their own destruction: The experience of freedom, if left to its own devices, leads to an insatiable desire for more of it, steadily severing individuals' attachment to family and faith, which these thinkers contend are the most reliable sources of the liberal spirit's virtues.

In fact, when properly formulated, these two opinions reflecting the optimism of the Left and the pessimism of the Right should be seen as opposite sides of the same coin. Free institutions do tend to teach toleration, generosity in the understanding of others, an appreciation of reason's limits, and self-restraint in the short term for the sake of long-term self-interest. But if undisciplined and unbalanced by other principles, freedom eventually causes toleration to morph into rigid neutrality between competing goods. It transforms generosity in the understanding of others into the presumptuous conviction that one understands other people's beliefs and needs better than they do and that one therefore should legislate to bring their conduct in line with their true interests. It fosters a desire for freedom from reason and its limits. And it opens the door to an excessive focus on calculating the best means for the satisfaction of desire, which soon crowds out calculations of the satisfactions in fulfilling one's duty and eventually renders invisible the claims of duty that transcend calculation.

Why does the liberal spirit overreach? In part, it does so because to overreach is human. In part, it believes that freedom is made more secure by acquiring more of it. In part, it overreaches because the enjoyment of freedom pushes against and wears down not just the claims of this or that authority but the claims of all authority, save for that of the freely choosing individual. We must not assume, however, that we are at the mercy of freedom's overreaching. In a free society, freedom creates the conditions under which we can bring our passion for freedom under control and discipline it to serve our purposes. Such an undertaking depends upon the awareness that our liberalism never fully embraces or exhausts our humanity. It also depends upon emancipating our understanding of the liberal tradition from a variety of misconceptions with which it has become encrusted and then grasping the temptations to which the liberal spirit is perennially prey. Such an undertaking is a preliminary to crafting policies, consistent with the principles of a free society, that safeguard the best interests of the liberal spirit—but, especially in the current clamor and confusion, it is an indispensable preliminary.

~

In our day, professors, largely representing the progressive wing of the liberal tradition, have taken the lead in promulgating a variety of misconceptions about the liberal tradition. These misconceptions obscure or simplify into nonexistence the tensions that flow from liberalism's fundamental premise, the natural freedom and equality of all. Although scholars sometimes sense the complexity, they prefer to devise stratagems to evade the conflicts among principles and goods that constitute the liberalism of our moral and political life. Their evasions, however, may prove costly, because the principles and goods that support freedom do not balance themselves, and we will not balance them wisely if we are lulled into disregarding the many and varied conflicts among them.

To move beyond the common simplifications, we must rejuvenate the distinctions that the professors have sought to collapse and reconstruct the working relations between rival principles and goods that they place in stark opposition. First, liberalism is not, as many scholars assert, the same as democracy. Many thinkers wish to erase the distinction between the two by incorporating into the idea of democracy standards of freedom, efficiency, fairness, security—indeed, all good things. They would make the term *liberal democracy* a redundancy. It is, however, not a matter of semantics to insist that liberalism adds something important to liberal democracy, awareness of which is diminished by dropping *liberal* from the name. That added something is the primacy of freedom, and that diminished awareness is of the ever-present potential for, and common reality of, conflict between popular will and individual rights. Scholars who fold their liberalism into their democracy contend that their progressive policy preferences are necessary to the full flowering of individual freedom and *therefore* are an expression of popular will, even when majorities to support the policies are nowhere to be found. Call this view the fallacy of the general will.

In fact, liberalism and democracy stand for competing, if related, principles. In contrast to liberalism, which puts freedom first, democracy puts equality first. Whereas liberalism is a doctrine about the limits that government must respect to ensure freedom, democracy proclaims that the people, with no particular limits, should rule.

Certainly, liberalism and democracy do have a critical affinity: Liberalism tends to think of freedom in terms of rights that are shared equally by all, whereas democracy tends to conceive of equality in terms of freedom to live as one pleases. Moreover, the experience of the past two hundred and fifty years strongly suggests that freedom is best protected democratically and that self-government is more just when constrained by liberal guarantees of individual freedom. But the individual rights of the liberal tradition impose a defining limitation on the people's, or popular, will, proclaiming as a matter of fundamental law that majorities, however strongly they may feel and however convinced they may be, may not enact certain policies and programs. Precisely where those limits fall must remain a permanent bone of contention, to be hashed out again and again as circumstances change, but both the permanence and the propriety of the debate are obscured if one equates liberalism and democracy.

Second, liberalism does not deny the claims of community. Nevertheless, an array of scholars have written as if freedom and community— or, more broadly, freedom and association—were thoroughly antagonistic and hopelessly irreconcilable. On the one side, in the name of liberalism, scholars argue that individuals are constituted by their capacity for free rational choice and that community is an external source of authority to which the individual's reason forbids him to submit. On the other side, in the name of communitarianism or civic republicanism—schools of academic political theory that arose specifically to challenge liberalism—scholars maintain that the free and rationally choosing agent is a fantasy, because all individuals are partly constituted by duties and attachments that are given and not chosen and because freedom is achieved not through individuals' private choices about how to conduct their lives but through the choices that citizens make in public through deliberation with their fellow citizens about government and public policy. The two sides collude in fortifying a false dichotomy between individual freedom and association. The collusion serves the interests of the liberal theorists who believe that freedom is not merely the supreme good for politics but the sole good. It also advances the ambitions of the communitarian and civic republican theorists who wish to establish a similar monopoly for their favored good.

The interests of the liberal spirit, however, are better served by understanding that a genuine tension exists between the claims of freedom and those of community and association, but not one so thoroughgoing that it precludes giving substantial recognition to the claims of both. To recognize that we are partly constituted by attachments and duties we do not choose is not to concede that individuals are incapable of reasonably questioning these attachments and duties or of rejecting them or placing them on a different, more considered, footing. Nor is it to deny that political deliberation is a good—indeed, that cooperating with fellow citizens to choose public policy and the laws of the land is an important aspect of individual freedom. Moreover, putting individual freedom first is not the same as proclaiming freedom to be the sole and self-sufficient good, in politics or beyond. Indeed, freedom and community or association can be mutually supportive. For example, individuals acquire the capacity for freedom, according to the makers of modern liberalism, in association. In *Some Thoughts Concerning Education* (1689), John Locke gives an intricate account of the role of education in inculcating the moral and intellectual virtues that equip individuals for a life of liberty; and in Locke's view, parents, within the confines of the fundamental association of the family, are responsible for ensuring that children receive this education. John Stuart Mill contends that flourishing voluntary associations through which men and women meet and learn to cooperate for mutual advantage render individuals more independent and liberty more secure. Even John Rawls, in the neglected third part of his masterwork *A Theory of Justice* (1971), argues at length that the family and the voluntary associations of civil society instill qualities of mind and character presupposed by a well-ordered liberal society.

Third, liberalism does not reject virtue. However, many scholars, both in the defense of liberalism and in the attack on it, parallel the common arguments that seek to drive a wedge between liberalism and community by insisting that the liberal tradition has little patience or place for virtue and that virtue has little patience or place for individual freedom. After all, liberalism was born in the revolt against the authority of the church and Aristotle, and the virtues were thought to revolve around the church's doctrine of human salvation and Aristotle's account of human excellence. So mustn't those who embrace individual freedom reject virtue, and mustn't those who cling to the virtues repudiate the type of political life that rejected the authorities who established the underpinnings of the moral life?

Something similar to what was said about the tension between freedom and community should be said about the tension between freedom and virtue: It is genuine, but rightly understood, it reflects a complicated relationship, not an insuperable opposition. As I have suggested, the liberal spirit is characterized by specific virtues, and the liberal tradition provides a compelling account of the virtues on which a free society depends. Moreover, in rejecting the political *authority* of religious faith and of Aristotle (and of other so-called perfectionist conceptions of man), one need not reject their truth or their capacity to instruct. For, to understate matters considerably, not every respectable understanding of faith requires religion to promote salvation through politics. And, to again understate matters, not every respectable account of Aristotle or of perfectionist ethics in general requires that the state inculcate the ethics that perfect man. The liberal constraints on the state's legislation of particular conceptions of human salvation or human perfection are even compatible with the conclusion that some virtues on which the liberal state depends are better grasped by religious faith or the Aristotelian tradition of ethics.

Fourth, and closely connected, liberalism is not based on skepticism. That liberalism is so based is often put forward proudly by academic liberals and advanced contemptuously by their critics. Academic liberals think that skepticism about the human good is good for liberalism because it frees the doctrine from dependence on controversial opinions about human nature and the content of a good life. They suggest that a foundation in skepticism provides a built-in safeguard against attempts to legislate morals: if liberalism is based on skepticism, how can it possibly promote one conception of the good life over another? Critics retort that because it is grounded in skepticism, liberalism cannot begin to do justice to the full range of human emotions, passions, and moral judgments, which necessarily reflect opinions about what is right, proper, and fitting for a human being.

In fact, liberalism is firmly grounded in the belief in the natural freedom and equality of all human beings. This fundamental moral premise is at once descriptive and normative. Whether this premise is demonstrable by reason, it is liberalism's most basic affirmation, its first principle, and its nonnegotiable starting point. It colors all that we say and think and do. The element that is erroneously interpreted as the liberal tradition's fundamental skepticism is in fact the tolerant, generous, and reasonable stance toward alternative conceptions of the good life that grows out of liberalism's fundamental premise. The liberal spirit tolerates differences of opinion about matters of ultimate importance because it believes in the equal freedom of all to make such judgments.

Fifth, liberalism is not an obstacle to securing the rights of minorities and women. Critics are keen to point out liberalism's various compromises with oppression and discrimination throughout American history and quick to conclude that liberalism has been the principal cause of the denial of property, power, and status to women and minorities. In the United States, the paradigmatic case is that of African Americans. They have had to overcome the Constitution's legal protection of slavery; the Supreme Court's pre–Civil War decision in *Dred Scott v. Sanford* (1857) holding that blacks were property; the Court's post–Civil War decision in *Plessy v. Ferguson* (1896) that affirmed that states could maintain separate but equal public facilities for whites and blacks; Jim Crow laws; and today, the excruciating challenge of inner-city poverty, which itself has roots in the legacy of American slavery and discrimination. Women, too, have had to struggle to attain equal rights. They lacked the right to vote until passage of the Nineteenth Amendment in 1920; throughout American history, they suffered legal disabilities such as the lack of the rights to make contracts and to hold jobs; and public opinion conspired with law to deny them standing, access, and opportunities. Because liberal institutions have harbored bigotry and have been enlisted in schemes of oppression, some conclude that liberalism is irredeemably tainted and must be overthrown.

Yet in the fight to attain equal rights, liberalism, far from being an obstacle, has been minorities' and women's most reliable ally. Discrimination on the basis of race and sex predates the advent of liberalism, and these injustices persisted in the United States long after the rise of liberalism—despite, not because of, liberal principles. Indeed, at every step in the battle to overcome legally enforced discrimination, minorities, women, and their friends have enjoyed their greatest successes when they appealed to liberal principles. And even when opponents of discrimination have appealed to nonliberal principles or, indeed, when they have poured scorn on liberalism—as have the student movement of the 1960s, postmodern theorists, and radical feminists—their appeal could gain a respectful and sympathetic hearing because of most citizens' liberal conscience.

Sixth, liberalism does not falsely promise to remain neutral among competing conceptions of the good life. This canard has its origins in the misguided effort by academic liberals, which had its heyday in the 1970s and 1980s but is still going strong in many precincts, to show that maintaining neutrality toward different ways of life lay at the heart of liberalism. On behalf of this claim, they devised elaborate thought experiments to show how state neutrality is possible—and why it is necessary for the state to aggressively redistribute goods or, to the contrary, why it is mandatory for the state to scrupulously avoid redistribution in order to honor neutrality. Their critics delighted in demonstrating that every such thought experiment, no matter how ingenious, presupposed the good of autonomy, or a life organized around the principle that individuals should live in accordance with ends that they have chosen for themselves. In other words, contended the critics, academic liberals posited neutrality as the primary principle for government because it serves the interests of the autonomous life.

The debate about liberalism's neutrality, however, has been poorly conceived. The critics are right that the doctrine of neutrality presupposes the goodness of freedom, but they are wrong to think that the liberal tradition is somehow at fault for not coming clean or for breaking its promise. In fact, the doctrine of neutrality is the invention of Anglo-American post-1960s academic liberalism, and the larger liberal tradition makes no such representations or promises. It sees the determination to promote a single conception of human perfection or vision of religious salvation through the force of law as a major threat to freedom. It fully expects that a political society grounded in the natural freedom and equality of all will be distinguished by its openness to human diversity and by the value it places—both to the individual and to the wider society—on "experiments in life," in John Stuart Mill's phrase. Although this stance may look like neutrality, it isn't. Individuals whose fundamental beliefs give less primacy to individual choice, to say nothing of those who see celebration of individual choice as a revolt against God or a betrayal of the nation and those who long for theocracy or despotism, will certainly be at a disadvantage in a free society. For this situation, liberalism need offer no apology. Although liberalism cannot and does not require neutrality, liberal respect for individual choice does counsel toleration. Toleration calls upon individuals to live with and respect the rights of others, including the rights of those who embrace ways of life of which one might disapprove, so long as these individuals are willing to respect the rights of others. Laws that put toleration into practice will, by design, certainly make life harder for individuals whose way of life requires them to enshrine in public law their religious ideals or conceptions of moral perfection.

Seventh, along the same lines, liberalism does not invest the state with responsibility to make individuals autonomous or give it authority to perfect citizens' powers to make rational choices about moral and political life. The idea that the state has such responsibility has been advanced by so-called perfectionist liberals. They criticize the idea of liberal neutrality but do so on behalf of the liberal state's supposed affirmative responsibility to emancipate individuals, through thoroughgoing public education, from the deadweight of religion, tradition, parental authority, and the accidents of personal experience. They do not go so far as to argue that individuals must be forced to be free, but they do sometimes envisage a contest over children's souls between parents and a secular and secularizing state. Without such state intervention, argue perfectionist liberals, citizens cannot fully enjoy their liberties, or deliberate reasonably about public affairs, or effectively maintain the political institutions characteristic of a free people.

The liberal tradition, however, does not suppose that all individuals are cut from the same cloth, nor does it require that state education make all individuals in the same mold. To the contrary, it counsels that the state lacks the authority and the competence to promote human perfection, including the liberal interpretation of perfection. The state is not prohibited from imposing educational requirements on children. There are jobs to be done in a liberal state, and an educated citizenry is needed to perform them. To maintain a liberal state, however, it is not necessary that every citizen be a virtuoso of enlightenment sentiment and critical reasoning. Indeed, that way lies a state-induced conformism. It is enough—it is in fact a great good—for the liberal state to secure sufficient freedom for individuals, with the help of others, beginning with one's parents, to perfect themselves.

Every misconception that encrusts the liberal tradition represents an effort to overlook the interplay of competing principles and goods. To be sure, we would have fewer sources of confusion and instability if liberalism and democracy were one and the same, if the claims of liberalism and those of community were entirely irreconcilable, if liberalism and virtue were utterly antagonistic, if liberals by definition couldn't legislate morals because their fundamental moral and political beliefs were devoid of moral content, if liberalism could be advanced as a principal source of the oppression and discrimination suffered by minorities and women, if liberalism could be applauded for its commitment to the doctrine of neutrality or condemned for its betrayal of it, and if the autonomous individual were the only individual liberalism could respect. But the suppression of crucial distinctions and the promulgation of false

dichotomies, often under the initiative of liberals themselves, is for contemporary liberalism a still greater source of confusion and instability.

~

The greatest source of instability in the liberal spirit is the momentum that
freedom develops in a free society. Public opinion and popular culture
sing freedom's praise. Social and political institutions absorb its imperatives and give voice to its demands. Private life is permeated by it. Progress
in freedom gives new meaning to the virtues that epitomize the liberal
spirit: It dissolves toleration into indifference or neutrality; it dissipates
generosity into busybodiness or bossiness; it unravels reason and leaves
in its place creativity and self-assertion; and it collapses enlightened self-
interest into petty selfishness. By placing the individual at the center, freedom also creates fertile ground for the growth of age-old vices, particularly narcissism, vanity, and sanctimoniousness. At every turn, the spread
of freedom emboldens the liberal spirit's inclination to expose and over-
throw the claims of arbitrary authority. However, as the claims of freedom themselves acquire authority in a free society, the liberal spirit has
difficulty limiting its campaign against authority to that which is arbitrary. Or rather, with each new success, the liberal spirit comes closer to
viewing all authority as arbitrary. Eventually, the liberal spirit turns upon
the authority of freedom itself, attacking the very source of its moral
standing. Thus does postmodernism arise out of the sources of liberalism.

We can see freedom's momentum in the unfolding of the liberal tradition. Early on, the liberal spirit, as exemplified by Locke, rebelled
against arbitrariness in the exercise of political authority, the authority
exercised by the state over the individual. Later, in Mill's age, as liberalism attained maturity, the liberal spirit increasingly chafed at authority
in the moral realm as well, targeting more directly the claims of public
opinion, clergy, and parents to issue authoritative judgments about how
others should live. In our day, as liberalism has grown both more aggressive and more complacent, the liberal spirit not only has found
threats to freedom lurking everywhere but also has demanded that the
state rather than the individual take responsibility for rooting them out.
The next frontier is the constraint imposed by our biology. Astounding
developments in the realm of biotechnology are encouraging the liberal
spirit to see natural constraints on human life as arbitrary and capable
of being overcome, if individuals so desire, by drugs, surgery, gene ther-
apy, and genetic engineering.

There is reason to worry, however, that the relentless breaking down of barriers in the political, moral, and natural realms poses a threat to freedom by destroying the conditions for its humanly satisfying exercise. For freedom has roots in our nature, depends on the maintenance of order in our affairs, and receives its highest justification in the ends it enables us to pursue. Yet the advance of freedom can also subvert our understanding of our natures, our respect for the imperatives of order, and our willingness to view any ends as authoritative.

Freedom's self-subverting tendencies create a paradox: Freedom depends upon a variety of beliefs, practices, and institutions that are weakened by the increasingly forceful reverberations of freedom throughout all facets of moral and political life. Some more traditional conservatives say that such weakening is the baleful and inevitable consequence of modern freedom. Some more radical progressives contend that this so-called baleful weakening is really a long-overdue liberation. But both the traditional conservatives and the radical progressives see only what they want to see. Freedom's self-subverting tendencies are real, but they are not the whole story. They are inseparable from progress in freedom and, indeed, are inseparable from freedom's self-correcting powers. The freedom that brings traditional authorities and institutions into question creates an opportunity to reconsider their function and foundation. Indeed, freedom's self-subverting tendencies are the objects on which the liberal spirit currently needs to focus its self-correcting powers—capitalizing on its ability to stand back, take a fresh look, discipline passions, ferret out prejudice, and assess its situation reasonably.

Consider first the realm of education. Education is indispensable to preparing citizens for the rights and responsibilities of freedom. Instilling in children a sense of good and bad, forming their principles, and generally directing their education is itself an expression of parents' freedom (limited by the rights of children, which are enforceable by the liberal state). The state also has its responsibilities. In the United States, all children must attend school through their mid- to late-teenage years. At the elementary level, basic education focuses on reading, writing, and arithmetic. As students move from grade school through junior high and high school, the mission generally expands to include instruction in the history and ideas that form the basis of the students' political society. In the United States, because of its universal principles, schools also seek to educate students in the history and ideas of other peoples and places. As an obligation that falls equally upon all young people, schooling helps form manners and moral sensibility, or mores. At higher levels, a liberal education—the general study of history, literature, art, philosophy, the social sciences, and the natural sciences—enlarges the perspective, refines the moral sensibility, and deepens the understanding. This focus makes for more responsible individuals, capable of bringing under their control a wider range of decisions that affect the kinds of lives they live and the kinds of people they will become.

But freedom's progress also hollows out education. It undermines parental authority, treating parents' efforts to pass on their way of life as attempts to bind their children to the past. Increasingly, the liberal spirit comes to see education as itself an arbitrary authority, intruding impermissibly on the self's right to live and interpret the world as it sees fit. Educators respond by adopting a progressive thrust for schools. No longer will schools teach truths; instead, they will prepare students to decide for themselves what is true, despite the fact that basic literacy and general knowledge of the world are preconditions for evaluating rival truth claims. Eventually, this approach turns schools into forums in which students are invited to make and express their own truths. The result is the opposite of a liberal arts education, for an educational system devoted to making each student the highest authority on truth locks in ignorance and shelters inherited ways of viewing the world. Moreover, by affirming that the writings and thoughts of the past are less important than individuals' feelings in the present, schools cut students off from the history of human political and intellectual achievement.

In a free society, work, or wage labor, provides the material means by which individuals make themselves self-sustaining. Work is driven by necessity: We must put bread on the table and maintain a roof over our heads. But under the auspices of freedom, work becomes a badge of honor. For most of us, jobs are the most sustained activity in public life: They serve as a conspicuous symbol of our personal independence and as a mark of our ability to care for ourselves and to take responsibility for our lives. Work channels ambition and competitiveness into undertakings that benefit society. It calls upon and fortifies necessary virtues such as discipline, industry, cooperation, and the calculation of long-term benefit. And for those employed in skilled labor or as professionals, mastery of craft in work provides a sense of pride and the pleasure of developing one's powers. Moreover, by opening the workplace to all regardless of class, race, or sex, the claims of freedom humanize the world of work.

But freedom becomes increasingly uncompromising, demanding that work be thoroughly rewarding so that we do not experience work as a form of servitude. The effort to meet this uncompromising demand threatens the functioning of other parts of a free person's life. Especially as work becomes increasingly attractive and fulfilling, we allow it to consume more of our time and energy. It encourages the neglect of private and public affairs. It squeezes vital realms—friendship and family, community and the arts, charitable work and politics—into smaller and smaller compartments. Moreover, however attractive and fulfilling it may become, work is still an exchange of pay for labor; therefore, the more we work, the more we tend to equate reward and worth with financial remuneration. And by rightly opening the workplace wide to women, the ethos of freedom ensures that both sexes will imbibe large doses of the code of commercial conduct every working day and then willy-nilly bring back into the home greater quantities of the cold spirit of calculation.

Romantic love, in a liberal age, occupies a commanding position in the hearts of men and women. When one authoritative good after another loses its luster, romantic love offers the hope of a taste of the transcendent in the here and now. Romantic love has roots in the powerful push and pull of sexual desire and in the abiding human longing to be loved for who one truly is. It gains standing as freedom progresses. By releasing individuals from the obligation to marry a mate of somebody else's choosing, remain in an unhappy marriage, or for that matter, marry at all, freedom provides the opportunity to search the world as long as one has breath for one's one true love.

But freedom also undermines romantic love by imparting lessons of impermanence and by establishing systems of separateness. Aided by the invention of the birth-control pill, which for the first time in human history cheaply and effectively separated sex from reproduction, freedom teaches us to postpone permanent relations: Before we can know that we have found our one true love, we (women as well as men) must experiment vigorously. Otherwise, how will we know what we have missed or be sure of what we have found? Yet the dream of one true love depends upon the idea of exclusiveness, and how can affections that we widely share also be exclusive? Moreover, the more we pile up experiences in dating and mating, the more we build up systems of separateness and learn to think of ourselves as independent agents capable of entering and exiting relationships at will—and the more we cultivate exactly the opposite of the heart's orientation in love, which longs for forever. Having raised the stakes for romantic love, freedom also undercuts the conditions for its attainment.

Family offers a fixed point amid the turbulence and uncertainty of a free society. It serves as a haven in a heartless world. Whereas public life puts one endlessly to the test of merit, the family gives its members unconditional acceptance and love based not on what one has achieved but on who one is. It permits the domestication and maturing of romantic love. It is the fundamental social unit in which children first learn to love and be loved, receive protection during the long period in which they are unable to care for themselves, and acquire the emotional, social, moral, and intellectual training necessary to eventually take responsibility for themselves as fully functioning adults.

But freedom also frays the fabric of family. It loosens the ties among family members and across generations by inclining individuals to see their essential responsibility as to themselves. It suggests to men and women that they should put their work or their pleasure ahead of duties to family members, in part by reducing those duties to calculations about benefits, in part by instilling a preference for going it alone. It induces parents to regard children as investments, the caring for whom must be weighed against the time and energy they take from work and leisure. As people delay marriage to find themselves before they commit, and as they squeeze family commitments to conform to their professional aspirations, family size falls, depriving children of the education that comes from sibling solidarity as well as sibling rivalry. At the same time, the standard internal structure of the family—one mother and one father—increasingly comes to be a matter of private choice, paving the way for the normalization of families with one parent, two mothers or two fathers, or other combinations growing out of the routinization of divorce and increasing comfort with diverse sexual preferences. These developments, in turn, lend more support to the reduction of family's meaning to a matter of private choice. As mobility separates grandparents from grandchildren, more elderly people are deprived of the joy of children, and more children are deprived of grandparents' love.

Biblical faith lends support to the idea, central to the era of freedom, that each individual has special significance. One does not have to believe that liberalism represents a secular and political interpretation of biblical faith to appreciate that the moral premise of natural freedom and equality of all is fortified by a religion that proclaims that all men and all women are created in God's image and are holy because He is holy. Moreover, communities of worship that rest on biblical faith provide a critical source of the individual discipline and self-restraint necessary for free individuals to set wise limits so that they can live well together. And such communities help choreograph life, endowing the routine of everyday with larger significance, allowing individuals to give and take solace, and honoring life's cycles and venerable turning points.

But freedom also puts faith on the defensive. God's will or law is primarily known through tradition and through the imperfect human beings who must preserve and transmit it. But of all forms of dependence, dependence on the will of other human beings sits most uneasily with the liberal spirit. It is one thing to submit to God; another, to submit to those who purport to interpret His will or law, especially in a world that daily furnishes rival and incompatible accounts of it. Emboldened by freedom, individuals endowed with the liberal spirit seek to go beyond the faith of their choice to create rituals and observances that better reflect their distinctive sensibility and understanding. However, as religion loses its ground in anything outside the individual's imagination, it loses the authority to discipline the soul and set boundaries for conduct. Some see this development as progress and even try to make a religion out of choice or, to use a popular formulation for the radicalization of choice, to engage in self-creation. This sanctification of individual will comes close to the temptation of idolatry that traditional religion warns against.

Modern science serves freedom by greatly expanding human powers. It enables us to draw energy from natural resources, produce and distribute vast amounts and a great variety of material goods, communicate at long distances, travel quickly and in comfort, cure disease and prevent illness, and in innumerable ways improve the quality of daily life. It is also an exhilarating exercise of man's rational faculty, in which progress depends on the determination to push the outside of the envelope and to constantly advance the limits of knowledge.

But freedom amplifies the core elements of the scientific sensibility: the determination to surpass limits and to achieve mastery over nature. This amplification puts science on a collision course with ethics, which is based on an appreciation of limits. Science teaches that no limit deserves respect, save perhaps the safety of individual scientists and their human subjects. But because science cannot explain in its own terms why even those limits are worth respecting—the natural freedom and equality of all cannot be verified experimentally—it slowly erodes respect for the individual. Scientists may want to produce results that benefit humanity, but the goal of benefiting humanity draws no support from the scientific point of view. Indeed, science's assumption that the world is strictly explicable by cause-and-effect relations tends to obscure the uniqueness of human beings and to reduce us to objects for study and manipulation.

Energized by freedom, science encourages individuals both to think of themselves as sovereign over all of nature and, at the same time, to consider themselves subject to nature's unvarying laws, as are all other objects in the universe. But a free man is neither master nor slave.

The paradox of freedom at work in the realms of education, work, romantic love, family, faith, science, and elsewhere is not set in motion by some perversity or pathology that sneaks up behind and seizes upon the liberal spirit. Rather, it springs from the inherent instability of liberalism's fundamental moral premise. The naturally free and equal individual is sovereign, because his freedom signifies that he is his own highest authority. At the same time, the naturally free and equal individual is a subject, because his sovereignty rests on a premise that commands the recognition of the equal sovereignty of all others. Hence, a free society is composed entirely of sovereign individuals and entirely of subject individuals because each is always both. As a consequence, the liberal spirit is simultaneously radically aristocratic and radically egalitarian. This multiplicity can be extraordinarily fruitful, preparing the liberal spirit, for example, to appreciate the world's many-sidedness. It can also be a recipe for disaster, inclining the liberal spirit to divide sharply against itself.

Ours is the era of equality in freedom. Our freedom encourages us to cast aside arbitrary authority and topple unjust hierarchy, but it also undermines the just claims of political order and moral excellence. It allows for the severance of onerous bonds of association, but it also separates and isolates. It is the touchstone of our equality, yet it permits and indeed encourages competition, fair and unfair alike, which results in vast disparities in wealth, power, and glory. It gives us opportunities to develop our gifts, makes us responsible for ourselves, and infuses us with a sense of humanity and rights that we share with all people, while loosening the claims of honor, virtue, and duty. It encourages us to search for love while impairing our capacity to sustain it. And it eloquently exalts choice and then falls silent about the actions and ends that are choice worthy, opening the disconcerting possibility that choice is all.

The promise and the dangers of our era are indissolubly connected. The more freedom we have, the more we want. And the more we get, the greater the potential for weakening freedom's foundations in moral and political life. However, the circumstances that unleash freedom's self-subverting tendencies also create opportunities for the exercise of the liberal spirit's self-correcting powers, which primarily consist of the free mind's ability to understand its interests and devise measures to secure them.

When the free mind turns its attention to our present predicament, it is likely to conclude that the liberal spirit's best interest is to conserve something of its origins. Thus, we must reacquaint ourselves with the liberal tradition's teachings about freedom's foundation in our nature and freedom's material and moral preconditions. In returning to the roots of liberal tradition, we may well discover that we must go beyond the liberal tradition. In other words, we may find that to be bound to one tradition is contrary to the liberal spirit's own imperatives and realize that the liberal tradition, much as we owe it, cannot offer the last word on who we are and what we can and should become. Returning to the liberal tradition's roots and reaching beyond its horizons will enable us to think more comprehensively about the purpose of freedom and to formulate laws and policies that can sustain it.

Improving by conserving the liberal spirit is easier said than done. But the doing first requires the saying, and to say something useful, we must understand the challenge.

2

The Contemporary Critique of the Enlightenment: Its Irrelevance to America and Liberalism

JOHN PATRICK DIGGINS

Who would have thought that today, in the first years of the twenty-first century, America would still be ravaged by intellectual wars that were supposed to have been resolved in the eighteenth century? During the Enlightenment, the French *philosophes* assumed that reason had triumphed over faith, and in Philadelphia in 1787, the framers of the Constitution were so confident about "the new science of politics" that they saw no need to invoke God in the document. The antagonism between the advent of science and older institutions of religion seemed to have been settled by allowing each to go its own way. Science would attend to the natural world of empirical fact, the realm of the "is," and religion would deal with the moral world of ethical conduct, the realm of the "ought." Thus, the authors of *The Federalist* wrote the Constitution not to tell the American people what they ought to do; on the contrary, they predicted what Americans would do, and they determined why controls are necessary to regulate human behavior. The future of the young American Republic, Alexander Hamilton emphasized in *The Federalist* No. 1, depended upon "reason and reflection" to construct a "machinery of government" to make up for the imperfections of human nature, which James Madison called "the defect of better virtues." In the beginning of U.S. history, American liberalism, trusting science more than religion, took its stance with skepticism.

The surprising irony of our time is that although European postmodern intellectuals criticize the liberal Enlightenment for being too innocent about human nature, American Christian fundamentalists criticize it for being too pessimistic in leaving religion back with the Middle Ages. Fundamentalists seek not only to bring religion back into public life but to ground their view of the nature of the universe in scriptural explanations of the origins of life. The contemporary argument for "intelligent design" seeks to bring religion back into the Enlightenment by rendering Charles Darwin's theory of evolution compatible with creationism. In past centuries, religious thinkers such as Blaise Pascal questioned the Enlightenment as a philosophical stance, arguing that it failed to answer questions about the meaning of life. Today religious fundamentalists seek to partake of the Enlightenment by treating matters of faith as scientifically valid. But they do so at a time when both the promises of the Enlightenment and the status of science have been discredited. In contemporary academic culture, liberalism has been put on trial, falsely accused of crimes it never committed, and the charges originated in France.

～

The Enlightenment, that glorious eighteenth-century era of philosophy, science, reason, virtue, progress, and the universal rights of man, has fallen on hard times. It seems to be facing a cerebral death in the very "City of Light" that brought it to life.[1] Recent European thought has blamed the Enlightenment for fostering racism, slavery, imperialism, sexism, censorship, political and cultural elitism, the tyranny of consensus, Eurocentrism ("cultural cannibalism"), and even the rise of twentieth-century fascism and communism. The fall of communism has also been blamed on the Enlightenment: introducing the spirit of enterprise two centuries ago, the *philosophes* betrayed their mind and committed "treason."[2] Presumably, a skeptical stance toward the promise of reason and virtue will save us from the political sins of modern history. Contemporary European thinkers who make such claims have no idea how skeptical were the framers of the American Constitution. The only possibility of freedom, we are told by the anti-Enlightenment thinkers, lies at the margins, with those who resisted reason and the rationalization of society. This scenario seems a little strange to those of us who have heard it before. An Emersonian America is familiar with the notion, later articulated by Nietzsche, that the modern mind is submissive when it should be subversive. The spectacle of the cringing "last man," more fearing than daring, is part of American literature as well as part of European philosophy. But did the western Enlightenment really carry the seeds of modern barbarism?

Curiously, in American intellectual history, those who started out as critics of the Enlightenment and of America's political foundings, particularly Charles A. Beard and Carl Becker, eventually concluded that the revolt against reason led to totalitarianism; hence, they found themselves reembracing the Enlightenment and the "generalities that still glitter" to bring the past to bear as America entered World War II. The two eminent historians once criticized the Declaration of Independence and the U.S. Constitution as either intellectually deceptive or politically reactionary. When faced with Hitler and the Third Reich, they embraced America's historical institutions as the world's last best hope for liberty. They assumed, as did many American intellectuals, that the Enlightenment was still alive and well and that the struggle against Nazism was a struggle between a culture devoted to reason and the rule of law and a culture that thought it was witnessing "the decline of the West," to borrow the title of Oswald Spengler's much-misunderstood book.

In the eighteenth century, the West was seen as in ascendancy, and the Enlightenment emerged as the proud vision of the future. Yet the Enlightenment in America had its ironies. If we take a brief glance at that episode in history, the familiar categories of the older progressive scholarship, developed by Vernon L. Parrington, no longer seem to make sense. Author of the three-volume *Main Currents in American Thought*, Parrington juxtaposed the Enlightenment with Calvinism and, as well, posed Jeffersonian agrarianism against Hamiltonian mercantilism, assuming that one side stood for reason, virtue, progress, and freedom, and the other for sin, power, greed, and oppression. But consider this paradox. The very exponents of the Enlightenment who championed democracy and equality, leaders like Thomas Jefferson and Patrick Henry, were also the leaders who defended slavery on the presumption of white superiority. In contrast, the critics of the Enlightenment who remained skeptical of democracy and equality, figures like John Adams and Alexander Hamilton, opposed slavery and, in the instance of officer Hamilton, even advocated arming Afro-American plantation slaves during the Revolution. The conservative Calvinist and the Federalist were the ones who, at the time of framing and defending the Constitution, took a stand that can be called "the counter-Enlightenment," and they continued to scorn slavery and the exploitation of fellow human beings. The progressives, the Jeffersonian Republicans, were the ones who continued to invoke the Enlightenment and who defended the French Revolution even as it entered the years of terror. And while defending the bloody revolution in France and the execution of the king and queen, Jefferson as president saw no problem, no embarrassing inconsistency, in hailing revolution in France while supporting Napoleon's crushing the struggle for black freedom in Haiti and reimposing slavery in 1802. As president prior to Jefferson, Adams befriended the black revolutionary and former slave Toussaint L'Ouverture, had his administration appoint a consul general to Haiti, and planned to open up trade relations. The conservative president sided with a noble insurrection; the liberal, with a military despot.

Southern racial phobias may partially explain this irony. But such curious positions raise a question that has stymied the study of intellectual history. Is there a connection between a person's philosophical outlook and his or her political stance? Do the ideas we hold shape our behavior? One scholar, convinced that conduct follows directly from thought, that action derives from theory, was Hannah Arendt, author of the controversial *The Origins of Totalitarianism*. As is well known, Arendt had been a student of Martin Heidegger, and her first writings show the traces of a Germanic existential angst. But with the publication of *On Revolution*, she began to take a positive interest in the American founders, especially John Adams. Earlier, she had drawn parallels between Hitler's Germany and Stalin's Russia, all the while remembering that what happened in Europe did not happen, or even begin to happen, in the United States. Some academic radicals have criticized her for harboring both the idea of totalitarianism and the idea of American exceptionalism. But Arendt is relevant to a discussion of the Enlightenment not only because she pointed out that America knew how to end a revolution and how to preserve liberty by institutionalizing it in the Constitution. Actually, she was profoundly ambivalent, as was Abraham Lincoln, about the possibility that the "lost treasure" of liberty could survive simply through the mechanistic devices of the division of power, as though the ideals of the Declaration could be fulfilled in the Constitution.

What makes Arendt even more relevant today is that even though she had been a student of Heidegger, she continued to believe in the Enlightenment as well as in classical philosophy, never losing hope in the power of mind and thought to bring about a better world. She was well aware of the obsessions of her fellow German exiles, who believed that the Enlightenment "project" had come to bitter fruit in modern mass society, with its uncontrolled technological advances, trivialization of religion and art, mechanized killing, one-dimensional mentality, and banalization of evil. Nevertheless, Arendt continued to believe that philosophy matters, that ideas have consequences, and that the status of the mind is not simply a fiction, a "metaphysics of presence," to which we can afford to remain indifferent. In *The Human Condition*, even though she lamented the Enlightenment's turning away from her beloved Greek idea of classical citizenship, she brought her knowledge of Aristotle and Augustine to bear upon modern thinkers like Marx and Veblen, who valued labor over politics. Just before she died, Arendt was working on a series of three books, and the titles are revealing: *Thinking, Judging,* and *Willing.* She went to her grave convinced that humanity's cognitive capacities gave meaning and value to behavior. And, she believed, with the atrophy of such capacities comes the horror.

THE ENLIGHTENMENT AND TOTALITARIANISM

The horror of the Holocaust led some scholars to look to Arendt's three questions in interpreting the experience: "What happened? Why did it happen? How could it have happened?" One answer to the last question may lie in the tortured reflections of Primo Levi, the Italian novelist and medical doctor who survived Auschwitz. Levi tried to understand what manner of thinking could have driven his prison examiner. "The man facing Haftling 174517," writes Alain Finkielkraut, referring to Levi's prison number, "executes his task with the force of an intellect, both simple and formidable, indifferent to the reasons why; the examiner cares only about the methodological and operational, responding with equal ease to every question that begins with *how.* How to make him contribute? How to kill him? How to use him? How to get rid of him? Against this absolute functionality, even usefulness does not help. In Doctor Panwitz's [the examiner's] soul, instrumental reason wins out over moral arguments, facts over common sense. This victory is the essence of his madness."[3]

Those who see the Enlightenment culminating in twentieth-century totalitarianism often cite the split between science and philosophy, technique and truth—between the how and the why, the is and the ought. Somehow reason, once looked upon as an exercise in curiosity, awe, and wonder, had become a systematic technique, no longer the vessel of truth but a means of organization, domination, and control. Such are the roots of the idea of "instrumental reason."

That term was bandied about by German Marxist exiles in America, who used it as a weapon with which to criticize democratic America as well as Nazi Germany. Ironically, the Marxists derived the term from Max Weber, who, though worried about the estrangement between ethics and power and between integrity and success, nonetheless admired America and saw Puritanism as an "everlasting heirloom" to modern liberty. Weber even advocated Germany's adopting Anglo-American political institutions during World War I, even though Germany was at war with both England and America. (His wife later destroyed some of these writings so they would not fall into the hands of the Nazis.) Like Lord Acton and British scholars, Weber saw a vital connection between religious conviction and political freedom. In our present era, when all "rights talk" is regarded as rhetorical maneuver without philosophical foundations, we would do well to recall that Weber could value ideas that had served an important historical purpose. "How can anyone possibly save any remnants of the 'individualist' freedom in any sense?" he wrote in *Economy and Society*. "It is a gross self-deception to believe that without the achievements of the Rights of Man any one of us, including the most conservative, can go on living his life."[4] Weber saw that the Enlightenment erred in assuming that reason could replace religion, but he also saw that certain values that evolved from both religion and reason, from the spiritual quest for meaning and the scientific need to see the world on its own terms, remain as a legacy that should not be ridiculed out of existence by the theoreticians of the academy.

If the alleged relationship of the Enlightenment to modern fascism is problematic, its relationship to modern communism is perverse. The familiar story sees Rousseau's idea of the "general will" turning up in Robespierre's dictatorship of virtue, and both conceits supposedly culminating in the Gulag.[5] A little more than a half century ago, at the outbreak of the cold war, New York intellectuals were at a loss to explain where Stalinism came from given that it had no foreshadowing in the writings of Karl Marx (though Bakunin and the anarchists warned of the dangers of bureaucratic collectivism). Years ago, I was absorbed in tracing a lively debate that went on for more than a decade between Sidney Hook and Max Eastman. Why did Marx's hopes for democratic socialism degenerate into Soviet totalitarianism? Hook blamed the phenomenon on Lenin's theory of a party vanguard and the "dictatorship of the proletariat," but Eastman, anticipating our recent "new philosophers" in France, traced the disease to none other than the philosophy of Hegel and the fetish of the dialectic, an idea that Edmund Wilson picked up in the last pages of *To the Finland Station,* in which his faith that the "cunning of reason" was coming to Russia suddenly turns to ashes. In England, Karl Popper wrote *The Open Society and Its Enemies,* tracing totalitarianism to Plato and Hegel. The ravages of Hitler and Stalin put philosophy on trial and called into question some of the easy assumptions of the liberal Enlightenment.

In recent times, even Asian communism has been blamed on western philosophy. Some of the armed teenagers in Cambodia's Khmer Rouge represented "the foot soldiers of Sorbonne ideologues," Robert Kaplan wrote in *The Ends of the Earth.* The journalist had in mind Khieu Samphan and a coterie of Cambodians, born in the 1920s and 1930s, who were exchange students in Paris. Their leader was Saloth Sar, the son of a well-off landowner who later called himself Pol Pot. The Cambodian students were converted to Marxist-Leninism, and Samphan argued in a doctoral dissertation that cities and towns were inhabited by "parasites" who should be moved out and used for forced agricultural labor. The "killing fields" saw the slaughter of a million Cambodians. Particularly suspect were scholars and intellectuals; anyone wearing eyeglasses was shot on sight. Ninety percent of the country's medical doctors were murdered between 1975 and 1979. Babies were bashed to death against trees. All this mayhem was in the name of a political idea first formulated in a doctoral thesis.[6]

To blame the liberal Enlightenment, or even the counter-Enlightenment, for such barbarism leaves the impression that those who passionately believe in freedom can also delight in its degradation. But Marx can no more be blamed for Pol Pot than Nietzsche can be blamed for the SS. Nietzsche was critical of mass phenomena, including the mystique of nationalism and the curse of anti-Semitism. Nazism rested on a psychology of fear and hate in which the German people projected their anxieties onto others and believed that the fatherland and the *fuehrer* were in sole possession of the truth. Nietzsche, like Weber, insisted that emotions such as vanity and racial prejudice needed to be faced and subdued. The same dynamic occurred in Marxism. Karl Marx saw himself as an heir of the Enlightenment, but what would he make of a doctoral dissertation that claimed the future of history lies with the tillers of the soil in the countryside and not with the industrial proletariat in the cities of the world? No doubt Marx would recall his admonition against "the idiocy of rural life." One might legitimately say that Marx and Nietzsche failed to value sufficiently the heritage of liberalism and thus left history vulnerable to the appeals of communism and fascism. But lately the liberal Enlightenment itself is made to stand in judgment for the terrors of the twentieth century. Marx, however, continued to believe in the progressive potential of science and history, and Nietzsche's desire to see the rebirth of tragedy indicated that he still believed in individual human possibility, in striving rather than succumbing. In what do our contemporary postmodernists believe?

It may come as a surprise that the two leading European postmodernists of our era, Michel Foucault and Jacques Derrida, are far from the scourges of the Enlightenment that the public seems to think. Just before his death in 1984, Foucault was finishing his multivolume *History of Sexuality,* and he appreciated philosopher Denis Diderot's struggle with the problems of truth and opinion and flesh and spirit. Although Foucault has been dubbed "the French Nietzschean" for his preoccupation with power, he might be called a "half-way *lumière"* because his theory of oppression, which refused to specify an oppressor, left room for struggle and liberation and hence can be interpreted as in keeping with the eighteenth-century doctrine of the rights of man. As for Derrida, he once ran into the American sociologist Todd Gitlin in Spain and asked him what he was doing there. "I'm here to defend the Enlightenment," replied Gitlin, who was in the country for a conference. "Everyone should defend the Enlightenment," responded the influential French theorist.

The Enlightenment has many sides, and one wonders where Foucault and Derrida wish to stand. Would they uphold the primacy of reason, or would they point to the illusions of reason that the earlier counter-Enlightenment had allegedly exposed (long before some of our contemporary postmodernists did)? Oscar Wilde once observed that one cannot reason anyone out of what they have not reasoned into. Some Enlightenment thinkers and postmodernists might agree with him. Postmodernists make us aware of the limits of reason, but no one was more aware of this debility than John Adams. Adams remained convinced that the young American Republic must avoid relying not only on the Enlightenment but on classical philosophy, Renaissance humanism, and even Christianity itself. Neither virtue, rhetoric, knowledge, nor love can be counted upon to guide the country. When we consider Adams, as we shall, we may appreciate that this old-fogy New Englander has some things in common with today's Parisian deconstructionists.

THE AMERICAN AND FRENCH REVOLUTIONS

The status of the Enlightenment is inextricably tied up with the status of the French Revolution. Conservatives often claim that the Enlightenment fostered the optimistic ideas about human rationality that lost sight of skepticism and led to the terror of the Revolution and Bonapartist despotism. In the eighteenth century, radicals argued that the Enlightenment was insufficiently enlightened and lacked optimism, a view that caused them to draw back from placing all trust in the masses. Conservatives placed faith in past traditions and historical institutions, whereas radicals trusted the future to democracy and the mystique of popular sovereignty.

Ironically, the postmodernists criticize the Enlightenment for precisely the ideas—embracing universal theories and values that would impose a deadening uniformity on the rest of the world—that some French *philosophes* sought to have America adopt. Condorcet, Mably, Turgot, and others criticized the U.S. Constitution for its devices that aimed to control popular democracy, particularly its establishment of an upper-house senate and a strong executive office. Such devices, the French contended, simply continued British political institutions, reflecting British social realities, especially aristocracy and monarchy, that did not exist in America. Why is a young America trying to control old phantoms from the past? "I would like," Mably wrote to John Adams,

> that every ten or twelve years you would celebrate as your most solemn holiday the day when you had declared that you were set free [*affranchi*] from the yoke of England. After having rendered thanks to the sovereign master of the universe for the favors you fully and happily enjoy, that joy should reign in all the countries of the confederation; that it bring all the citizens together in peace and pleasure; that the magistrates and wealthy join the multitude; that such gatherings of Saturnalia demonstrate the great image of equality; that representatives of each republic renew with pomp your alliance between the branches of Congress; that the people learn to love their country and their superiors; that God be invoked to have the people observe religiously the laws, defend the Union and submit their judgment to the rules of justice. Having the knowledge and position, we must impress upon them the most respectable truths of which we have need, and that the multitude does not comprehend.[7]

How could American leaders impress upon their followers ideas with no basis in the real world? In the passage above, Mably is asking Adams to celebrate a consensus, a sense of unity, patriotism, respect for law, religiosity, and social solidarity that the framers could not count upon when constructing the Constitution. Perhaps unknown to the *philosophes,* they themselves were perpetuating the assumption of unity and harmony that had actually been the mystique of monarchy. Today the critique of the Enlightenment by the postmodernists could well apply to past French thinkers, some of whom did indeed assume that all sorts of people and social classes could be subjected to a common political culture and thus required only a single national assembly. Adams and the *Federalist* authors, not the French, rejected the notion of consensus and saw the need to structure political institutions to deal with conflict. One reason the contemporary critique of the Enlightenment is irrelevant to America is that the framers rejected the possibility of unanimity and saw factional rivalry as inevitable. They identified liberty neither with the social solidarity espoused by French thinkers nor with the civic duty espoused by classical thinkers. Instead, they identified liberty with diversity. Many scholars have observed that the framers failed to foresee the emergence of political parties. More pertinent is their recognition of the ineluctability of factions and their resulting view that division and opposition are legitimate. If not multiculturalism, certainly multicontentialism began with the U.S. Constitution. Liberalism has its origins in conflict, not consensus.

To the American framers, the problems that the Enlightenment, or at least some of its proponents, promised to resolve—power, conflict, the vicissitudes of opinion, and the debilitating *incivisme* of egoistic materialism—were permanent aspects of the human condition that could not be eliminated but could possibly be limited by a well-devised machinery of government. This government would have no clear source of sovereignty and no indisputable, incontestable, irresistible center of power. In proceeding toward the careful division of power, Americans proved to be better Montesquieuians than the French themselves. In developing their constitutions in the early 1790s, French revolutionary leaders ignored and even ridiculed Montesquieu, believing that he, like John Adams in America, merely sought to perpetuate institutions that belonged to the old order. Cannot Americans understand, wrote Condorcet, that the French had to declare their rights before they possessed them, and hence the older political structures had to make way for new possibilities for the regeneration of a political society? Those who, like Adams and Montesquieu, sought to bring constitutional devices to bear upon the passionate movement of events had to face Robespierre's taunt: You want to end the revolution before you have truly had it.

Although the French believed that they were breaking radically with the past, in one instance they were carrying it forward like an unfelt curse: the concept of sovereignty continued to perplex social thought for centuries to come. Although the idea of sovereignty was originally associated with monarchy and even despotism, French revolutionary thinkers assumed they could democratize it; later, socialists and syndicalists would hold the same view. Jean Jacques Rousseau located sovereignty in the people; Abbey Sieyes, in the nation, which he saw as a mystical force with a will of its own. "A nation cannot decide not to be," he announced, in language that would have confounded the framers, who were trying to bring a nation-state into being so that America would not be what Hamilton called "an awful spectacle."[8] Adams once observed that when he read Rousseau, he felt like "getting down on all fours."[9] No wonder. Rousseau's idea of sovereignty requires a willing suspension of disbelief. Sovereignty, declared Rousseau, could neither be alienated, delegated, nor represented. It could only express itself in the "general will," which also contained the sovereignty of reason. If Hamilton had read Rousseau, he would have seen the philosopher's idea of sovereignty as a prescription for tyranny fueled by paranoia. "There is in the nature of sovereign power," he wrote in *Federalist* No. 15,

> an impatience of control that disposes those who are invested with the exercise of it to look with an evil eye upon all external attempts to restrain or direct its operations. From this spirit it happens that in every political association which is formed upon the principle of uniting in a common interest a number of lesser sovereignties, there will be found a kind of eccentric tendency in the subordinate and inferior orbs by the operation of which there will be a perpetual effort in each to fly off from the common center. This tendency is not difficult to account for. It has its origin in the love for power. Power controlled or abridged is almost always the rival and enemy of that power by which it is controlled or abridged. This simple proposition will teach us how little reason there is to expect that the persons entrusted with the administration of the affairs of the particular members of the confederacy will at all times be read with perfect good humor and an unbiased regard to the public weal to execute the resolutions or decrees of the general authority. The reverse of this results from the constitution of man.

Hamilton saw that sovereignty and freedom are incompatible. The exercise of absolute sovereignty in the realm of power breeds its own antagonistic rivalries, and there is "little reason" to expect that rulers will rule wisely and justly. Contemporary critics of the Enlightenment, in contrast, claim that thinkers placed too much trust in reason and looked to philosophy to provide the knowledge that would enable democracy to master power. But Madison's *Federalist* No. 49 suggests just the opposite: that private conscience may be appealed to, but the collective mind remains unresponsive to reason. Why cannot America, protested the antifederalists, the opponents of the Constitution, forget all the mechanisms of the Constitution and simply put its trust in the rational mind and the rule of law? "The reason of man," Madison replied, "like man himself, is timid and cautious when left alone, and acquires firmness and confidence in proportion to the number with which it is associated. When the examples which fortify opinion are *ancient* as well as *numerous*, they are known to have a double effect. In a nation of philosophers, this consideration ought to be disregarded. A reverence for the laws would be sufficiently inculcated by the voice of an enlightened reason. But a nation of philosophers is as little to be expected as the philosophical race of kings wished for by Plato."

As we move beyond the eighteenth-century Enlightenment and into the nineteenth century, "the voice of enlightened reason," which the *Federalist* authors left strangled in skepticism, proudly reappears in the writings of Karl Marx. Both the premises and the promises of the Enlightenment continue in Marx, not only in his belief in science and technology but in his view of the progressive development of history and the upward movement of human consciousness. When the stages of history are working themselves out and history is moving toward socialist revolution, said Marx, philosophy will be "the head" of that movement and labor will be its "body." Sovereignty now moves from the people in general to the proletariat in particular, whose mission is to "negate" all the alienating forces that have historically oppressed humanity.

It is no secret that many of our European postmodernists were brought up on Marxism, but their faith in human possibility was not what appealed to American students and academics; it was their profound doubts about hopeful change and progress. Several of the European postmodernist (or poststructuralist) thinkers were writing as early as the 1920s and 1930s, but only in the 1970s and 1980s did their thoughts catch fire in America. The postmodernists appealed to the post-Vietnam generation of Americans because they appeared as the authorities of failure, sages and gurus who claimed to know why the predicted events failed to happen, why the working class cannot be expected to make a revolution, and why students need to come to terms with a society supposedly dead from the neck up. If Marxism saw the proletariat as potentially victorious, postmodernism saw radical students and academics as potentially helpless and endowed them with the consolation of victimhood. What presuppositions of postmodernism stem from the Enlightenment, and how relevant are these ways of thinking to the American Enlightenment?

"CRITICAL THEORY" AND THE ENLIGHTENMENT

Contemporary postmodernists are not the first to take on the Enlightenment. Before our time, there had been, even in America, criticisms of the eighteenth-century Age of Reason. The New England transcendentalists criticized the Constitution for its mechanistic foundations that left little role for intellectual leadership, and they found John Locke's philosophy inadequate because of his emphasis on property and his dictum that things could enter the mind only by way of the senses. A later generation of thinkers upheld the philosophy of pragmatism while looking skeptically upon the Enlightenment; they saw the theory of the social contract and of natural rights as fictions and believed that historic liberalism left America with an atomistic individualism that had no place in John Dewey's "beloved community." But the transcendentalists and pragmatists were only mildly concerned about history and its intellectual legacy in the eighteenth century.

The real assault on the Enlightenment came with the arrival of German-refugee intellectuals to America in the 1930s. Associated with the Frankfurt Institute for Social Research, this group of scholars first settled in at Columbia University before heading to Brandeis and the University of California. Representing several disciplines, they established a school of thought known as "critical theory," which took hold in several academic fields as a new and exciting way of looking at the phenomenon of knowledge and power. Or so it seemed.

The embrace of critical theory is a cautionary exercise that makes us aware of the limits to knowing, the mind's conditions of possibility, and the need for rational faculties to undergo self-interrogation. Although some critical theorists became interested in mass society and popular culture in America, their early publications dealt with philosophy and intellectual history. Two documents pertinent to this discussion are Max Horkheimer's essay "The End of Reason" and Horkheimer and T. W. Adorno's *Dialectic of Enlightenment*, both of which appeared near the outbreak of World War II.

The German authors held that reason, the foundational concept of the Enlightenment, must be scrutinized to determine its real purpose. At one time implying *theoria*, or inquiry, the looking into things in the spirit of curiosity, awe, and wonder, reason underwent a transformation with the Enlightenment and turned from theory to practice as philosophy allowed itself to be shaped by the principles of science. Empirical science attempts to know the world by experimenting upon it and transforming it. In concert with science, reason becomes rationalization, a means of organizing the world to better control it; and the human subject, unconscious of its alienation from the phenomenon of power, is no longer answerable to reason. Horkheimer confronts us with the "pragmatic significance" of reason's fate in the modern world. Reason, he insists, has become functional, instrumental, efficient,

> and in this sense is as indispensable in the modern technique of war as it has always been in the conduct of business. Its features can be summarized as the optimum adaptation of means to ends, thinking as an energy-conserving operation. It is a pragmatic instrument oriented to expediency, cold and sober. The belief in cleverness rests on motives much more cogent than metaphysical propositions. When even the dictators of today appeal to reason, they mean that they possess the most tanks. They were rational enough to build them; others should be rational enough to yield to them. Within the range of Fascism, to defy such reason is the cardinal crime.[10]

This passage contains some strange reasoning about reason. For the American pragmatists, philosophy liberated the Enlightenment from its "metaphysical propositions," from its Cartesian deductions and otiose (to use Dewey's favorite term of denigration) fixations. Pragmatism emerged in American history as progressive and hopeful. But the critical theorists regarded it as a philosophy not of democracy but of domination, "cold and sober." Yet a further dimension to critical theory has occupied some French deconstructionists. We might call this aspect the knowledge-power conundrum; it runs through the pages of *The Federalist* as well as the halls of the Sorbonne.

The Enlightenment has been criticized not only for instrumentalizing knowledge but for holding out the promise that knowledge itself is capable of comprehending and controlling power. The *philosophes* assumed, we are told by the postmodernists, that to be authentic, knowledge must be validated under conditions of noncoercion and open, unconstrained inquiry and verification. By definition, then, the advent of knowledge is the opposite of power and can thus challenge it. But such assumptions are illusory, according to the postmodernists, because instrumental reason is itself power and it exercises sway in feats of organization, persuasion, manipulation. Does this conundrum subvert the premises of the American Enlightenment? Can the value of liberal theory survive the assault of critical theory?

To read the *Federalist* authors and the writings of John Adams is to become aware that knowledge makes no such claims about mastering power. Knowledge is rarely granted the status of objectivity or uncoerced validity. On the contrary, it is always compromised, indeed "corrupted," by the "interests and passions" that govern it; thus, citizens may be unable to arrive at a sense of the public good by means of rational deliberation. The framers of the Constitution hardly endowed people with the capacity of prudential reason and fair-minded deliberation. The same applies to the people's representatives, who could seldom be counted upon to rise above their factional loyalties. On legislative controversies, the framers expected that those who deliberated would be agents of their own cause and thus could deliver at best partial and biased judgments. As Madison wrote in *Federalist* No. 49: "The *passions,* therefore, not the *reason,* of the public would sit in judgment. But it is the reason alone, of the public, that ought to control and regulate the government. The passions ought to be controlled and regulated by the government." In seeing the people moved by passion and hoping that the government could be guided by reason, Madison knew he was walking a theoretical tightrope. Thus, in *Federalist* No. 51, he stated the dilemma candidly: "In framing a government which is to be administered by men over men, the great difficulty lies in this: you must first enable the government to control the governed, and in the next place oblige it to control itself. A dependence upon the people is, no doubt, the primary control on the government; but experience has taught mankind the necessity of auxiliary precautions."

A postmodernist could readily jump on this passage to accuse the framers of naïveté in thinking that whereas people may be irrational and passionate, government and its structures could be guided by reason. Granted, *The Federalist* sees something close to a Newtonian design, which may rest on the science of balanced forces and equilibrium. Hamilton writes of "symmetry" and "orbits," and Adams, in his three-volume *A Defence of the Constitutions of the Government of the United States of America,* assumed that political power followed a geometric pattern of triangularity and that America would be composed of three distinct social strata (aristocracy, democracy, monarchy) that would need to be balanced through countervailing institutions. Nonetheless, such "auxiliary precautions" are necessary because reason cannot fulfill the role that the European Enlightenment assigned it: taking the place of religious faith—and thereby promising a new human nature freed from the stain of sin and capable of goodness and virtue. On the contrary, the authors of *The Federalist* had to operate with "the defect of better motives," in Madison's words, the premise that, on the whole, political man is driven by irrational emotions and desires and thus is unresponsive to reason. Nowhere in *The Federalist* or in the writings of Adams is the suggestion that the presence of knowledge itself will be sufficient to control power. The element that renders power manageable is the balance of forces that enables one class or faction to resist the encroachments of another class or faction. Power, in short, is to be controlled not by knowledge but by the counterpoised mechanisms of power itself. "Take but degree away," Adams loved to quote Shakespeare, "untune that string / And hark! What discords follows! Each thing meets / In mere oppugnancy . . . Then everything includes itself in power."[11]

When one reads the poststructuralists of our time, one discovers several respects in which America's founding political philosophers anticipated poststructuralist ideas and theories. The claim that all knowledge is power, and that it expresses itself not so much through the free, self-determining activity of the rational mind as through the presence of controlling institutions is an idea not exactly alien to the founders. To paraphrase Burke, every time a British institution coughed or sneezed, the American colonists sniffed the threat of conspiracy against their liberties. As Bernard Bailyn points out in his seminal *The Ideological Origins of the American Revolution,* fear and suspicion of power gripped the colonies no matter what the intentions of Parliament and the Crown. And when the colonists took to their muskets, they did not have to wait for Nietzsche to tell them that truth resides in power. Nor did John Adams have to wait for Michel Foucault to tell him that knowledge is power. Why, after all, did he try to warn his country that a superior, educated American aristocracy would "swallow up" the lower members of the House if not isolated in the Senate? Foucault, Jacques Derrida, Jean Baudrillard, Jean Francois Lyotard, and other postmodernist theorists have been hailed as "the masters of suspicion" because of their various insights into the deceptions inherent in ready claims of knowledge and their ability to perceive the silent operations of power. But long before our cultural heroes of Paris, the *Federalist* authors warned America to beware of "ingenious disquisition" and the claims of anyone denying "love for power." In their writings, they elevate suspicion to the pitch of perception.

DECONSTRUCTING MACHIAVELLI

Perhaps we can attribute the framers' skepticism about the heady claims of the Enlightenment to their reading of David Hume, with his liberal skepticism that reason could be anything other than a slave to passion, and to the lingering pessimism of Calvinism. At times, Jefferson's writings on democracy and human nature take on a chirpy optimism that is more platitudinous than profound. But there remained in the writings of Hamilton, Madison, and Adams a kind of tragic wisdom in dealing with a humankind incapable of transcendence yet willing to aspire to progress. What might they have made of the contemporary poststructuralist critique of the Enlightenment?

The first charge of the poststructuralists is that the Enlightenment considered itself "logocentric," assuming that pure, transparent reason operates in human faculties and that the human self is the reference point of reason. Instead, they believe, we should see that because we have no access to unmediated knowing, we cannot know the truth. We should thus face our predicament and cease our desperate pursuit of something we cannot attain. For centuries, the human subject has remained under the illusion that finding truth is an act of uncovering or recovering, because the rationalist mind presupposes the presence of what it is looking for (Heidegger) and treats as objective discovery what is actually an imposed interpretation (Nietzsche). Yet the things we believe are not found but made, invented rather than uncovered, a matter of persuasion rather than proof. And the beliefs exercised and imposed reflect not the search for truth but the will to power, with words like *liberty* and *freedom* concealing the domineering motives behind them. After such knowledge, philosophy should recognize its antiessentialist and antifoundational predicament, for there is no essence behind any existing phenomena, and no basis, antecedent reality, or prior existence on which knowledge could be said to rest.

Finally, the poststructuralists describe "the linguistic turn" in modern thought, the conviction that all human cognition is inescapably verbal, with no reference to a reality beyond the text. Words signify not nothing but almost everything and anything. In this view, older philosophers and literary critics assumed they were looking for truth when they were only writing words about words, manipulating metaphors, alternating verbal images. Rhetoric, Stanley Fish argues, masks its own rhetorical nature; knowledge turns not on what is said or written but on how it is presented as an act of persuasion. Deconstruction aims to reveal these hidden assumptions, showing us the ways in which a proposition or statement comes to be regarded as true—not because it corresponds to the object it names but rather because its utterance adheres to convention, to the norms that govern writing.

Is there anything in poststructuralism that would cause the framers and defenders of the U.S. Constitution to reconsider their premises? They were essentialists and foundationalists to the extent that their belief in natural rights had its basis in "Nature's Law and Nature's God," to use the expression of Jefferson, who also believed he was propounding "self evident" truths in the Declaration. But God is not mentioned in the Constitution, and Adams dismissed Tom Paine's appeal to nature as the "idiocy" of the ideologue.[12] Indeed, in *The Federalist,* all debates about the design of the new republic are lacking in self-evident properties. Its authors said they wrote with "trembling anxiety" because they were forced to acknowledge how rarely "a political truth could be brought to the test of mathematical demonstration."[13]

Some American thinkers made the linguistic turn more than two centuries ago. In his voluminous *Defence of the Constitutions,* Adams brings to light the covert assumptions of Machiavelli's *History of Florence,* demonstrating that the text contradicts itself despite its author's intentions. "One is astonished at the reflection of Machiavel, 'such was the spirit of patriotism among them in those days, that they cheerfully gave up their private interest for the public good,' when every page of his shows, that the public good was sacrificed everyday, by all parties, to private interests, friendships, and enmities." Adams sought to expose the rhetorical devices and linguistic maneuvers that concealed the reality that Machiavelli refused to admit in pandering to the Florentines: that power eluded his grasp because his "pious exhortations" about civic virtue excluded the darker truths of Christianity. Adams, in short, deconstructs Machiavelli by showing how he represses "what he very well knew were the effects" of a human nature subjected to original sin.[14]

Perhaps Adams saw Machiavelli not as Leo Strauss did, as the "teacher of evil," but as Reinhold Niebuhr might have read him, as the philosopher who pretends to deny evil in the people so that he can make them feel good enough about themselves to rise to civic pride. How to read Machiavelli is, of course, a matter of endless interpretation in the history of political philosophy. In Adams's view, the Florentine and his heirs were trying to sustain an unworkable classical politics. Isaiah Berlin, however, saw in Machiavelli a harbinger of modernism for whom the future of liberalism depended upon skepticism, tolerance, and pluralism.[15]

Like Adams, *The Federalist* authors were also aware of the deceits of rhetoric and the vagaries of language. We cannot, Madison advised in No. 37, rely completely on linguistic expression to get at the truths of politics or religion, for three impeding distortions can occur: "indistinctness of the object, imperfection of the organ of conception, inadequateness of the vehicle of ideas." Written and spoken language is scarcely transparent, wrote Madison in his Humean mode. "When the Almighty himself condescends to address mankind in their own language, his meaning, luminous as it must be, is rendered dim and doubtful by the cloudy medium through which it is communicated."

Some critics of the Enlightenment presume to know history better than history knew itself. Denying full conceptual consciousness to the *philosophes,* they want us to realize that reason cannot recognize its own servitude. This corrosive perspective characterizes not only the Marxist text *Dialectic of Enlightenment* but also the graceful essay *The Heavenly City of the Eighteenth Century Philosophers,* written in the 1920s by the American liberal historian Carl Becker. But the two works have a telling difference.

The Germans depict the Enlightenment as bent on the technological conquest of nature, which brings about the "disenchantment of the world"; reason becomes objectified and is turned into an instrument of control. The American characterizes the Enlightenment not as sinister but as innocent, naively denying sin and human depravity and looking to reason and virtue. In Becker's analysis, the Enlightenment saw itself as escaping the Middle Ages when, in fact, it merely perpetuated the emotions of the era, substituting reason for faith and the authority of nature for the authority of scripture. Whereas Adorno and Horkheimer saw the Enlightenment as a chilling dehumanization of the world, Becker saw it as a fervent reenchantment that subliminated reason to enable the modern mind to face the existential issues of life that once had been left to the church. Recent research on the French Revolution indeed shows the people and their leaders sacralizing a cult of reason in ceremonies and festivities that served as baptismal rites in the regeneration of society.[16] Becker would hardly be surprised to see that the events in France did not repeat in America, and Adorno and Horkheimer would probably regard the turmoil in the streets of Paris as animism run amuck, the masses in the grip of supernatural spirits, the curse of "false consciousness." But the views of the brooding German thinkers and that of the whimsical American represent different takes on the same phenomenon. One perspective saw the essence of the Enlightenment in domination; the other saw it in delusion.

It is easy, perhaps too easy, to show the *philosophes* assuming that they had solved problems whose intricacies and mysteries had eluded them. The more striking view is to look at the problems they addressed and honestly left unresolved, issues so confounding that we are still trying to deal with them today in fields like psychology, sociology, political theory, and intellectual history. Approaching the two realms of thought in this spirit of humility, we may see more continuity than rupture. The Enlightenment and postmodernism share a problem that its thinkers faced but could hardly solve: the problem of desire, some elusive object that can never be attained. This riddle has perplexed thinkers from John Locke to Jacques Lacan.

THE OBSCURE OBJECT OF DESIRE

Thomas Jefferson's well-known letter to Maria Cosway, which came to be titled "The Head and the Heart," is only one of many documents that call into question the charge that the Enlightenment suffered from logocentrism—the assumption that reason is a self-determining faculty capable of grasping its object and, in knowing others as well as itself, it knows what it wants. Jefferson's poignant twelve-page letter shows he is in agony about not knowing what he wants; he is caught between reason and emotion, with his mind's self-control about to give way to the overpowering passion of romantic love. It remains unclear whether Jefferson had anything other than a platonic affair in Paris with the married Mrs. Cosway, an accomplished artist born in Italy and raised in England. But he was madly in love with her, and one wonders how he would take to our contemporary postmodernists' telling him that the self is problematic because a lover cannot regard himself as the source of his own desires.

The easy morality of French women posed a problem not only for Jefferson but for Adams and other Americans in Paris, though not for the swinging Ben Franklin or the libertine governor Robert Morris, who shared a mistress with Talleyrand. Prostitutes in the streets, courtesans in the salons, trysts in the carriages—what was a Calvinist to do! Adams's daughter was told by a French lady that mothers sent their young girls to a convent to be raised far removed from the influence of *mauvaise femmes*. But not only women had questionable morals. The daughter remembers how "very much disgusted at the match" her father was, finding himself sitting next to an eighty-year-old ambassador married to a sixteen-year-old.[17]

Adams and Jefferson were convinced that a successful revolution in France was unlikely not only because of the inherited vices of the ancient

regime but also because of the lax *moeurs* of the female sex. A half century later, in *Democracy in America,* Tocqueville tended to reaffirm this
view when he insisted that America's political success was due not to its
institutions but to people's shared values and to women's propriety, both
before and after marriage. Tocqueville may have been a little optimistic
about the happy state of women in America, but earlier some American
leaders listened closely to what women had to say. Adams's relation to
his wife, Abigail, documented in David McCullough's best-selling *John
Adams,* is a remarkable romance that age could not wither. Adams was
also in contact with politically active women such as Mercy Otis Warren, and he responded in the margins of Mary Wollstonecraft's *French
Revolution* with a compendium of observations on her views of the
event:

M.W.: It is difficult to determine which was the most reprehensible, the
folly of the Assembly, or the duplicity of the King.

A.: The duplicity of the Assembly was greater than that of the King.

M.W.: The occasions of remarking that the Frenchmen are the vainest
men living often occur . . .

A.: Whether the French are the vainest men or not, English melan-
choly pride would behave as ill or worse in a revolution.

M.W.: As the world is growing wiser, it must become happier . . .

A.: This is the burthen of her song. If the world grows wiser, it will
grow more sensible of the emulations of the human heart and
provide checks to it.

M.W.: The improvement of the understanding will prevent those baneful
excesses of passion which poisons the heart.

A.: The understanding will only make rivalries more subtle and scientific, but the passions will never be prevented, they can only be
balanced.[18]

The many references to pride, vanity, and the passions of the heart
suggest the limits to reason as a faculty of reflection and control. The literature of the Enlightenment, European as well as American, is thick
with texts that sought to prove that desires reside in the heart not the
head and that the sources of the self lie not in reason but in sensations
and emotions. Voltaire wondered how unhappiness could overcome him,
rendering the rational mind helpless to improve his mental state.
Franklin had the opposite problem, the temptations of delight. During
the day, Franklin noted, he could dedicate himself to civic responsibility; at night, duty gave way to desire and virtue gave way to wine,
women, and song.

The view that Enlightenment thinkers saw reason as a means of control and even domination is unconvincing when we appreciate the extent to which they were troubled by the opposite, by a human condition that could barely deal with self-control, a rational mind that proved incapable of taming the emotions, and the drives of desire with no voice to guide action toward the desirable. Enlightenment thinkers, in short, had to deal with an issue that classical philosophy assumed it had successfully addressed. Aristotle believed that we could know ourselves by understanding our actions and giving reasons for them. One need not be concerned with what one has, Socrates advised, only with what one is. Desires can be either disciplined or fulfilled, for we can know the good as that which is proper to "our essence." Many Enlightenment thinkers could no longer partake of such essentialist thinking. With the Scottish Enlightenment's emphasis on property, a person's possessions define what one is. Some thinkers even doubted the classical imperative to "know thyself" because they believed the self had been conditioned by sources beyond itself. Young Ben Franklin, certain that he had inherited no innate self, simply invented one and reinvented it for each occasion and, in doing so, gave Americans advice on how to get ahead.

The contemporary critique of the Enlightenment mistakenly claims that the philosophy of the time had turned into technique: thinkers became interested only in the how and not in the why. To the contrary, the Enlightenment recognized that with the waning of authority, the learned thinkers would have the responsibility of explaining why we do what we do and what we should do when we don't know what we should do. Eighteenth-century thinkers, as well as some who came before, became absorbed in the question of motivation, "the springs of action." John Locke, for example, went back and forth between the idea of natural law, which obliges us to think and act from moral reasons, and the idea of natural right, which allows us to think and act primarily in our self-interest. But the deeper drive that moves one to act and labor is neither a law nor a right; it is "the uneasiness of desire," which implies the absence of satisfaction, a want or need asking to be fulfilled. In this respect, Locke was a hedonist (an apt label for one whose ideas would shape America's political culture). One is moved to act by the prospect of pleasure and the avoidance of pain, and by the hope of reward and the fear of punishment. But Locke found himself in debates with fellow philosophers, as our contemporary Lockean scholars have pointed out.[19] At stake was the idea of freedom. For if action is motivated by uneasiness, "a disquiet of body and pain of mind," then action must proceed from a person's need to relieve some discomfort. If so, is the will determined by what it consciously wants or by an unconscious source from which it is trying to flee? Human action can scarcely be regarded as voluntary when behavior is running away from that which moves it. Nor can it be regarded as rational. Desire itself cannot explain a person's actions unless it has an object, something that the individual pursues consciously and purposefully.

That the mind may be shaped by forces beyond itself suggests that a Lockean philosopher would be at home with contemporary schools of thought. But when today's postmodernists tell us that the mind must be seen as a "social formation," is not this thesis, so trendy in our present academic "discourse," remarkably similar to the outlook of some eighteenth-century thinkers? Consider John Adams's *Discourses on Davila* and Denis Diderot's *Le Neveu de Rameau (Rameau's Nephew)*.

Although one text is an essay in history and political philosophy and the other is a work of prose fiction, both deliver the same message: the human self is a social phenomenon developed out of the need for recognition by others. To be neglected, overlooked, and disregarded is intolerable. The deepest drive of humankind is to be looked at and, above all, to be looked up to. This impulse toward emulative approbation forges "the constitution of the mind," Adams observed, and it variously expresses itself in the individual's "desire to be seen, heard, talked of, approved, respected," in the "passion for distinction," and in the gratification of "this universal affection for the esteem, the sympathy, admiration and congratulation of the public." Where Adams saw human nature craving recognition, Diderot depicted the self in a continual exercise of cynical manipulation, posturing, and role-playing to achieve the same results. As Hegel noted when he read *Rameau's Nephew*, here we have the first modern expression of alienation. The self is estranged and at the mercy of forces exterior to itself; it acts and is acted upon, all the time posing and pantomiming; it is *colpoteur*, selling and hawking, inventing and recasting its image, shadow upon shadow. In a departure from the French Cartesian tradition, Diderot implies that the mind is not a self-contained faculty capable of discovering truth by analyzing and defining. Instead, it is a masked performance and society is its stage, which the audience must build.[20]

Adams and Diderot might well be welcomed not only by today's postmodernists but also by the new historicists, who also study history to portray how human agents shape their lives and identities in a given social context. But the idea that thought and action consist of nothing other than the demand for recognition remains disturbing. Does this need suggest that we seek others' approval because we cannot approve of ourselves? As Santayana wrote in *The Life of Reason,*

> What others think of us would be of little moment did it not, when known, so deeply tinge what we think of ourselves. Nothing could better prove the mythical character of self-consciousness than this extreme sensitiveness to alien opinion; for if a man really knew himself he would utterly despise the ignorant notions others might form on a subject in which he had such matchless opportunities for observation. Indeed, those opinions would hardly seem to him directed upon the reality at all, and he would laugh at them as he might at the stock fortune-telling of some itinerant gypsy.[21]

Taking Santayana's advice, which applies to private life, would be fatal in politics. The *Federalist* authors emphasized that politics turns on opinion and impression, as did Machiavelli when he taught us that politics is not about what we know but about what we see. The American founders also believed that reputation is everything and that great leaders aspire to fame and glory, with Hamilton claiming that "fame" and "honor" are the ruling passions of better minds. Although they recognized that America would never have an aristocracy such as the European class of inherited status and privilege, they did hope that America might be guided by noble ideas. But—and this is a big but—they did not count on this outcome. Madison predicted in *The Federalist* that "enlightened statesmen will not always be at the helm"; Adams, who insisted that "avarice is a meaner passion than ambition," warned that wealth could very well come to dominate politics; and Hamilton, who looked to the "rich, well-born, and able" for leadership, worried that democracy would become the theater of the demagogue who runs after government by running against it. Here, our conservative framers presaged the radical postmodern sensibility of our time.

Are the postmodernists closer to the truth in advising us that there is no truth because the world turns on appearances and, equally disturbing, that there is no reality because life is lived in response to rhetorical strategies and persuasions? Philosophy and its quest for truth and wisdom came to an end at 1600 Pennsylvania Avenue long before it suffered an analytic death at the Sorbonne. Hannah Arendt once envisioned political life as the last opportunity to revive interest in classical philosophy as well as civic virtue, and she lamented a modern America mired in consumption and mindless sensation. But few eighteenth-century Americans looked upon the "din of politicks" as elevating, and in many respects, Adams and Diderot anticipated the shape of modern politics: a performance based on image management, opinion ratings, campaign financing, spin, and whatever other actions are necessary to, in Adams's words, "flatter the passions of the people." The thing that killed truth was not philosophy and its demands for rigor but politics and its lust for success. Niccolo Machiavelli's legacy needs to be updated with the advice of Vince Lombardi: in politics, as in football, winning isn't everything; it's the only thing.

3

Liberalism and the Conservative Imagination

JENNIFER BURNS

Over half a century ago, liberals and conservatives skirmished on the pages of the nation's leading opinion magazines about the definition of the word *conservative*. More than mere semantics, the argument centered on what it meant to be conservative and who would determine the parameters of conservative identity. Now, revisiting that mid-twentieth-century debate promises to illuminate what it means to be liberal, for the conflict highlights core liberal values in the storied time of liberal dominance. In the 1950s, liberals welcomed conservative social values but frowned on the accompanying economic ideas. In place of the conservative emphasis on laissez-faire and business, they defended the ability of government action to ameliorate social problems and advanced a reasoned yet passionate conception of the common weal.

Since then, liberal reaction to conservatism has almost entirely reversed itself. Liberals now share some of conservatives' suspicion of the federal government. Many gladly embrace the "neoliberal" economic agenda of free trade, low taxes, and low regulation they found so troubling at midcentury. And they have become extremely reluctant to credit conservatives with wisdom or salience in the realm of cultural or religious values. Naturally, much has shifted in the United States during the past fifty-odd years, with the intervening years giving rise to a host of moral concerns that were unimaginable before the 1960s. Still, it is worth revisiting the time when both liberals and conservatives articulated a robust set of nonmarket values. Conservatives, through their embrace of the free market, have weakened their hold on these ideals. Liberals, for a variety of reasons, have also let these values lapse into disuse. The time is ripe for liberals to rediscover and restate the beliefs and priorities that animated their first vigorous critique of conservatism. In so doing, they may be able to converse more easily with Americans who both sympathize with the conservative claim to uphold the nation's most cherished values and are receptive to liberal economic policies.

When self-conscious, articulate, and ambitious "new conservatives" first appeared in the postwar years, liberals greeted them as valuable contributors to political and social debate. Reviewing Peter Viereck's *Conservatism Revisited* (1949), the book that inaugurated a vogue for conservatism, Dwight Macdonald told readers of the *New Republic* that the work was "useful and clever" and wrote, "the defect of Viereck's book, curiously enough, is that it is not deeply conservative enough."[1] Similarly, Arthur Schlesinger Jr. praised Viereck's work in the *New York Times Book Review* as "a brilliant political essay."[2] Other titles of the New Conservative movement, such as Clinton Rossiter's *Conservatism in America* (1955) and Russell Kirk's *The Conservative Mind* (1953), also received a warm reception from liberal reviewers.[3] A flood of articles appeared in liberal opinion magazines appraising and evaluating the New Conservatism. Although writers not infrequently criticized aspects of the "conservative revival," the overall reception was respectful and even welcoming.

Much of this endorsement was instrumental. Liberals had worried for years about their one-sided dominance of political discourse. In the introduction to *The Liberal Imagination* (1950), now remembered primarily for its gibe at conservative ideas, Lionel Trilling actually bemoaned the absence of conservative voices in America. He wrote, "It is not conducive to the real strength of liberalism that it should occupy the intellectual field alone."[4] Trilling cited John Stuart Mill's engagement with Samuel Taylor Coleridge as a model that liberals should follow. Wrestling with the ideas of an opponent would only strengthen liberal thought, Trilling argued. Similar intentions were telegraphed by the title of a 1950 *New York Times* article by Schlesinger, "The Need for an Intelligent Opposition."[5]

This pragmatic endorsement aside, midcentury liberals also evinced genuine appreciation for conservative thought. After the wars, revolutions, and disillusionments of the previous decades, temperance and prudence emerged as newly important virtues. Macdonald wrote in his review of Viereck, "In an age where technology is as dynamic and destructive as it is today, there is much virtue in one who simply *conserves*, who tries to slow down the machinery a bit."[6] Similarly, Schlesinger defined conservatism as a "grand" British tradition and, reviewing a book about John C. Calhoun for the *Nation* in 1950, wrote, "A time of perplexity creates a need for somber and tragic interpretations of man. Thus we find Burke more satisfying today than Paine, Hamilton or Adams than Jefferson, Calhoun than Webster or Clay."[7] These sentiments were also manifest among rank-and-file liberals less illustrious than Macdonald and Schlesinger. A writer in the *Bulletin of the Association of American University Professors* (AAUP) argued that "the conservative of today is the twentieth-century humanist," and hoped that the new conservative strength could usher in "an era of human dignity in which men could once more live as self-respecting individuals within a meaningful community of ordered values."[8] This receptivity to conservatism's more pessimistic view of mankind came partly from the influence of neo-Orthodox theology. But the New Conservatism also meshed well with a liberal phase of self-criticism and introspection that had arisen in the postwar years, particularly after the midterm electoral defeats of 1946 and the presidential contest of 1952.

Moreover, liberals' position of cultural dominance meant that they could afford to be indulgent toward conservatism, which appeared as little more than a side curio that might spice up intellectual life. As conservatives would bitterly complain in the ensuing years, liberal discourse was marked by an unconscious assumption of enduring superiority. Schlesinger thought a revitalized conservative party would be desirable, and he generously allowed that it "might even win an election now and then."[9] Liberals framed themselves as natural arbitrators of the good and the true, generously welcoming quaint, fuddy-duddy conservatives to the national conversation. That conservatives were not true contenders for intellectual leadership was made clear by the constant characterization of conservatism as a "mood" or "temper" rather than a true political philosophy.[10]

Liberals could appreciate conservatism as an intriguing yet utterly harmless mood because in the early 1950s, conservatism had yet to harden into a clearly defined ideology. During these years, the right was wracked with internecine conflict and could hardly claim to offer a coherent political program until it settled its internal disputes. Not until the early 1960s would Frank Meyer's doctrine of fusion unify traditionalists, libertarians, and anticommunists under one banner. Before this settlement, even the definition of the word *conservative* was up for grabs.[11] Thus, what liberals praised as conservatism was, in reality, only one part of the larger coalition that would come to be known as American conservatism. In fact, liberal affection for traditionalist conservatism, as showcased by the praise of Viereck, Rossiter, and the other New Conservatives, was a conscious effort to elevate traditionalism over the libertarianism and crude anticommunism that also vied for the conservative label.

By the mid-1950s, perceptive liberals had begun to sense a genuine threat in the nascent marriage of libertarianism and traditionalism. Arthur Schlesinger Jr. was the most prescient. As far back as 1950, he had noticed several variants of conservatism in circulation. Schlesinger was deeply suspicious of conservative receptivity to business, and he made the first effort to define "true" conservatism as distinct from the advocates of laissez-faire. He wrote, "Conservatism is not the private property of the National Association of Manufacturers. It is not a device for increasing the short-run security of business. It is rather a profound sense of national continuity, stretching deep into the past and forward into the future, and providing a protective membrane for all the people of society."[12] In Schlesinger's view, conservatism was an organic vision of society that valued reciprocal obligations, emphasized social and national responsibilities, and was entirely compatible with state-run welfare programs. Thus, economic individualists and dedicated opponents of the New Deal could not justly claim the label of conservative.

As different pieces of the future conservative coalition drew closer to one another, liberal criticism increased, and soon the very definition of the word *conservative* became hotly contested. Like Schlesinger, other liberals began to suspect they were being offered a kind of bait-and-switch ploy. Writing in 1953 in the *Western Political Quarterly,* Brandeis professor Gordon Lewis noted the many meanings of conservatism and commented, "The critic of the enterprise may perhaps be pardoned for suspecting that, when all the sound and fury are over, he is really being offered nothing much more than the defense of the present order of a self-satisfied and unimaginative American capitalism."[13] Many liberals, unwilling to let conservatism be so easily redefined, mounted a valiant effort to distinguish true from false conservatism. Status still clung to the word *conservatism,* so making such an effort seemed worthwhile.

Perhaps the best example of this definitional struggle came in Clinton

Rossiter's *Conservatism in America,* which labored to separate false, lowercase "conservatism" from true, uppercase "Conservatism." To Rossiter, Conservatism was an honorable creed descended from Burke that "accepts and defends the institutions and values of the contemporary West." Rossiter styled himself as a Conservative following that definition. And he attacked false American conservatism as unworthy of the name, for this conservatism had committed the "chief intellectual sin" of embracing individualism and "economic Liberalism."[14] Like Schlesinger and other liberals, Rossiter was comfortable with the social and cultural values typically attributed to conservatism but blanched at its economic agenda. By calling himself a Conservative, Rossiter hoped to carve out a political position that blended Burkean social values with American realities.

Rossiter's efforts touched off a virulent reaction among other claimants to the conservative moniker. Reviewing *Conservatism in America,* Gerhard Niemeyer wrote sarcastically, "It is once again fashionable to call oneself a conservative—provided, of course, one does not stray too far from the liberal fold." Niemeyer criticized Rossiter's imprecision in his definitions of conservatism, particularly his failure to understand that American conservatives were primarily concerned with the dangers of the federal bureaucracy. But even he was hesitant about laissez-faire, writing, "The alliance is accidental and should not obscure the profound differences between conservatism and laissez faire economism." Niemeyer himself was a conservative crusader for small government yet also a critic of capitalism—a seemingly impossible position, which existed for a brief moment during the ideological flux of the 1950s. Still, unlike liberals, Niemeyer did not find laissez-faire odious enough to sever his ties to movement conservatism.[15]

For liberals, perhaps the clearest danger signal came in 1955 with William F. Buckley's founding of *National Review,* a magazine that embodied both the emerging conservative fusion and the willingness of conservatives to stake their claim on the traditional terrain of liberals, the opinion magazine. The immediate negative reaction to *National Review* showed how deeply liberals rejected conservative economics, even while welcoming conservatism as a social or political philosophy. This gap was most obvious in the reaction of Dwight Macdonald. Though Macdonald had praised Viereck's traditional conservatism, he had nothing but derision for *National Review*'s blend of libertarianism, religious traditionalism, and anticommunism. He excoriated the magazine as "scrambled eggheads on the right," calling it amateurish, dull, long-winded, and perverse. "Here are the ideas, here is the style of the *lumpen*-bourgeoisie, the half-educated, half-successful provincials . . . who responded to Huey Long, Father Coughlin, and Senator McCarthy," Macdonald scorned. *National Review* was "pseudo-conservative" and advanced a "crude patchwork of special interests." He concluded, "We have long needed a good conservative magazine. . . . This is not it."[16] By embracing free-market economics, traditionalist conservatives had lost the respect and influence once granted them by liberals.[17]

But with *National Review,* one faction of midcentury conservatives gained a powerful new way to assert their understanding of conservatism. In an intemperate 1956 *National Review* column, Yale political scientist Willmoore Kendall went on the offensive against the popular New Conservatives, dismissing them as "Trojan Horses" of liberalism. He criticized Peter Viereck for telling his audience "how to be conservative and yet agree with the Liberals about Everything," while writing that Rossiter "went Viereck one better: he could make you feel ashamed of yourself if you were *not* both conservative and Liberal."[18] Kendall argued vigorously for a conservative position that was clearly distinct from liberalism. This conservatism would combine traditionalism and free-market economics; staunchly independent and proudly oppositional, it would have no need or desire for liberal praise. The battle was joined.

Much as Trilling had anticipated, the slow development of conservatism into an ideology, rather than a mood, forced liberals to articulate their own principles and beliefs. Of course, Trilling's idea sounded better in theory than practice, and there is little evidence that liberals welcomed the new strength of conservatism (rather than "New Conservatism") as salutary for its own sake. They wrote with utter seriousness against a dangerous and wily opponent. But in retrospect, like Trilling, we can be grateful for this moment of conflict, for it resulted in a clear paper trail of midcentury liberal values, principles, and beliefs. The residue of this conflict is somewhat dusty, and necessarily incomplete, but is a valuable resource nonetheless.

The liberal defense against conservatism sounded two main themes worth revisiting today: a belief in the efficacy of human effort to change society for the better and a stirring articulation of nonmarket values. The first theme dominated the early 1950s and responded as much to neo-Orthodox theology as to the New Conservatism. Sensitive to criticism that liberalism succumbed too easily to utopian visions of social planning, liberals defended a middle road that avoided both impractical idealism and complacent inaction. In a printed debate with Russell Kirk,

Schlesinger wrote, "It is preposterous to suppose that we cannot continue to improve the conditions of American life in sectors of weakness—and to argue this is not to argue that man or society is perfectible, only that degrees of happiness and security are important."[19] In a similar vein, Temple University professor Gaylord Leroy admitted the past failings of liberalism but refused to relinquish liberal belief in human efficacy. In the AAUP bulletin, he wrote, "If the liberal was in error in telling us that man had a power he lacked, the conservative is guilty of much the same error when he tells us that man lacks certain powers he unquestionably has." Leroy criticized conservatives for indulging in sentiment and seeking to "escape the challenge to act by telling themselves that action is useless."[20]

The responses of Schlesinger and Leroy limn a moderate position still worth defending. Liberals today could respond to the neoconservative critique of government programs with a similar commitment to the power of human effort. Indeed, the stubborn popularity of Social Security in the face of Republican assault indicates that Americans do appreciate the ability of the government to manage and ameliorate large-scale social problems, such as poverty among the aged. The Social Security debate also indicates that many Americans harbor a corresponding doubt about the reliability of the private sector when it comes to critical areas of social policy. Defending human agency and effort may be easier than many liberals assume. And the necessity of doing so has particular urgency in the current time of environmental crisis.

The more dominant theme of the midcentury debate, which retains special relevance, was liberals' articulation of nonmarket values. This theme had two primary points of emphasis. First was a willingness to challenge businesses' ability to serve as a fair-minded arbitrator of national interests. Not only were midcentury liberals willing to alter the outcomes of market competition to serve a wider public good (primarily through redistributive taxation), but they questioned the basic ability of business to lead national affairs. Liberals found New Conservatives far more palatable than proponents of laissez-faire, for the New Conservative emphasis on tradition and continuity was an implicit argument against the legitimacy of upstart merchants and bankers. Such attitudes could shade easily into snobbery about the *nouveau riche*, and when coupled with an emphasis on intellectualism, could taint liberalism with a veiled elitism. But this elitism was tempered by liberals' deep commitment to the idea of a commonwealth.

This second liberal theme of the commonweal or national good, evoked in response to resurgent conservatism, is particularly remarkable because after a brief moment of popularity, it was rarely articulated again. At midcentury, liberals spoke in a confident, sure voice about the interests of the nation as a whole. They confidently criticized the behavior of capitalists without impugning capitalism, and their tone was steady, not defensive. Since then, these attitudes have been mocked from both the right and the left as complacent centralism and a false consensus that papered over the realities of American life. But without a robust sense of the public good, liberalism has little to do but carp at business. Surely, such carping has its uses, for as a dominant feature of American life and a thoroughly human institution, business will always behave in ways that call for criticism and correction. But liberals also need to offer a positive idea of what America can do and be. In the 1950s, as they fought back against the first surge of conservatism, liberals articulated such a vision.

This vision was a by-product of the more immediate struggle against the conservative threat. Schlesinger, a prolific commentator on current events, was one of liberalism's most active combatants. As a historian with a fondness for analytic precision, Schlesinger directed his ire primarily at conservative misuse of the British conservative tradition. But underlying this criticism were Schlesinger's own liberal beliefs, which emerged clearly in his attacks upon conservatism. Russell Kirk was one of his favorite targets, for Schlesinger found Kirk to be a rank hypocrite in his willingness to accept the alliance with business despite his clear aristocratic and communitarian sympathies. In a fiery 1955 attack upon the New Conservatism, which he called "the politics of nostalgia," Schlesinger singled out Kirk. Citing his characterization of federally provided school lunches as "totalitarian," Schlesinger wrote, "If there is anything in contemporary America that might win the instant sympathy of men like Shaftesbury and Disraeli, it could well be the school lunch program. But for all his talk about mutual responsibility and the organic character of society, Professor Kirk, when he gets down to cases, tends to become a roaring Manchester liberal." This tendency, however, went beyond Kirk, for American conservatives more generally, "when they leave the stately field of rhetoric and get down to actual issues of social policy, they tend quietly to forget about Burke and Disraeli and to adopt the views of the American business community."[21] To Schlesinger, American conservatism was little more than a smoke screen to advance the economic interests of business. It was dangerous because the business community, incapable of seeing beyond its own short-term interests, would provide poor political leadership.

In a way almost unimaginable today, Schlesinger questioned the ability of business leaders to run national life. For Schlesinger, the problem was not so much that conservatives were conservative but that they were capitalists. American conservatism, as it was emerging, was the conservatism of plutocracy, not aristocracy. He wrote, "Conservatism founded on money is fickle, selfish, and irresponsible; its chief object is to protect what it has and, if possible, to make more." However, he was willing to grant that aristocratic conservatism might be different: "The aristocrat, ideally at least, wants to protect the poor because in the end he regards the nation, rich and poor alike, as one family."[22] Astonishingly, Schlesinger, a committed democrat, came close to defending hereditary rule in his article. But this gesture was a mere rhetorical flourish, for underlying Schlesinger's relative friendliness to the Tory position was his belief that British conservatives, like American liberals, saw society as an organic whole and were willing to make economic sacrifices to ensure the well-being of all members of society. He cited British Tory measures on behalf of factory workers and the career of Winston Churchill, suggesting that these activities were analogous to the efforts of the Roosevelts, Stevensons, and Harrimans in the United States. Schlesinger pointed out proudly that these civic-minded American aristocrats were to be found among liberals, not conservatives. Though Schlesinger's intent in this essay was merely to flay conservatism and highlight its deficiencies, in passing his essay helped define the liberal conception of society.

A more explicit statement of liberal values came from August Heckscher, whose 1947 book *A Pattern of Politics* placed him in the New Conservative camp.[23] Heckscher might have been a New Conservative, but a 1953 essay made clear he had would have little in common with the emerging conservatives of *National Review*. Early on, Heckscher recognized the changed meaning of conservatism and the developing fusion between libertarianism and traditionalism. He echoed many of the criticisms voiced by other liberals. American conservatives only claimed to be conservative; they ignored the noble spirit of British Toryism in favor of Manchester economics; and so forth. But Heckscher's essay was not so much critical as elegiac, for he lamented what conservatism had lost when it allied itself with laissez-faire. In such an alliance, conservatives would never offer a romantic yet reasoned, almost literary defense of the government and the state. So Heckscher did so instead.

Heckscher began his essay by confronting conservative economic values. Whereas he agreed with the conservative critique of bureaucracy, he thought conservatives were wrong to argue solely in terms of dollars. Heckscher sympathized with the idea that an expansive federal bureaucracy could have a detrimental effect on local communities and the traditions of American life. But conservatives largely ignored this more subtle point and attacked centralization in the terms of its economic cost: "The point was almost never made that the rapid and revolutionary developments in Washington were, in their total impact, a blow against the free, independent, varied, and self-governing life of the American community. This was the true basis for a conservative critique. Bureaucracy may have been expensive, but that was not the real trouble with it." Though conservatives claimed to be defenders of community, they did little to develop a positive understanding or defense of it in their work. Instead, they focused entirely on economic questions, thus confining their concern to a select segment of the population. But, for Heckscher, this narrowness belied a fundamental misunderstanding of conservatism, for "not only is welfare—the welfare of all the citizens—a supreme end of the government; it is a concept made familiar by the authors of the Constitution and basic to every sound conservatism."[24] Here was a bold and positive statement about the purposes of government that was entirely at variance with conservative ideals: government was to maintain the welfare of all its citizens as its supreme end. This view might have seemed a basic concept of civic life. But faced with the growing ranks of opponents who denied and attacked this basic tenet, Heckscher took the time to elucidate a fundamental liberal belief.

Warming to his theme, Heckscher emphasized how conservatives, ironically, betrayed their historic roots as they turned against the state in favor of the free market. According to him, there was a venerable conservative/Republican tradition, descending from James Madison and continuing through the Whig Party, the Homestead Act, and the present Eisenhower administration, that "had a strong respect for federal power, wielded responsibly for a good end. It upheld the states, not as a means of thwarting national action, but as viable communities where citizens could be cultivated and loyalties engaged."[25] Essentially, Heckscher was arguing for the moral superiority of the East Coast, patrician wing of the Republican Party, as opposed to the more libertarian factions from the western and Sun Belt states. In 1953, this segment of the Republican Party remained vigorous and strong. But as Heckscher and Schlesinger seemed to intuit, it faced a formidable challenge from its own grass roots. Fearing that conservatives were abandoning their historic beliefs, Heckscher felt compelled to reassert the worth of this Republican tradition.

Although he identified his ideas as conservative, Heckscher presented a vindication of state action that stands today as essentially liberal testimony, for it contains a vital confirmation of human efficacy and the positive role of government. Although he criticized Manchester economics, Heckscher was no frothing socialist. Rather, he believed that government is essential to capitalism because it can soften and soothe the blows of the free market. Heckscher's words have meaning for us today because they speak to the continuing reality of capitalism's dominance. And they are also extraordinarily eloquent:

> Individuals must know that preventable catastrophes will not needlessly be let fall upon them, that the worst of fortune's ills will be alleviated out of the common store, and some floor will be placed under the normal and predictable hazards of a lifetime. It is in such a framework that true enterprise flourishes and that opportunity is more than a word.[26]

Heckscher's ideas speak to the uses to which an affluent society can put its wealth. In his view, government does not hobble the winners or carelessly squander its citizens' resources. Rather, it makes the game of capitalism fair and competitive and does what it can to minimize the inherent risks of life. The market remains a primary institution but is not sacrosanct. As Heckscher acknowledged, the values that he highlighted were fast being abandoned by conservatives. Today, they lie unclaimed.

The liberal effort to wrest the word *conservative* from its laissez-faire and McCarthyite custodians underlay much political commentary in the 1950s, for the semantic tug-of-war cut to the heart of both liberal and conservative identity. Although Heckscher and Schlesinger were two of the most penetrating commentators on up-and-coming conservatism, their arguments were echoed by less famous writers in the liberal ranks.[27] The debate also profoundly shaped—and obscured—the ways in which intellectuals on the left understood the right. Traces of the discussion appear in Daniel Bell's edited volumes *The New American Right* (1955) and the revised *Radical Right* (1963), for decades the most influential scholarly works on the American right.[28] In his contributions to these volumes, historian Richard Hofstadter refused to concede the label *conservative* to the populations he analyzed. Instead, Hofstadter called his subjects "pseudoconservatives," a distinction that gains its full meaning in the context of the New Conservative revival and debates about the word *conservative*. Hofstadter was unwilling to use the word *conservative* because, like most liberals of the time, he understood the term to mean something very different than anticommunist crusaders and free-market disciples.

Although the sudden liberal preoccupation with conservatism in the 1950s foreshadows the anguished debates that erupted after the 2004 election, to review the ideological conflicts at midcentury is to peer into a curious looking glass in which present realities are almost entirely reversed. Fifty years ago, conservative economic ideas outraged liberal sensibilities, yet their social and cultural values elicited little negative comment. To today's eye, the minor role of religion in the 1950s liberal counteroffensive is striking. Very few commentators of the time mentioned the conservative emphasis on religion, and even fewer offered any criticism.[29] They made scant effort to carve out a secular realm of political discussion or to attack conservatives for their religiosity. Midcentury liberals seemed to assume that religion was a natural and unremarkable ingredient in political and social discussions. Perhaps this silence is unsurprising for the era, when leading liberals like Schlesinger celebrated the theological insights of Reinhold Niehbur, and more radical segments of the Left also drew upon Christian writers to articulate their social vision. But it is certainly worth noting that when liberalism was most robust, it was also entirely comfortable with religion.

Liberals fought long and hard to prove that their ideological opponents misused the word *conservative,* but by the 1960s, the battle had been lost. By then, conservatives had managed to redefine the word so that it referred almost solely to traditionalists comfortable with the despised Manchester economics. A conservative was now someone who called for both an unfettered free market and a return to tradition, however bizarre such a position seemed to liberals. *National Review* had been one of the first steps in this libertarian-traditionalist fusion. An unmistakable sign of victory came with Barry Goldwater's *Conscience of a Conservative* (1960), cowritten with Buckley's brother-in-law, L. Brent Bozell. This best-selling book definitively established the new meaning of the word *conservative* both in the American vernacular and in the American political scene. After its publication, there would be no more New Conservatives, only conservatives.

Evicted from the conservative fold, where did homeless would-be Burkean conservatives go? Some of them restated their arguments, even as they realized the cause was lost. Rossiter reissued *Conservatism in America* in 1962, newly subtitled *The Thankless Persuasion* to reflect the beating he had taken from the Right. Viereck was even more explicit in his new subtitle, republishing *Conservatism Revisited* (1949) in 1962 with the addition of *Book II: The New Conservatism—What Went Wrong?* His second edition noted the changed meaning of the word *conservative* and asked, "What is it, triumph or bankruptcy, when the empty shell of a name gets acclaim while serving as a chrysalis for its opposite?"[30] Disconnected from both the refigured conservative movement and centrist liberalism, writers like Viereck, Rossiter, and Heckscher faded into obscurity. The values they had championed did the same. Liberals, now focused primarily on the cultural and social struggles surrounding civil rights, had less interest in economic questions. Writers who were first known as New Conservatives but were willing to ally with free-market promoters, or at least to overlook the conflict between capitalism and their social beliefs (like Russell Kirk), became plain old conservatives and gravitated to Buckley's *National Review* or other outposts of movement conservatism.

As conservatism redefined itself, so too did liberalism. Through the 1960s, liberalism's traditional emphasis on economic questions and the role of the state gave way to a concern with social questions—in Daniel Bell's phrase, liberalism moved from class to culture.[31] In large part, this shift came at a time when a host of newly important moral issues, from racism to sexism, and much later, sexual orientation, staked their claim on liberal sympathies. The legitimacy of these concerns is beyond question, and the liberal response is one to be proud of. Conservatives entirely missed the boat on racial and sexual discrimination, as the more truthful among them freely admit.

But if liberals' movement away from economic concerns and the role of the state is understandable, it is also unfortunate. Paradoxically, when they turned to culture, liberals lost the ability to understand how conservatives connected with a larger audience, for they stopped taking conservative arguments seriously. In the 1950s, liberals took time to respond to the conservative challenge and elucidated their own positions on the issues at stake. Since then, they have largely avoided doing so. As David Plotke points out in his introduction to the 2002 reissue of *The Radical Right,* "Parts of the left often tried try to weaken [the conservative] position by pointing out the apparent tension between the aversion to state action in economic and social welfare policies and a willingness to use government to defend traditional cultural values. This strategy was more clever than effective. Its proponents often made their critique in place of a substantive response to either half of the right's perspective."[32] By failing to engage the Right's arguments, liberals have found themselves mystified by the popularity of conservatism.

Liberals in the 1950s might not have been so surprised, for they understood some aspects of conservatism's appeal. If today's liberals were more familiar with certain conservative values—mainly the idea of permanence and the need for caution in undertaking social change—they might, at the very least, better understand the opposition that many of their policies and attitudes have engendered. And one can both understand and disagree with the conservative viewpoint, acknowledging that social change may be disruptive and threatening to many while asserting its necessity. This position, after all, was the one liberals maintained during the civil rights era. But without understanding the conservative reluctance to embrace change, particularly top-down change, liberals isolate themselves from widespread, natural popular reactions, leaving them open for conservatives to exploit. Liberals can recover some of the midcentury sense that change should occur slowly, with an eye on preservation and gradualism, even as they keep their belief in reason and progress. As they defend the possibilities of social transformation, liberals can restate their older belief that human beings have the ability to assess their society's needs and to effectively address the most pressing problems.

Perhaps more importantly, in the midcentury debate, liberals can discover a sense of civic identity, civic pride, and language of the commonweal that has almost entirely vanished from contemporary discourse. One might argue that this conception of the commonweal or the greater good is hopelessly outdated and will never achieve popularity. But liberals can profitably take a page from the conservative playbook in this regard. Conservatives at midcentury cared little that their ideas were unpopular. Indeed, they used their sense of marginalization to form a powerful oppositional culture and to cement themselves into one relatively coherent, or at least peaceful, ideological movement. After giving all parties a thorough hearing, they smoothed out or minimized internal disputes. Then they used a formula that was brilliant in its simplicity: Repeat the message. Who would have thought, fifty years ago, that capitalism would be so popular and government so demonized? Simple messages, repeated often, take on the appearance of timeless wisdom. And, indeed, the conservative critique of liberalism contained seeds of truth; many liberals were elitist, complacent with their power, and blind to other sides of human nature. But liberals, too, have wisdom on their side. In addition to faulting all the ways conservatives have led us astray, they would do well to emphasize the positive messages of liberalism. There is more to life than money. And investments in the common stock can improve all our lives. These messages are worth repeating again and again until they, too, seem to be common sense.

As I write these closing words, New Orleans lies under water, its citizens homeless and desperate, the rest of the country and the world shocked and embarrassed at the paucity and ineffectiveness of the American government's response to the disaster. Hurricane Katrina provides an obvious object lesson about the need for a vigorous, competent, active state, and for a government that can attract the best and brightest to its ranks because national service is considered an honorable calling rather than a patronage giveaway. The storm triggered a feeling throughout the land that might be called conservative in the sense that midcentury liberals conceived it—the idea that the nation is akin to family and that the more fortunate find meaning and reward in caring for those buffeted by fate or foul weather. If conservatives will not, or cannot, argue for these values, then liberals must.

PART TWO

LIBERALISM AND AMERICAN VALUES

4

Liberalism and Belief

ALAN BRINKLEY

We live in an age of belief. In the United States, as in much of the rest of the world, passionate faiths compete for the allegiance of citizens, inviting them to form deep and unshakable convictions. Banishing doubt, men and women of faith conduct their lives with the certainty that those who disagree with their religious, moral, economic, or political beliefs are profoundly misguided, if not evil.

In this rush to certainty, liberalism quakes and at times collapses, its adherents unable and unwilling to embrace fundamental dogmas of their own and incapable of effectively challenging those who do. Liberals in our time, and indeed through most of the history of liberal thought, have rejected most unexamined faiths and insisted on subjecting ideas to the test of experience. In an age of belief, this rational skepticism is, to its many foes, unacceptable. Understanding the potency of this issue, anti-liberal politicians have exploited it effectively, labeling liberals weak, in-decisive, inconsistent—rudderless "flip-floppers" with no clear values and no "moral compass" to guide them.

Not only those hostile to liberalism lodge such complaints. Many disappointed liberals are themselves highly critical of the present state of their own politics. These critics are not simply the countless disheartened liberals who are frustrated most of all by liberalism's political failures and who blame them on the craven timidity of Democratic politicians. Liberal philosophers and intellectuals have also offered damning critiques of the basic premises of liberal thought.

The historian Christopher Lasch, for example, moved from left-leaning liberalism in the 1960s to a harsh critique of many of its premises beginning in the 1970s; ultimately, he challenged one of the underlying assumptions of Enlightenment thought, the idea of progress itself. Toward the end of his life, he began searching instead for social models of community life, both in the present and in the past, that by most definitions would be considered decidedly illiberal. "Progressive optimism," he wrote, "rests, at bottom, on a denial of the natural limits on human power and freedom, and it cannot survive very long in a world in which an awareness of those limits has become inseparable." Such optimism is, he claimed, a form of "wishful thinking" and must be held up against a different and, to Lasch, morally more attractive alternative: a vision of community as represented by, among others, lower-middle-class ethnic cultures. Populism, not progressivism or liberalism, he claimed, is the basis for a viable future, precisely because populism has been skeptical of optimistic visions of the future and modern liberalism's commitment to social progress. In Lasch's vision, moral individuals are those who accept the limitations the world places upon them and perform the roles assigned to them by the accidents of birth and circumstance. Such people do not, as so many progressives do, rebel against the restrictions imposed by birth, family, community, and workplace. Nor do they see as their principal goal the improvement of their own or their family's material circumstances. A morally successful life resembles, instead, an acceptance of duty in which individuals take responsibility for their own lives, do useful work, and expect little of the larger world.[1]

The political theorist Michael Sandel has offered a less provocative but no less challenging critique of liberal theories of justice. Those theories, most prominently articulated by John Rawls, argue that what constitutes justice is a fair distribution of goods among peoples—a distribution that rational men and women would choose if they had no knowledge of their own circumstances. Such people would, presumably, consider how they would fare if they were among the least-favored members of a diverse society and would thus construct a system of distribution that would benefit everyone. But such systems, Sandel argues, cannot by themselves create a just society, because liberal justice presupposes only a process of distribution—a concept not of the community but of the market—and thus not a real vision of a social or moral good. Justice of

this kind is not irrelevant to a good society, he argues, but it is not sufficient to create such a society. A presupposed and shared conception of
the good must exist to give content to any theory of justice. The route to
such a conception is not through the liberal theory of rights but through
another political tradition deeply rooted in American history: republicanism, which embraces the kind of self-government that includes "de-
liberating with fellow citizens about the common good and helping to
shape the destiny of the political community." Republicanism of this
kind "cannot be neutral toward the values and ends its citizens espouse."
The republican conception of freedom requires those who embrace it to
take a stand behind a strong conception of civic virtue.[2]

The problems with liberalism, these relatively sympathetic critics
argue, are the absence of an animating faith or passion, the weakness of
the liberal concept of community, the fragility of all liberal moral claims
in the face of utilitarianism and contingency. In this view, they share with
critics from the right a yearning for deeper and more solid moral underpinnings for liberal values and goals.

Such criticisms are particularly hard for liberals to answer because
they strike at the core philosophy that has animated modern American
liberalism since at least the beginning of the twentieth century: pragmatism. William James, who with John Dewey is rightly considered the father of American pragmatism, took issue with the reigning philosophical idealism of his own time (strongly defended by his Harvard colleague
Josiah Royce) and attacked the notion that there are fixed beliefs that can
and should be passed unquestioned from one generation to the next. Belief, James argued, must be tested by experience. Even the most deeply
held convictions of a society might be discarded if they fail to answer the
needs of their time. The battle between faith and pragmatism, which
many liberals believed was settled in their favor in the middle decades of
the twentieth century, is now alive again. For liberalism to flourish in
such an environment, it must present a case for itself that neither rejects
belief nor embraces dogmatism.

The history of liberalism in the twentieth century suggests clearly that
this is not an impossible task. The pragmatic core of liberal thought in
that era did not preclude robust convictions and broad popular support.
For much of the century, in fact, liberals were a far greater magnet for
people of passion and faith than were their conservative critics. In the
first decades of the twentieth century, it was progressives who animated
public life with their passionate calls for reform, social justice, and a social gospel, and with leaders—Theodore Roosevelt, Woodrow Wilson,

Robert La Follette, and many others—who inspired adulation and intense loyalty.

Throughout the Great Depression and World War II, Franklin D. Roosevelt and the New Deal offered ideals, goals, and powerful beliefs that inspired millions of people to support them and thousands to flock into government to work on their behalf. As recently as the 1960s, liberalism seemed to many Americans to have vanquished the Right altogether. And although we now understand that assumption to have been deeply mistaken, we cannot underestimate the enormous, if ultimately fragile, power of the liberal alliance with the cause of racial justice and civil rights and the tremendous moral power it brought to liberal politics.

During these years, American conservatives presented a grim public face defined by sour resentment of and embittered opposition to the liberal order. Some struggled, largely in obscurity, to create a coherent set of beliefs with which to challenge liberalism, but their progress was slow and frustrating. So marginalized did they feel that they began to refer to themselves as the "remnant." Their philosophical efforts, some of considerable intellectual importance, were virtually unknown outside their own small circle. Even as astute a social critic as Lionel Trilling could unfairly but understandably dismiss conservatism in 1950 as "irritable mental gestures which seem to resemble ideas."[3] Conservatives had yet to learn how to bridge the gulf between an intellectual commitment and a popular movement. The great popular passions in the United States through most of the twentieth century were, in short, inspired predominantly by liberal beliefs, not conservative ones.

Much has changed since the end of World War II, and even more since the 1960s, and it is worth asking why liberalism has lost so much of its purchase on the loyalty and commitment of its once-vast constituency. Clearly liberalism's roots in utilitarianism cannot alone explain this remarkable change. Other, more historically specific events have contributed much more to liberalism's current dilemmas.

~

One core belief that animated liberalism through much of the first half of the twentieth century was a strong belief in economic justice, rooted in a deep concern about corporate power. Hostility to monopoly power was a major part of the early twentieth-century progressive agenda. Finding and empowering the "forgotten man" was a central goal of the

New Deal. "Freedom from want" and "freedom from fear" were the most original and resonant parts of the Four Freedoms by which Franklin Roosevelt tried to define American war aims; they were part of an effort to tie that most resonant of American ideas—"freedom"—to a vision of economic justice and uplift.

Both progressivism and New Deal liberalism also contained a strong belief in the wisdom and virtue of "the people." Progressives worked to create political vehicles—direct primaries, referenda, the recall, woman suffrage, and other democratizing efforts—by which power would flow away from parties, bosses, machines, and corporations and into the hands of citizens. The New Deal, although not notable for political reform, identified itself—through its policies and its cultural symbols—with the "common man" (workers, farmers, and others) and received strong and even passionate support from such people in return.

Progressives and New Dealers also had a strong belief in the positive value of the state. Liberalism had begun in the eighteenth century as a challenge to the autocratic power of the state, and twentieth-century liberals never wholly relinquished the fear that state power could become tyrannical and dangerous to liberty. But in an era in which great private institutions were wielding enormous, seemingly unchecked power and were themselves endangering the autonomy and liberty of citizens, liberals looked to government—and as the twentieth century progressed, increasingly to the federal government—as a countervailing power. Large corporations seemed in danger of becoming the Leviathan, and the state, they believed, was the only instrument capable of protecting the interests of citizens in an advanced capitalist society. Liberals embraced this idea unapologetically and enthusiastically in the first half of the century, when they were at the height of their influence and success.

Liberals in the first half of the twentieth century also benefited in many ways from a continuing, if often uneasy, association with the Left. Most liberals remained hostile to utopian ideologies, opposed socialism and communism, and rejected the sometimes radical or violent methods that some groups on the left advocated. But they also shared many concerns with socialists, communists, and other radicals. Liberals and the Left worked together at various times in supporting organized labor, attempting to improve the lives of impoverished immigrants, opposing racism at home and tyranny and aggression in the world, and defending personal freedoms. This uneasy alliance with the Left was not always a happy one, but it helped liberalism convey a sense of robust democratic fervor and a passion for social justice.

And finally, liberals drew strength—and conviction—during many of those years from their commitment to liberal internationalism, a series of principles that would, they believed, help move the world in the direction of democracy and peace. First articulated by Woodrow Wilson and then revived and translated into a series of consensual war aims by Franklin Roosevelt, these principles helped shape the most important conceptual project of postwar international relations: the containment policy that defined the cold war. On the surface, containment bore little relationship to Woodrow Wilson's visionary model of a self-policing international system. The policy of containment assumed a continuing struggle between two ideological systems that both sides believed could end only with the destruction of one system or the other. But containment was a response not just to the fear of communism that penetrated almost every area of American life. It was also a moderate alternative to the Right's proposals for far more aggressive and dangerous responses to the cold war. Containment advocated restraint through its acceptance, at least in the short term, of communism's present boundaries; its right-wing critics called for forthright action to "roll back" the present boundaries of communism, by military means if necessary. Containment embraced multilateralism and relied heavily on international organizations, albeit with the expectation that the alliances and institutions with which the United States was allied would follow America's lead. The Right called for America to act unilaterally in the world, without inviting the constraints of allies and without ceding even token authority to the United Nations or any other international organization. Some terrible things happened in the name of containment during the more than forty years in which the policy shaped American foreign actions (especially in Vietnam), but many far worse things would likely have happened without it. In any case, containment gave liberals—and indeed the nation—a coherent framework for thinking about the cold war and for undertaking a broad strategy of international engagement.

All these qualities—the belief in economic justice, the support for popular democracy, the faith in the positive uses of the state, the ability to draw productively from the fervor of the Left, and the vision of defending American security fused with a commitment to a democratic world—helped give liberals conviction and enabled them to convey confidence, belief, strength, and passion in fearful times—to assure citizens that they were not only committed to their interests but also able to serve them. The slow decline of liberalism since its heyday in midcentury is, in part, the story of liberalism's retreat from all these commitments. That retreat began, but did not end, with the liberal response to World War II and the early years of the cold war. In those years, liberal intellectuals and politicians adjusted their beliefs in several ways.

First, they retreated from some of their more robust views of the potential of the state, chastened by their reactions to the strong states that had produced war and genocide during the war itself—Nazi Germany, Fascist Italy, Imperial Japan—and others that they believed continued to threaten aggression and practice tyranny in the postwar years, most notably the Soviet Union. The longtime warnings of the Right about state power—restated with tremendous power by the economist Friedrich Hayek in his best-selling wartime polemic *The Road to Serfdom*—began to attract some followers on the left as well; and although liberals certainly did not give up on the state, many began to look for relatively restrained and indirect ways for the federal government, in particular, to shape society. Hence came the tremendous attraction of Keynesian economic management to liberals in the 1940s and 1950s and beyond. Keynesianism permitted the government to manage the economy without intruding directly into the workings of capitalist institutions. And hence too came the choice, out of the large array of programs with which the New Deal had experimented, of various forms of social insurance, most of which (with the significant exception of Aid to Dependent Children and related "welfare" programs) were reasonably simple to administer and required no extensive monitoring of employers or workers. It is not surprising that the most popular and durable social programs of the past seventy years have been Social Security old-age pensions and unemployment insurance, which work largely through the tax codes and a reasonably simple, if vast, distribution system.

Liberals remain, of course, the principal defenders of government in the United States, and some continue to urge far more aggressive uses of state power than those the country's leaders have attempted in recent decades. But they are, on the whole, apologetic defenders—quick to concede the dangers of state power ("The era of big government is over") and slow to make a strong, positive case for its value.

Just as totalitarian regimes caused liberals to reconsider their identification with the state, so too these regimes encouraged liberals to reconsider their belief in the essential virtue of the "common man" and "the people" as their natural allies. To the postwar generation of liberal theorists, popular commentators, and political figures, one of the great questions facing the modern world was how fascism and communism had cemented their grip on multitudes of apparently willing followers.

What caused so many people to embrace bigotry and fanaticism? And if people freely embraced these things, what did their embrace suggest for the future of popular democracy? Of course, many liberals and others throughout the world argued that the rise of totalitarianism was not the result of popular democracy but the product of its suppression. Many, however, believed otherwise and began to develop both explanations and strategies to prevent such horrors from occurring again.

Fear of unmediated popular democracy produced one of the most distinctive features of the intellectual and scholarly landscape of the 1950s and 1960s: a vision of the people as "the mass." "The sense of a radical dehumanization of life . . . ," Daniel Bell wrote (with considerable skepticism) in 1955, "has given rise to the theory of 'mass society.' One can say that, Marxism apart, it is probably the most influential social theory in the Western world today."[4] Nazi Germany and Soviet Russia, many members of the liberal intelligentsia argued, were only extreme examples of a much wider problem: the capacity of any citizenry to fall under the sway of demagogues and ideological fanaticism in ways that undermined both liberty and democracy.

The widespread belief among American liberals that the great Red Scare of the 1950s was the product of a spontaneous popular frenzy (rather than, as was actually the case, the product of the combined efforts of anticommunist bureaucrats and ambitious politicians) reinforced their concern that "mass politics" and "mass man" were dangerous forces. Those forces, they argued, must be contained within a democratic system in which "educated elites," as Bell called them, could mediate between the passions of the people and the realistic needs of a modern democracy. Many "consensus liberals" in the 1950s tended to look at dissent and radicalism as signs of dangerous ideological absolutism that might threaten America with the same tragedies that Germany and Russia had endured. Reinhold Niebuhr, the great liberal theologian, looking back with distaste on his own earlier attraction to millennial vision wrote, "The rise of totalitarianism has prompted the democratic world to view all collectivist answers to our social problems with increased apprehension. . . . A wise community will walk warily, and test the effect of each new adventure before further adventures." The capacity in men's souls for evil "that no human institutions can control" suggested that nations needed to consider ways of constraining popular power, not enhancing it.[5]

Closely related to this uneasiness with popular democracy was growing wariness of the Left. If McCarthyism demonstrated the capacity of fanaticism from the right to corrupt democracy, communism seemed to many liberals to reveal a similar capacity on the left. Few liberals did much to defend the Left from the ravages of the Red Scare. Even fewer lamented the diminished power of the Left in its wake. Instead, mainstream liberalism in these years sought to distance liberals not just from communism but from any kind of ideological politics that might threaten the pragmatic center that now seemed crucial to the survival of democracy.

One of the defining documents of this new relationship between liberals and the Left was Arthur M. Schlesinger Jr.'s *The Vital Center,* published in 1949. Schlesinger articulated the growing sense among centrist liberals of his time that little difference existed between fascism, which most Americans had consistently loathed, and communism, which some Americans had once romanticized. Absorption with the challenge from the Right, he warned, "has made us fatally slow to recognize the danger on what we carelessly thought was our left—forgetting in our enthusiasm that the totalitarian left and the totalitarian right meet at last on the murky grounds of tyranny and terror." With what he considered the dismaying example of Henry A. Wallace's 1948 Progressive Party campaign freshly in mind, he took pains to explain how erstwhile allies had become significant adversaries. The "progressive," he warned, had refused "to make room in his philosophy for the discipline of responsibility or for the dangers of power" and had thus "cut himself off from the usable traditions of American radical democracy." He had "rejected the pragmatic tradition of the men who, from the Jacksonians to the New Dealers, learned the facts of life through the exercise of power under conditions of accountability." Instead, progressives had developed sentimental attachments to dangerous myths such as "the mystique of the proletariat" and the inevitability of progress. Indeed, Schlesinger argued, at the core of the progressive "illusions" was not so much a mistaken agenda as an ominous "need for faith."[6]

Daniel Bell's much-misunderstood 1962 collection of essays, *The End of Ideology,* became another touchstone of the liberal retreat from "faith" and "passion." Bell did not entirely support this retreat and indeed called explicitly for a return to at least some form of utopian thinking. But he did echo Schlesinger's discomfort with the absolutism of "the ideologue." The most important purpose of ideology, he argued, was "to tap emotion." Ideology rejects "abstract philosophical inquiry" and becomes instead a "secular religion." Therefore, the exhaustion of these ideologies was a welcome development: "Few serious minds believe any

longer that one can set down 'blueprints' and through 'social engineering' bring about a new utopia of social harmony." Instead, he concluded,
"there is today a rough consensus among intellectuals on political issues:
the acceptance of a Welfare State; the desirability of decentralized power;
a system of mixed economy and of political pluralism." This stance was
in welcome contrast to the ideologies of the past, which rested on a facile
faith in improbable "certainties"—what William James once called "the
faith ladder."[7]

~

American liberalism entered the 1960s stripped of many of the deep beliefs that had once animated it. By 1960, it was once again a cool, pragmatic, hardheaded position (Schlesinger himself called it "tough-
minded") that was skeptical of passion and committed to leadership by
enlightened, educated elites. It was closer in some ways to its nineteenth-
century counterparts in America and Britain than to the age of the New
Deal. And yet liberalism in the early 1960s retained considerable power
and for a time became again—as it had been in the 1930s—so commanding in its control of American politics that it seemed to have vanquished all serious opposition. The new strength of liberalism in these
years came in part from the continued weakness and marginality of the
Right; in part, from the heightened tenor of the cold war and the eager-
ness of liberals to compete more intensively with the Soviet Union; and
most of all, from the sudden and unexpected emergence of one of the
great moral projects of the twentieth century: the civil rights movement.
Many white liberals, John F. Kennedy among them, were hesitant at first
to embrace the campaign for racial justice, fearing the passions and conflicts that it promised to unleash. But the moral example of protesters
facing murderous violence in the South aroused the nation and drew the
president, the Democratic Party, and the liberal world more generally
into a deep and heartfelt commitment to the cause. Lyndon Johnson's
landslide reelection in 1964 was not just a repudiation of his outside-the-
mainstream Republican challenger but an endorsement of the newly vigorous and morally grounded liberalism evident in the Democratic commitment to the civil rights movement. (It was also, of course, a warning
of Democratic troubles to come. Johnson's failure to carry the Deep
South—whose white voters did not share the rest of the nation's commitment to the civil rights crusade—was the first sign of a partisan re-
alignment that would ultimately greatly strengthen the Republican base.)

The 1960s reintroduced into American politics many of the convictions that had animated the New Deal: the skepticism of corporate power, the celebration of popular will, the faith in the wisdom of the state, the robust relationships with the Left, and the belief in the power of liberal internationalism to reshape the world. But many mainstream liberals embraced these convictions uneasily and repudiated some of them altogether as their fragile alliance with the Left crumbled in the face of growing militance and extremism. By the end of the decade, the moral intensity of liberal belief that had flowered in the early 1960s was largely gone. And even the Left, soured by the Vietnam War and its inability to force political change, had turned away from the state and from economic reform toward a largely cultural agenda. This agenda helped fuel the "identity politics" that proved incapable of producing robust coalitions among liberals or sustaining the liberal relationship with the Left. Even the cold war lost its power to arouse passion and conviction once the Vietnam War divided the nation and discredited many of the tenets of containment as liberals had understood them. Many liberals turned away from the vigorous internationalism of the postwar era, convinced that no American engagement with the world could be anything but exploitive and militaristic. And, of course, the 1960s also helped mobilize the Right in ways that, by the mid-1970s, had made it once again a powerful, conviction-driven rival of liberalism, which had become increasingly uncertain of its beliefs.

For more than thirty years since the end of the 1960s, liberalism—and the Democratic Party that has been its vehicle—has suffered more defeats than victories and has lost much of the vast constituency that once made both the creed and the party dominant. There are many reasons for this decline, some of them admirable. The liberal alliance with the civil rights movement alienated not only the South but many working-class and lower-middle-class people; but no one, I hope, would argue that this loss of constituency was too high a price to pay for supporting racial justice. The cost of taking other principled liberal positions—supporting gender equality, abortion rights, and gay rights, and opposing the death penalty, unjust wars, and the intrusion of religion into politics—has also been high, but probably unavoidable. Nevertheless, liberalism today is not known as much for these moral commitments to unpopular issues as it is for a drab, relativistic pragmatism and a commitment to sectarian interest groups and identity issues. The challenge is less to reconsider liberal positions on controversial issues than to determine how to make liberalism inspire the same kind of deep loyalty and commitment that contemporary conservatism now does.

One of the great challenges facing liberals is how to reconcile liberalism's pragmatic roots with a system of belief that can give liberalism the confidence and conviction to compete with the highly coherent world view of the Right. The Right has chosen tenets that its adherents consider to be incontestable truths, and it defends them unwaveringly regardless of their utility. The liberal position must be different. It must argue that deep, passionate, and durable conviction is compatible with liberalism's rejection of rigid dogmatism. It must demonstrate that robust belief can coexist with a willingness to question all creeds when circumstances demand it. That stance is, in fact, one that virtually all societies eventually must take, whether they admit it or not, no matter how rigid and dogmatic their belief systems may be. Straussians and other proponents of certainty would scorn such a view and argue that without timelessness and universality, convictions have no moral weight. But liberals can argue that beliefs need not be eternal to be morally compelling, that convictions can be strong, even lasting, without abandoning the possibility that circumstances may someday require their reconsideration. Relativism should not mean that any principled belief is unworthy of respect, only that no belief is forever immune to questioning. In *A Theory of Justice,* John Rawls writes, "What justifies a conception of justice is not its being true to an order antecedent to and given to us, but its congruence with our deeper understanding of ourselves and our aspirations, and our realization that, given our history and the traditions in our public life, it is the most reasonable doctrine for us. We can find no better charter for our social world."[8]

Even a contingent position like Rawls's leaves room for the long-term survival of powerful convictions. Thomas Kuhn, similarly, suggests that powerful paradigms, utterly convincing to generations of people, can survive for long periods before succumbing to shifts in understanding that may obviate earlier convictions. The search for moral truth, even for a kind of moral certainty, is not a dishonorable, or illiberal, quest. But the belief that such truth should be forever impervious to challenges or change is a mistake that liberals must strive to avoid.[9]

Looking back on the history of modern liberalism, one can see many vibrant convictions of the past that no longer seem relevant to our own era. Times change. Needs alter. Old possibilities close, and new ones emerge.

We can no longer imagine a society of small-scale producers unencumbered by large-scale organizations, as the populists once did. We cannot assume that government is always wiser than the private sector, or that the federal government is always more trustworthy than state ones. We cannot expect to revive the economic planning mechanisms with which the progressives and the New Deal flirted, and we can no longer assume that Keynesian devices will be sufficient to ensure prosperity in our increasingly globalized world. But certain legacies of previous eras of liberalism remain available to liberals today, even if they will need to take new forms to serve the needs of our time.

Corporate power remains an important issue, and the assumption of recent years that the private sector should be outside the reach of government already seems ludicrous in the face of the business scandals and failures of recent years. Eliot Spitzer, the New York attorney general, was elected governor of New York in 2006 precisely because he was so aggressive as attorney general in challenging corporate malfeasance.

Listening to and communicating effectively with ordinary voters—working-class and lower-middle-class families who were once fervent Democrats and have now become far less reliable supporters—is an indispensable part of rebuilding a liberal coalition. Liberals need not adopt the Right's cynical pandering to the worst prejudices of citizens in order to build their own relationships with the people whose economic fortunes have been grievously damaged by the economic changes and public policies of the past several decades. A commitment to helping such people, and understanding their circumstances, could, and I believe should, have as much moral weight as a commitment to minority rights.

Defending the state is a more difficult task than it once was, both because government's ability to influence events has diminished in this age of international corporate power and because its capacities have been deliberately eroded by leaders with an ideological hostility to its exercise of almost any nonmilitary powers. But few liberal hopes can succeed without a state that can advance the interests of the many with the same enthusiasm that the present government advances the fortunes of the few.

And although alliances with the Left—even in its present diminished state—come with a political cost, an inflexible hostility to the ideas and goals of the Left could be equally damaging to liberal prospects. Richard Rorty, as passionate a defender of liberal pragmatism as there is, argues persuasively in *Achieving Our Country* that liberalism shares many basic commitments with the Left and that neither group should draw an artificial boundary between itself and the other.[10] In recent years, portions of the Left have kept alive commitments that many liberals have cavalierly abandoned: concern about growing economic inequality, support for the imperiled union movement, and calls for corporate accountability.

Perhaps most important in our present, troubled world, liberals have a critical role to play in restoring the once-deep commitment to a form of internationalism that is rooted in a vision of democracy and peace and implemented through vigorous partnerships with allies and international organizations. Liberal internationalism was once a powerful and alluring vision to generations of Americans, and at its inception in 1918, it was an idea that entranced much of the world. In the 1960s and 1970s, the Vietnam War and other, accumulated cold war excesses made many liberals turn away from internationalism and embrace, instead, a vague isolationism that made any projection of power into the world seem an act of imperialism. But liberalism in its heyday did not reject principled American global leadership. Liberals should, and do, vigorously oppose the aggressive unilateralism of today's Right. But they should not at the same time wholly reject their own legacy of internationalism.

One consistent criticism of the liberal creed is its preoccupation with rights. And, in fact, an abstract commitment to rights that is unconnected to a vision of a good society and a just community can be an arid basis for political commitment. But through most of its history, liberalism has fused its commitments to rights with a commitment to social justice and enlightened progress. Rights are not simply a vehicle for empowering individual interests and desires. They are also the basis for a community's commitment to its collective well-being. Many of the great moral achievements of American history—the end of slavery, the battle against fascism, the struggle for racial equality, the empowerment of women, indeed the very revolution that created the United States and established the philosophical basis on which we have attempted to shape our nation ever since—have rested largely on a conception of rights that goes well beyond narrow individual preference.[11]

Liberalism that can muster a real majority and do more than tinker with the agenda of the Right requires both sound policies and strong convictions. Fighting belief-based politics with tactical maneuvers and pragmatic compromises is a recipe for continued frustration. This strategy may produce occasional victories at moments when the failures or excesses of particular leaders produce a demand for change. But it will not change the underlying dynamic of our political world, which consistently draws voters to the right when all else seems equal.

A liberal belief system need not, indeed cannot, rest on faith in eternal and uncontestable truths. To allow it to do so would be to betray one of liberalism's core beliefs—that ideas exist in a context and must be continually reexamined. But a liberal belief system can reflect, as it has in the past, genuinely deep, even passionate commitments to ideas that may not be appropriate for all time but are principled, robust, and effective faiths for our time.

5

Liberal Tolerance at Middle Age

NEIL JUMONVILLE

Since World War II, liberals have been justifiably proud that toleration has grown in the United States under the direction of liberal
presidents, clergy, social-service directors, novelists, college-
admissions committees, and filmmakers. But this tolerance has two distinct parts. The first is tolerance of other racial, ethnic, and religious
groups.[1] The second is tolerance of individual and cultural attitudes,
principles, and actions. I address the second in this essay. The toleration
and acceptance of others so evident in contemporary America, the first
category, is one of the lasting benefits of the 1960s cultural revolution.
Yet with this great success has also come resentment about the lack of
boundaries and principles that liberal tolerance of the second category
has produced in American culture. Distress at the lack of cultural limits
has prompted many Americans to overlook liberalism's great success in
furthering racial diversity. Ironically, liberalism has experienced great
success yet also sharp criticism since the 1960s—and both its success and
failure have been the result of forbearance. Employed without proper
limits since the mid-1960s, liberal tolerance has become embarrassingly
flabby and has backfired and helped undermine the national commitment to liberalism that existed a half century ago. Liberals' reputation
for being willing to abide anything and oppose nothing has fueled the

American public's appetite for conservative leadership. Currently, America is experiencing liberal tolerance at middle age, wheezing and out of shape, unprincipled, and without its former strength and vigor.

The form of tolerance that permits or encourages individual attitudes and lifestyles to be out of the ordinary is one of the principles to be cherished in America. This variety of tolerance, such as that of Ralph Waldo Emerson or John Stuart Mill, sometimes takes the form of indifference to the opinions or actions of others. In other instances, it embraces relativism, adopting an open attitude that indulges contradictory viewpoints, "a hesitancy to pass value or 'truth' judgments on individual or group beliefs," or an "epistemological skepticism leading to an endorsement of various lifestyles."[2] It is the forbearance of someone who, as a matter of principle, puts up with an attitude, opinion, or behavior that she doesn't like in another person. It's the patience of an individual who acts pleasantly oblivious when talking to someone whose ideas or habits offend him. It has a long history that reaches back at least to J. Hector St. John de Crevecoeur's comments on American tolerance in his *Letters from an American Farmer* (1782).

This form of tolerance is one of the best impulses encouraged by the 1960s. But each generation might do well to establish through public discussion a rough idea of where its cultural boundaries are. For example, will society extend tolerance to those who oppose it, whether these opponents are neo-Nazis or terror groups? Are there some values that liberals will tolerate but not promote? Can a liberal civic culture exist in a society that tries to balance tolerance with general limits?

~

A representative case of middle-aged liberal tolerance gone flabby occurred in the mid-1980s when liberals responded to allegations that lyrics in some gangsta rap songs were harmful to the young. In this contest, liberals not only campaigned to permit gangsta artists to say what they wanted to (which is an important doctrine they were right to support) but also stumbled over each other in their rush to defend the worst of the lyrics from criticism or warning labels. In the ensuing face-off over whether labeling albums for their content constituted censorship, liberals held to few of the principles they followed when discussing violence in television programs or films. The previous generation of liberals had frequently recommended regulating television programming to discourage depictions of violence, particularly during times when children typically watch, or at least had sought to provide parents with a rating system for the shows. They felt very differently, apparently, about an art form that was far more corrosive to children. Are rating systems, one of the least intrusive sets of cultural boundaries, inconsistent with liberal tolerance?

The battle over gangsta rap arose when Tipper Gore, who liked Prince's songs "Let's Go Crazy" and "When Doves Cry," bought the album *Purple Rain* for her twelve-year-old daughter. Prince and other artists whom Tipper first objected to were not gangsta rappers, of course, but still she was disturbed to find that the lyrics of the song "Darling Nikki" described a girl masturbating with a magazine. In May 1985, Tipper, the wife of Tennessee senator Al Gore, and Susan Baker, wife of James Baker III, along with a few other distraught parents, founded the Parents Music Resource Center (PMRC) to educate and inform others about the music sold to their children.[3] The Senate Commerce Committee, which included Al Gore, held a meeting in September in which the senators heard from witnesses such as John Denver, singer Dee Snider of Twisted Sister, and Frank Zappa, all of whom were afraid that the hearings were part of a plan to silence free expression.[4]

In fact, the PMRC opposed passing legislation to solve the problem and instead asked the record companies to label offensive albums voluntarily with warning stickers, which they agreed to do. The PMRC joined with the National Parent-Teacher Association in a call for a rating system that would help parents identify entertainment material that contained profanity, sex, or violence. The resulting labeling system soon was alleged to be ineffective because it lacked standard language and because the labels were often the same color as the album and were not especially visible. By 1990, at the prompting of retailers, police departments, and others, record companies made the labels more uniform and prominent and used the wording "Explicit Lyrics—Parental Advisory."[5] From the beginning, the arts community denounced Tipper as a rogue exponent of Victorian sensibilities, cast her as a lieutenant in Jesse Helms's crusade against wanton culture, and lampooned the labeling issue on *Saturday Night Live* in a skit in which Jon Lovitz played Satan as a congressional witness who argues for free speech.[6]

Tipper Gore should have been grateful that the musicians who offended her in 1985 were only soft-core singers such as Prince, Cyndi Lauper, Madonna, and Sheena Easton, because a scant few years later, gangsta rap, performed by groups such as N.W.A. (Niggaz With Attitude), landed in her children's world with a menacing, swaggering, crotch-grabbing thud. Song titles from N.W.A. included "To Kill a Hooker," "Findum Fuckum & Flee," "One Less Bitch," "I'd Rather Fuck You," and "A Bitch Is a Bitch."

The tune "She Swallowed It" is representative N.W.A. fare. It's a story about a "bitch" who screwed the entire rap group, a "ho" who laid so many of the gangsta crowd that the rappers bet on who she'd do that kind of "shit" with next. In fact, this "dumb bitch" would use her tongue on your "asshole," and if you collected a bunch of "niggaz," the stupid "bitch" would let everyone "rape her." Most girls say they wouldn't "suck a dick," but if they try it, they can't resist it, because almost all "bitches" really "love that shit" even though they deny it. The rappers know the truth, "so fellows," the next time one lies saying she doesn't "suck a dick," you should "punch the bitch in the eye." When you've knocked "the ho" down, then get on top of her, "open up her mouth," put your cock in, begin humping her face, and she'll get the point and "start doin' it on her own."[7] Such is the kind of material that Tipper wanted to label but not censor.

In 1994, Congresswoman Cardiss Collins, chair of the House Subcommittee on Commerce, announced another round of hearings on gangsta rap lyrics. Collins, a Democrat from Illinois, declared, "I am among many of our African-American leaders who are concerned about the message this music is sending to our already beleaguered black youth," and, she added, "I think we have a responsibility as black women to at least speak out and be heard about the kinds of music our children listen to and the kind of music that they buy." But, she emphasized, "I remain steadfast in my opposition to any abridgment of First Amendment rights."[8]

In the course of this controversy, some liberals and leftists were more offended by the parental warning labels than about the explicit lyrics and considered the labels racist. Is criticism of gangsta culture illiberal? For example, bell hooks, distinguished professor of English at City College of New York and a prominent figure on the cultural left, argued that "a central motivation for highlighting gangsta rap continues to be the sensationalist drama of demonizing black youth culture in general and the contributions of young black men in particular." Deflecting the blame from those whose photos graced the albums, hooks charged that "the sexist, misogynist, patriarchal ways of thinking and behaving that are glorified in gangsta rap are a reflection of the prevailing values in our society, values created and sustained by white supremacist capitalist patriarchy."[9] Blaming N.W.A., then, was racist. Similarly, Keonna Carter, a student at the University of Virginia who had her thoughts on rap published on the university's American studies etext website, criticized the PMRC for suggesting that rap has filled "youthful ears with pornography and violence." Actually, she reported, rap is as all-American as our storied mythology of the West and is "just as American as apple pie." After all, television cowboys also used drugs (beer), violence, and pornography. "In short, rap music is not really being criticized for being too violent or profane," Carter complained, "it is being attacked because of who's saying it."[10] Criticism of rap, then, was merely racism skulking in disguise—which might come as a surprise to Congresswoman Collins, who worried that gangsta culture would undermine the values of the African American communities she represented.

When 2 Live Crew was tried for obscenity for its album *As Nasty as They Wanna Be* in October 1990, Henry Louis Gates Jr., professor of English at Duke University, was witness number three for the defense. He explained that "these songs have taken the worst stereotypes of black men and blown them up. And that is that we are oversexed or hypersexed individuals." Like the television character Archie Bunker, who was only a caricature, these songs weren't meant to be taken literally. "One of the brilliant things about these four songs is they embrace that stereotype," Gates continued. "They name it and they explode it. You can have no reaction but to bust out laughing. The fact that they're being sung by four virile young black men is inescapable to the audience. Everyone understands what's going on. Their response is to burst out laughing. To realize it's a joke. A parody." Gates paused. "That's p-a-r-o-d-y."[11] But over the past decade and a half, his explanation—that gangsta rappers' misogyny and violence are simply caricatures to free them from a false identity—has been increasingly difficult to swallow.

A contingent of black liberals were not so willing to laugh off the menace of gangsta rap. The National Association for the Advancement of Colored People (NAACP) defended the First Amendment rights of 2 Live Crew and stood against the group's prosecution in the censorship trial. But the organization also denounced the rappers' message. "Our cultural experience," said Benjamin L. Hooks, executive director of the NAACP, "does not include debasing our women, the glorification of violence, the promotion of deviant sexual behavior or the tearing into shreds of our cherished mores and standards of behavior." When 2 Live Crew member Luther Campbell appeared on a television talk show, the NAACP headquarters in Baltimore was overwhelmed with phone calls from people who, its leaders said, "took offense at his attributing these sentiments to black culture and wrapping it in the mantle of black tradition." Gates shrugged off the NAACP's concerns as simply part of a longer split among blacks, reaching back to the Harlem Renaissance, about whether black art has to serve the goals of black advancement.[12]

Meanwhile, many liberals thought Tipper Gore's labeling project was an act of censorship. Elliot Mincberg, the legal director of the People for the American Way, a liberal organization that has done much good, acknowledged that the PMRC supported only voluntary labeling of music, but, he claimed, "the fact that this kind of legislation doesn't explicitly prohibit the sale of these records does not immunize it from the First Amendment," because "the government seal of disapproval that these labels would apply, and the fact that the label has behind it criminal sanctions, is enough to have a substantial chilling effect on free expression."[13] A measure short of outright legal censorship, Mincberg suggested, could still discourage some consumers from buying a piece of artistic expression. But does this outcome—hesitancy to buy a product for children— have anything to do with censorship of expression or an abuse of the First Amendment? Again, the PMRC tried to preclude legislation that would censor. Jennifer Norwood, the group's executive director, hoped the labeling "would offset some of the legislation that is pending."[14] Thus, though the PMRC promoted "FYI" labels for parents and explicitly opposed censorship, many liberals treated the organization as though it were run by Roy Cohn.

The most interesting exchange on these issues occurred in 1993 between Danny Goldberg, the senior vice president of Atlantic Records and chair of the ACLU Foundation of Southern California, and Philip Berroll, a New York writer. Goldberg, who had organized a group to combat the PMRC's labeling proposal, warned that attacks on the entertainment industry for presenting violence and sex would end like medieval medical treatments: the cure would kill the Hollywood patient. And where was the evidence that entertainment corporations were influencing the population anyway? Goldberg said he had encountered only glib reports and unscientific statements that violent shows or music made people violent. Attempts to keep some material from the preadolescent public, as labeling of gangsta rap albums did, Goldberg called "blacklisting," which he noted was far worse than disapproval. "Criticism seeks to persuade the public not to consume a product," he pointed out. "Blacklisting seeks to make sure that they don't have the choice. Fighting communism was morally correct. Destroying the free speech opportunities of artists who were communists" was not.[15] But Goldberg missed the point, because labels do allow the public to consume the product, and they don't blacklist gangsta rappers—none of whom served jail time or were frozen out of their jobs for their lyrics. In fact, most gangsta rappers continued to get richer during this period. So Goldberg never explained how the labeling initiative paralleled the repression of communists in cold war America.

The difference between the Westerns of early television and current violence on the screen, Goldberg continued, is that now people bleed when they're shot, and, he said, referring to young viewers, "I'm not sure this is such a bad thing for them to learn." After all, he argued, the 1960s upheaval was partly a dismissal of the phony, rosy depictions of life that we had been spoon-fed for decades and that had turned us into a dreamy, disconnected culture. Real life is better, and we need to have the courage to face it. Few liberals would disagree with his general point, but many of them in the past have endorsed movie ratings so that parents can regulate the amount of violence their children watch before a certain age. With that fact in mind, we might ask him, Do we want the most violent and misogynistic rap life pumped through throbbing speakers into the bedrooms of young children so that they can memorize and chant lyrics about violence against women before they even know what the words mean? Goldberg admitted that he sometimes agreed with Tipper Gore about particular albums, but he complained that "I never understood what possible criteria could be used to label song lyrics in a way that addressed her concerns." Officials, he charged, have been confused and thus have occasionally denounced songs that actually oppose drug use. "Who," he asked, "is wise enough to label the thousands of variations on the ancient themes of sex, violence, religion, morality?"[16] The task is indeed difficult, but because a course is fraught with difficulty, should liberals shrug their shoulders and turn away, or should they produce pragmatically the best outcome that they can?

Philip Berroll, in contrast, said at the time that liberals had mistakenly allowed rigid allegiance to the First Amendment to erode their intelligence. Yes, liberals occasionally allow the stray libel or pornography case to proceed, but in almost all cases, liberals focus only on ferreting out and attacking whiffs of censorship in the air. The distasteful and dangerous result of such First Amendment absolutism, Berroll warned, was that its adherents accuse anyone who has the audacity to question the effects of culture on different portions of the population of being procensorship. Thus, they portray cultural questioners such as Tipper Gore, whether they are liberals or conservatives, as judgmental scolds who want to shovel their values onto others.[17] Berroll objected to the reckless conflation of all liberals like Tipper Gore with strident conservatives such as Donald Wildmon of the American Family Association (AFA), whose website declares, "AFA is for people who are tired of cursing the darkness and who are ready to light a bonfire."[18]

An analogous case is the contested exhibition of the photography of Robert Mapplethorpe and Andres Serrano in 1989 and 1990, in which howls of rage erupted throughout the land at the expenditure of public money to pay for Mapplethorpe's photos of gay sadomasochistic figures and at Serrano's photo of a crucifix submerged in urine. I drove from Boston to Hartford to see the exhibit on November 4, 1989, and I was not then nor am I now offended by the nudity, the child nudity, or the homoerotic element of the show. I'm not drawn to see photos, either of gay or hetero participants, of fisting (a person's arm pushed halfway to the elbow into another's rectum), one person urinating into the mouth of another, a penis with a finger lodged in it, or a bloodied penis bound onto a piece of wood accompanied by two traumatized and engorged testicles. I understand that this perspective is a personal matter and that my taste in nude photography might offend someone else. Although I disliked part of the show for its roughness, pain, and a few intensely personal acts I did not care to see, I enjoyed much of the exhibit and thought Serrano's *Piss Christ* was particularly good.

Much but not all of the controversy about this exhibit focused on government bodies' attempts to censor it. The partnership among liberals to fight censorship of the show was entirely laudable and necessary, the kind of crusade that liberals should be proud to mount. The related liberal struggle to shield the National Endowment for the Arts (NEA) from public and government attacks—attacks that could have forced the agency to cut grants to artists for work that transgressed community standards—was defensible, although not nearly as crucial. Liberal activists were right to oppose efforts to overturn the NEA's peer-reviewed awards to offending artists. But the public has a right to criticize an agency such as the NEA, as it has a right—and maybe the responsibility—to criticize the decisions of all government agencies. The public and government officials have the right to complain about projects erecting public statuary, after all, and the NEA has no exemption from this process.[19] As with gangsta rap, can liberals, if they choose, tolerate the Mapplethorpe show but not necessarily promote it? Can liberals fight to prevent censorship of the exhibit but vote against publicly funding it?

Some liberals believed that the exhibit should be supported simply because it broke preexisting cultural barriers and represented a beleaguered group of sadomasochists. Christopher Knight, an art critic for the *Los Angeles Times,* wrote, for example, that Mapplethorpe "pictured, with clarity, oppressive stereotypes created by the dominant, or 'straight,' society." The photographer portrayed "marginalized people," including "prodigiously virile" blacks. Sure, these compositions are "clichéd," Knight noted, but Mapplethorpe used stereotypes to convey a deeper meaning.[20] Those who didn't find the exhibit particularly intelligent or enlightening, in Knight's account, were mostly members of the "evangelical right" whose recent sex scandals had diminished their power. The devout hatched the idea of a moral war to repair the Right's image. "The reliable bugaboo of 'godless homosexuality' made a useful battleground, especially as the equally tried-and-true bogeyman of 'godless communism' had evaporated." To Knight, this sordid, furtive, conservative campaign was the real story behind the opposition to the contested show. Thus, Mapplethorpe was a political and cultural hero who had constructed, in the face of great opposition, a visual plea for freedom. Knight believed the exhibit's content was important, perhaps revolutionary. "His homosexual men flaunt themselves, sometimes enacting their social bondage in sadomasochistic garb." Thus, the exhibit was a good show, an important record of cultural bondage, one that liberals should see and support.[21]

The novelist David Leavitt made a similar call in the *New York Times* to support the show in order to endorse tolerance for "the other." The battle, as Leavitt described it, was promoted by those such as Jesse Helms, who wanted Nick-at-Nite neighborhoods where "the music is by Wayne Newton, the paintings are by Norman Rockwell, and sex takes place only between married men and women in beds at night." The attack on such shows, Leavitt reported, "has little to do with the arts at all, and everything to do with the extreme right wing's determination to terrorize an already ambivalent American population by manipulating its entrenched fears of anything foreign, unfamiliar or explicitly sexual."[22]

As the *New York Times* itself correctly summarized Leavitt's point in a sidebar, "The real target behind the attacks on the National Endowment is not obscenity but the dread of the nameless 'other.'"[23] Leavitt was right to oppose national resistance to gay culture and antigay expressions or policies as expressed by some critics of the exhibit. But should liberals always have to embrace or celebrate "the other," no matter its specific character? An automatic fear of "the other" is parochial and dangerous to liberty and the social fabric. An equally automatic embrace of "the other" is just as foolish and unwise. Liberals should decline to endorse unthinking destruction of cultural limits and barriers, and they should not hope a priori for society's eventual absorption of everything "other." One could either endorse or disparage the show while still opposing censorship.

Critic Luc Sante noted that no matter how foreign or unwelcome the photos were at the time, they would at some point be accepted into America's tolerant culture. "As unlikely as it might seem," he acknowledged, "they are even now creating the climate for their eventual acceptance, or if not acceptance then at least a blasé unconcern. After all, cultural taboos have in the past century tended to collapse not long after a furious battle for their maintenance was apparently won." A conflict such as the one over the Mapplethorpe exhibit weakens barriers, and the barriers fall after the cultural battle ends and the combatants drift away. "There will always be people who will claim that morals are somehow at stake, as well as advocates of bland tolerance and solemn universality," Sante continued, "all of them in their diverse ways trying to hose down art, but they will inevitably be bested in this task by the culture's boundless capacity for indifferent absorption."[24] Some of this generalized, indifferent absorption is fueled by the liberal ethic of unthinking tolerance, much of which has been institutionalized in the academic left in the past quarter century. But if liberals aren't able to oppose some elements of "the other," then how are any boundaries to exist? How can liberals ever set their own agenda? What is the meaning of a liberal value? Only more tolerance?

Camille Paglia likes to think of herself as the embodiment of the Dionysian counterculture of the 1960s, and, like Mapplethorpe, who she considers her "spiritual brother," she was raised Catholic. Paglia is no liberal, yet some of her reactions to the exhibit are useful for liberals to contemplate. She complained that "it injures Mapplethorpe to whitewash him, to deny his cunningly perverse motives, to turn him into a gay Norman Rockwell." The photographer has an open strain of Catholic-pagan iconography in his work that is brutal as well as erotic. "We must frankly face the mutilations and horrors in Mapplethorpe's sexual world," she said, "and stop trying to blandly argue them away as fun and frolics of 'an alternative lifestyle.' His grim sadomasochists are not lovable, boppy Venice Beach eccentrics on roller skates." Again, liberals, holding tight to their well-meaning tolerance, celebrated the photos as a breaking of boundaries, as though every barrier that falls is worthy of celebration if only because it has fallen. "It is foolish and naïve to claim, as has repeatedly been done," Paglia pointed out, "that the discomforting or painful features of Mapplethorpe's sexual tastes reflect the unjust oppression of a homophobic society." If such a force had existed, liberals would have had a tidy story of victory over oppression, with Mapplethorpe as an appropriate hero. Instead, she reminded us, "he saw and accepted the cruelty and aggression in our animal nature, our unevolved link with the pagan and primeval past. Mapplethorpe was not a liberal. Sadomasochism is not liberal. It is rigorously hierarchical and coldly ritualistic."[25]

As Paglia emphasized, "Mapplethorpe's liberal supporters do not understand him. His work is a scandal to all their progressive humanitarian ideals." In this era of liberal tolerance at middle age, tolerance is so freely pushed onto those who are willing to topple barriers that no one pays much attention to whether those falling barriers will smash fundamental liberal values such as comity, compassion, civility, respect, benevolence, generosity, concord, and solidarity. "Mapplethorpe's work, like Swinburne's," she noted, "demolishes the liberal worldview, with its optimistic faith in benevolent, egalitarian social and sexual relationships."[26]

In the cases of both gangsta rap and the Mapplethorpe photos, some liberals vocally opposed censorship, as they were right to do, but they also were against criticism or labeling of disputed work because they feared that such criticism would produce a change in standards or send a bad signal. "The greatest threat we face," complained Robert Storr, a member of *Art Journal*'s editorial board, in the Mapplethorpe case, "may not be court-enforced censorship but repressive decorum and general self-censorship."[27] But do liberals and intellectuals really fear occasional self-imposed restraint as much as they fear censorship? Should criticism of artists cease to shield them from doubt? In the gangsta rap controversy, Danny Goldberg suggested that criticism and labeling might silence artists. His and other responses show the fear of some in the intellectual community that criticism is death to creation and the belief that tolerance thus needs to be automatic and constant, with its windows wide open.

Yet the problem for some liberals goes beyond their confusion about what is censorship and what is not. Often they are gratuitously stupid about matters of simple cultural politics. A needlessly strong public embrace of N.W.A. or sadomasochism, for example, is a recipe for liberal political defeat.

∾

What transformed American liberal tolerance four decades ago? The principle of open tolerance had characterized the counterculture as far back as the Beats in the 1950s, whose dharma inquiries into the nature of life provided the soil for the growth of the hip counterculture a decade later. This spiritual quest against mass society and its consumer engine, led by such varied figures as Gary Snyder, Amiri Baraka, and Lenny Bruce, offered a complex collection of personal freedoms (tolerances) for the individual and resentful criticisms of American cold-war values. The important and necessary cultural revolution that broke the civilization like an earthquake in the 1960s was fueled partly by the civil rights movement, changing ideas about gender roles and equality, and resentment toward the government for ordering young men to fight in an unpopular war. In the 1960s, many liberals and leftists challenged traditional sources of authority, questioning why control was located where it was and asking whether the resulting pattern of dominance produced a healthy society. Were advertisements, corporations, school principals, military officers, or parents rightful sources of authority? Though the resulting changes in the 1960s were painful, they were useful and represented a Whitmanesque disregard for authority and privilege and a boundless sense of humanity that ignored racial and gender boundaries.

Though both the counterculture and the New Left wanted to achieve community, as was clear in the Port Huron Statement by the Students for a Democratic Society in 1962, many yearned for a lack of rules, for an antinomian enlightenment that, even in the presence of community, encouraged individuals to take their own paths and to pursue their own courses, to guide themselves by the Emersonian intuition within them.

The emphasis on tolerance was especially useful in the 1950s and 1960s, when the pall of a conservative, starched, crew-cut conformity attempted to seal the eyes, ears, and minds of Americans to anything outside the narrowly defined middle. America in the quarter century after World War II sometimes seemed Orwellian in its shuttered intolerance. But as the 1960s turned into the 1970s, with American cultural and political repression already blasted open by student radicals and baby boomers, unthinking tolerance no longer served an important purpose.

In the 1970s and 1980s, the liberal commitment to tolerance gained steam from the intellectual and cultural relativism filtering into universities, led by a wave of anthropological insights. One's judgment of cultural products depended on whether one subscribed to Matthew Arnold's "high" definition of culture as the product of symphonies and museums or to the "low" anthropological view of culture as practices, beliefs, and creations. Similarly, a person might judge a cultural product differently depending on whether he or she stood inside or outside the boundaries of a specific culture or was a member or nonmember of the culture. Tolerance increased, and, especially on matters of racial, ethnic, and gender diversity, this expanded view was a change for the good. Even so, a feeling was afoot in the country that liberalism had lost its sense of boundaries.

How does a society find its boundaries? What represents too much or too little tolerance? A similar question arose in the 1950s about how to find the proper level of nonconformity. For a decade or more, the literary critic Irving Howe, a founder and editor of *Dissent,* urged the intellectual community to be more nonconformist, because mainstream society, he argued, stood so unchallenged that intellectuals had to be a countervailing force. He proposed that the job description of an intellectual is to stand in opposition to power automatically because nonconformity is healthy for intellectuals and society. In response, however, the literary critic Granville Hicks charged that " 'blind unreasoning rejection' may be, as Howe says, 'healthier' than blind unreasoning acceptance, but it is not more intelligent.' " Similarly, the philosopher Sidney Hook warned Howe that to be appropriately intelligent, critics had "to discriminate, to make relevant distinctions," to be pragmatic.[28] The important factor, according to Hicks and Hook, was not whether one is a conformist or nonconformist but the position to which one conforms or does not conform.

In the same way, liberals today might choose to assert, in the spirit of Hicks and Hook, that unthinking tolerance is no more inherently intelligent and not always more beneficial than is unthinking intolerance. Tolerance for its own sake only begets more tolerance—which might be good or bad, depending on what we're tolerating. We need to apply tolerance thoughtfully and pragmatically, in pursuit of the goals we're trying to achieve in society. Liberals need to discuss the ends that liberalism embraces and then especially use tolerance in pursuit of those goals, even if in some limited cases the goal is to create more tolerance. Thinking about the boundaries of tolerance is one way to strengthen tolerance as a principle and to fortify liberalism as a political set of ideas. In the past quarter century, a commitment to tolerance as a primary value has pushed liberals into positions that they need not occupy, either on the basis of liberal principle or on the ground of political strategy.

6

Liberalism and Democracy: A Troubled Marriage

KEVIN MATTSON

For several years after the Supreme Court had decided unanimously that American schools must be desegregated in the famous *Brown v. Board of Education* decision of 1954, no one was clear, certainly not the Supreme Court itself, just how black and white students would start going to school together. In 1955, the Supreme Court justices spoke, in a decision that came to be known as *Brown v. Board of Education II*, of "all deliberate speed" in the process of desegregation, whatever that meant. Then, three years after the original *Brown* decision, a southern politician made a fateful decision and did something other southerners only dreamed of doing. Orval Faubus, governor of Arkansas, decided that all deliberate speed meant *never*. Faubus was prepared to send in the National Guard to prevent nine black students from entering Central High School in the town of Little Rock. Though he rescinded his promise to use the guard, mobs of white citizens took up his call and drove the black students away. Here was the first step in a campaign of "massive resistance." National battle lines were drawn.

President Eisenhower didn't want to send in federal troops but decided that a military presence was necessary to protect the nine black students and put the weight of force behind *Brown*. The only alternative seemed to be mob rule. And the pictures of angry, rock-hurling, sneering and spitting white parents were bound to get out around the world, making it difficult to portray America as the land of freedom during the cold war. African and Asian nations were already asking a challenging question: If America believes in democracy and equality, then how did it explain the mistreatment of black citizens in its homeland? Eisenhower made his fateful decision and sent in paratroopers; he brought the National Guard under federal control.

The situation had come to this: the use of military force, the mobilization of American troops against America's own citizenry, to ensure that African American citizens would have the full advantages of citizenship. Troops mounted and pointed bayonets at fellow citizens in the name of equality and national unity, the foundational principles of the American creed. The dreams of the national community trumped the will and passions of the local community. It had to be so. And liberals knew why.

~

Two thousand miles away from Little Rock, where mobs screamed and little black children huddled around federal paratroopers, a group of intellectuals chattered on within the provincial confines of New York City, doing what they always did, quarreling and debating over big political ideas. Their debates were often abstract and difficult for ordinary citizens to understand, but debate about Little Rock was different. Suddenly, intellectual discussion became focused.

Hannah Arendt, a German émigré intellectual known for often-opaque meanderings about political theory, decided to ask a very concrete question: "What would I do if I were a white mother in the South?" She answered, "I would deny that the government had any right to tell me in whose company my child received its instruction. The rights of parents to decide such matters for their children until they are grown-ups are challenged only by dictatorships."[1] There was that word *dictatorship*, which framed so many debates during the cold war. Arendt had famously defined the term in her important work *The Origins of Totalitarianism*. Now she applied it not to Nazi Germany or to Stalin's Russia but to an act committed by her own president, Eisenhower.

Arendt was no racist defender of the Old South; she was, after all, a German Jew who knew the brutality of anti-Semitism. She believed in racial intermarriage. "The right to marry whoever one wishes," she explained in the same essay about Little Rock, is an "elementary human right."[2] So Arendt's argument against school integration was bewildering to many. People had talked of the potential for "massive resistance" by white male southerners before, but Arendt was a German female Jew who hung out with liberal intellectuals of the time (her essay was originally published in the socialist publication *Dissent*). This résumé made her argument all the more challenging.

And it also made her argument difficult to follow at moments. Arendt moved quickly from asking the white southern mother's blunt question to doing what she had been trained to do: plot out abstract political theories. She believed that schools weren't the right places to wage a war for integration. Others had already suggested that the drafters of the Fourteenth Amendment, passed during the Reconstruction period, did not intend it to apply to public schools. But Arendt's argument looked beyond such constitutional issues. She sought to situate public schools in her overall framework of politics.

For Arendt, there were three spheres of life: the private, the social, and the public. Schools fit into the "social sphere," or in today's more fashionable terms, civil society, a realm in which citizens interact voluntarily with one another in institutions neither private (individual) nor bound by political laws (public). Arendt explained, "What equality is to the body politic—its innermost principle—discrimination is to society. Society is that curious, somewhat hybrid realm between the political and the private in which, since the beginning of the modern age, most men have spent the greater part of their lives." Arendt also placed "vacation resorts" in this social sphere, which helped her justify an argument against school desegregation. "If as a Jew I wish to spend my vacations only in the company of Jews," Arendt explained, "I cannot see how anyone can reasonably prevent my doing so."[3] Drawing out her vacation-resort analogy, she reasoned that parents have the right to say no to outsiders who want to tell them whom their kids can associate with.

Arendt maintained that when the state intervenes in the social sphere, citizens are right to resist. She was not surprised that all hell had broken loose in Little Rock. Self-determination had simply turned angry. "The arrival of troops," she explained, "did little more than change passive into massive resistance."[4] The sight of bayonets prompted the "massive resistance" unleashed in Little Rock.

This last point was disingenuous, and at her best, Arendt knew it. She realized that the United States had a long tradition of resisting the powers of the federal government without any prompting by federal action. Had troops really prompted the Little Rock turmoil, or could certain ideas in the realm of political theory have prompted the resistance, troops or none? Arendt herself spoke of "states' rights" and the idea that "the power structure of this country rests on the principle of division of power and on the conviction that the body politic as a whole is strengthened by the division of power." These were the ideas put forth by the anti-Federalists during debates over America's Constitution and by the great southern political thinker John Calhoun, who had argued for preserving a voice for southern political leadership even if it had no claims to a national majority. Arendt believed these arguments held lessons for liberals. "Liberals fail to understand," she wrote, "that the nature of power is such that the power potential of the Union as a whole will suffer if the regional foundations on which this power rests are undermined."[5] Little Rock taught liberals that lesson; it was captured in the faces of rock-hurling parents and in the words of a German émigré whose political language seemed to have southern hues.

~

If Faubus got a surprising defense of liberal equality from President Eisenhower, Arendt received something similar on the plane of ideas. Her talk of local self-determination—an argument she would later develop fully in her provocative book *On Revolution*—had turned scary when it appeared to support self-rule in the form of the mob. Liberals asked a basic question inseparable from the history of Little Rock: When was self-determination little more than mob rule? This was the inevitable question that Little Rock prompted. Fighting over this issue was not the battle liberals were hoping for; they believed that the national government was right to provide the key features of citizenship—including equal access to a decent education—to all citizens, no matter their race. Such was the doctrine in *Brown*. Nonetheless, history is rarely straightforward, and in supporting this ideal, liberals faced not just critics but grassroots mobilization against their ideals. Out of that struggle came some lessons for political theory in the long run.

As the historian David Chappell points out, white moderate segregationists in the South were often worried that their sophisticated arguments on behalf of "interposition" and states' rights could wind up "sacrificing order and respectability."[6] In other words, scratch the surface of sophisticated talk about local self-determination, and you might find a sweaty mob taking things into its own hands. In an article that chastised Arendt, the liberal public philosopher Sidney Hook argued, "One does not enforce law by mobs, except in Westerns."[7] The historian C. Vann Woodward, though his comments weren't directed toward Arendt, concurred with Hook. He explained, "The movement for racial justice must not be disbanded by the threat of disorder . . . nor intimidated by mobs and demagogues."[8]

Woodward's criticism was especially astute. He was not only a self-professed "liberal," as was Hook, but "even more, a southern white liberal."[9] He had also provided research that helped justify the *Brown* decision. Woodward supplied the National Association of Colored People's lead lawyer, Thurgood Marshall, with historical arguments that buttressed a case against school segregation. Afterward, he wrote the book that Martin Luther King called "the Bible of the Civil Rights Movement," *The Strange Career of Jim Crow.* And though Woodward did not frame his central arguments in this way, his book made clear why liberals could never defend Arendt's thinking on the Little Rock crisis.

Woodward enjoyed an ironic disposition toward American history, noticing contradictions and the odd twists and turns in the past. For example, he found perplexing the argument of many defenders of segregation that they were supporting local traditions (Arendt's arguments tended in this direction). They wound up articulating what he called "a laissez-faire bias" and relying on organic "folkways" as the basis of segregation.[10] From this standpoint flowed the idea that laws could not change the hearts and minds of people who were practicing customs that were local and organic in nature. Having studied the historical rise of segregation, Woodward could only laugh at these laissez-faire, localist, and tradition-based arguments. If anything, he pointed out, segregation grew out of the imposition of new laws in the 1890s—following a debate about other approaches to race relations, including the Populist Party's call to forge an alliance between poor blacks and whites and a viciously racist policy of lynching and murder practiced by the Ku Klux Klan that made segregation seem downright sensible. To hear people speaking now as if segregation were a sort of extralegal social practice coming from "folkways" made Woodward grimace. Where Arendt saw mobs defending their way of life—their ability to do what they had always done and to associate with whom they pleased—Woodward saw an ironic use of force to defend legal, top-down legislation.[11]

If Arendt's arguments as a German Jew were challenging, Woodward's arguments as a white southerner were more so. He hoped to protect his beloved homeland from the "bulldozer revolution," the 1950s tendency to make every place look the same—evident in uniform suburbs, the cul-

ture of television, and Muzak playing in corporation elevators. Woodward loved the particularities of his homeland. But equality mattered to
him too. And, he reasoned, "if Southernism is allowed to become identified with a last ditch defense of segregation, it will increasingly lose its appeal among the younger generation" and therefore simply be replaced
with more sensible values and principles.[12] Woodward accurately explained a basic liberal principle: that there is always a plurality of values,
some of which clash with one another. If the South's regional difference
and its faith in local control—the virtues Arendt championed—clashed
with the national principle of equality, so much for local control and regional distinction. Equality trumps democratic control.

The fact that Arendt discussed public schools in her article only drove
home this point about a plurality of values and the prerequisite of equality. First, public schools clearly are not equivalent to vacation resorts.
Certainly, schools are places where students associate with one another
in a social setting. But as Chief Justice Warren of the Supreme Court
pointed out during the *Brown* decision, schools are essentially government institutions.[13] They rely upon public taxes and are governed
by public laws. Moreover, the public schools that arose during the
mid–nineteenth century in America—long before the rise of the welfare
state in the early twentieth century—were the quintessential expression
of liberal values. They symbolized a citizenry's willingness to sacrifice for
one another and to provide all children with equal public goods. They
balanced a citizen's rights—a right to learn—with responsibility—the responsibility to pay back, through taxes, to the commonwealth. They captured the principle of equality more than any other government institution, at least during peacetime. Schools did so by making certain public
goods available to all—public goods that could ensure not just public intelligence but also a certain equality of opportunity.

By placing schools in the "social sphere," Arendt could make a major
leap and assert that the state had no right to meddle in school affairs.
Liberals reacted against her leap, precisely because they held faith in the
egalitarian promise of public schooling. Schooling was not just about an
individual choice but also about delivering on a social responsibility. Sidney Hook reasoned that Arendt's view led to the idea that "only the political sphere is the sphere of equality."[14] He suggested that equality
might be too important a value to contain in one sphere; it must be extended to the social sphere too. The political theorist David Spitz also argued against Arendt on this point, writing that "education is the most social, as it is the most socializing, of human activities." If Arendt admitted,

as Spitz believed she must, "that the community has a legitimate stake in the intellectual development of its citizens, on what ground can she maintain that the give-and-take among students, the exchange of ideas and attitudes and interests that is central to such associations, is not relevant to this concern?"[15] Indeed, Spitz believed that the community has a responsibility to apply the value of equality to its public schools. This view was a natural extension of the idea that motivated the creation of public schools in the first place.

Liberals believed essentially that a national responsibility to fellow citizens might have to trump the principle of local self-determination (for more on this idea, see Alan Wolfe's essay in this collection). Spitz pointed out that Arendt had built a one-sided version of the "federalist" vision, stressing only the local self-determination side. He pointed out that, contrary to Arendt's arguments, federalism's highest ambition was to create a unified nation. Combating Arendt, Spitz wrote, "Federalism is also a principle that strives to unite people; it creates before everything else a state that is *national* rather than parochial in character, that represents the common rather than the dividing interests of its citizens; and what is common to them all, what constitutes their bond of unity, is the complex of values that is spelled out in the Constitution." He used this nationalist argument to warn, "There is the possibility that while we delay [desegregation], private groups and state government will continue to subvert those same bonds of community as to destroy the Union from within."[16] The national community therefore has a responsibility to a minority within its borders that suffers from the sin and violence perpetrated upon it by the majority within a local setting.

In this area, we can benefit from looking at the ideas of one of the towering figures in postwar liberalism: the theologian Reinhold Niebuhr. He had bequeathed the intellectual scaffolding for Martin Luther King's theory of nonviolent direct action that would be put into practice during the mid-1950s. In 1932, almost twenty-five years before the Montgomery bus boycott, Niebuhr argued for nonviolent "coercion" through actions like "boycotts" as a "particularly strategic instrument for an oppressed group" like "the Negro race in America."[17] But when the time came to pursue this practice, as Martin Luther King did in 1955, Niebuhr had drifted away from his 1930s radicalism toward liberalism. And in the process, his belief in the importance of the national community had started to displace his trust in local grassroots action. Though he remained on the side of nonviolent action, his justification for civil rights started to shift.

The moral cache of the national community was the thing that mattered most to Niebuhr in the postwar years. He had watched the American nation vanquish fascism abroad, and he started to argue that nations had to be moral creatures as much as geographical entities (even though he thought it impossible for the nation to ever become singularly moral). When he heard of *Brown,* Niebuhr was cheered: "What is at stake in this whole enterprise is the contest between the moral sense of the national community and the local communities in which there are vestigial remnants of the slavery ethos."[18] Before King decided to shift strategy and move away from a local approach (promoting his cause city by city in the South) toward one that sought to attract press attention at the national level, Niebuhr had set out a moral vision of the nation that he believed should trump local communities. As reaction set in against *Brown,* he argued, "Absolute democracy is not necessarily a resource of justice. It sacrifices leadership to lay prejudice, and obscures the continuing and broadly based will of the national community to assert the immediate and particular will of the local community."[19] Thus, the national community's moral attributes must trump the value of participation at the local community level.

Niebuhr's was a liberal vision of democracy growing out of the debates surrounding Little Rock—a vision that balanced out a plurality of values but that also emphasized the core values of the nation-state against local practices to the contrary. In the end, to defend equality against the local wishes of Little Rock's citizens, coercion might be the only, albeit regrettable, solution. As Niebuhr explained, "No community can maintain its order if it cannot finally limit impulses by coercion."[20] The national community had to preserve itself against the disorder of the local mob. As Sidney Hook remarked, Little Rock was a "national disgrace," precisely because the acts of the mobs there threatened core principles in the nation's creed.[21] The crisis there seemed serious enough to justify doing something, even pointing bayonets at fellow citizens if necessary.

THE SYMBOLISM OF LITTLE ROCK

Danger lies in trying to build general principles out of extreme situations. But in trying to understand the relation between liberalism and democracy, studying the events in Little Rock helps a great deal. If the crisis there was just about a particular moment in the history of the civil rights movement, then perhaps we should not make too much of it. But in this case, the fear that a mob would determine who attended and who didn't attend a school crystallized a large, overarching theme in liberal thought. The tension between liberalism and democratic participation and popular self-governance had a long history.

Indeed, it went back to the founding of America. The authors of *The Federalist*—heroes to Reinhold Niebuhr—faced the challenge of forging a national community out of a polyglot set of colonies. In their arguments against anti-Federalists, they prompted some major questions about democracy, especially about direct forms of self-governance such as the sort that Arendt would come to champion. They were some of the first to question whether a liberal polity could always be in sync with direct citizen input into decision making. After all, they knew the American nation could not rely upon a military that was voluntary, called to order at will. They knew that America had too large an expanse of land to govern itself by assembling all its citizens in one space to debate and forge agreement on public matters. They knew that coordinating national energies required a more focused mechanism than a decentralized political structure would allow.

Instead, they plotted out a representative republic that would transfer power, in part, to those who sought political office. In their words, they wanted to "refine and enlarge the public views by passing them through the medium of a chosen body of citizens," chosen by the people themselves, of course. This structure was necessary not only to manage the political community effectively but also to face the cold realities of human nature. The Federalists raised questions about the capacity of human beings to govern themselves, without ever giving up on popular sovereignty. There was too much "passion" in human nature to entrust citizens with direct self-governance, and the "reason of man" is "fallible." As James Madison famously wrote, "If men were angels, no government would be necessary."[22] But impulsive ambitions would always make direct self-rule dangerous. The Federalists didn't foresee the crisis at Little Rock, but they came close.

This view of human nature continued to inform the liberal political vision. Liberals were often more optimistic than the Federalists originally were, but during the cold war and the era of the civil rights movement, they relearned the importance of asking questions about human nature. Indeed, how could they not as they saw the rise of Hitler, mass genocide, the gulag, Stalin's dictatorship, not to mention racism in America? Niebuhr drew from the Christian conception of sin to explain human nature. He believed that "man is" by definition "a finite and contingent creature" who rebelled against this fate. "This is the sin of man—that he makes himself his own end," rather than recognize God's perfection. For Niebuhr, the self-righteous desire to make oneself God became the root of much evil in the world. Drawing from Saint Augustine, Niebuhr argued that ambition and self-regard could never be eradicated. He believed that conflict is endemic to social relations because of self-regard. Certainly, human beings possess the ability to improve society through free will, but freedom always promises good *and* bad—creativity and love on one side and destruction and self-centeredness on the other. Therefore, liberals had to be constantly vigilant to prevent the baser tendencies of humans from corrupting the public good.[23]

No doubt, the angry mob captured the liberal fear more than anything else—from the Federalist fear of Shays's Rebellion (when farmers massed against Massachusetts's court system) to the liberal fear of Little Rock mobs. Liberals knew that citizens could turn irrational and hateful at the spur of the moment, even if they were blessed with the tools of Enlightenment. This fear took a new direction in the postwar years, as liberals, spurred on by the works of Hannah Arendt and George Orwell, noticed the effectiveness of totalitarian power during the twentieth century, largely based on the "discovery of propaganda."[24]

Even before the consolidation of Stalin's rule, liberals worried about propaganda. Walter Lippmann is a case in point. A leading progressive intellectual before World War I, he decided to support Wilson's war to "save democracy," and he helped write propaganda in support of the war. He then reflected on mass persuasion in his now-classic book *Public Opinion* (1922), written soon after World War I. Here, he argued that as democratic societies had to deal increasingly with international issues—with which people had little direct experience—errors in human judgment became more likely, as did leaders' ability to manipulate citizens' ideas. "The world that we have to deal with politically," Lippmann explained, "is out of reach, out of sight, out of mind."[25] More and more, citizens relied upon "images in their own head" to help them understand the outside world, and these images included what he called "stereotypes." Lippmann admitted that stereotypes—and prejudices—helped organize people's thoughts about news they received. He suggested you could never get along in life without making use of stereotypes; but he also thought that stereotypes could prevent clearheaded judgment about problems. He remained ambivalent about the potential to square democracy and liberalism.

Lippmann, as with the Federalists before him, never gave up entirely on democracy. He wanted a larger role for experts but never called for taking away citizens' right to vote. Nor did liberals give up on pursuing propaganda to persuade the American public of the need to take action. During World War II, liberals such as Archibald MacLeish, Elmer Davis, and Arthur Schlesinger Jr. entered the Office of War Information, writing and creating propaganda to persuade their fellow citizens that they needed to fight fascism. They hoped that liberal propaganda would be less manipulative than the sort used in fascist countries. But they still used propaganda and weren't entirely certain the citizenry would come to the right conclusions without it (they had reason for their fear because U.S. entry into World War II remained unpopular only until Pearl Harbor). Nonetheless, they never gave up on public opinion; they realized that the public needed to be convinced, and ideally wanted citizens to change their minds through participation in public debate. And part of this debate would have to be about the rightfulness of granting civil rights to all citizens in America, no matter their race. This battle was a battle of persuasion, ideally, but guns would be brought in if necessary.

If you combine fear of the often manipulative nature of mass persuasion with the fear prompted by a negative view of human nature, liberal faith in democracy became harder to conjure. Both fears culminated during the cold war in the nascent civil rights movement. After all, America faced a new enemy in international communism—an enemy that had agents within the country's borders that needed to be confronted. Communists were known to be deceitful—creating "front groups" that lied about their support to infiltrate organizations and recruit new members—and saw "civil liberties" as little more than protections of bourgeois property rights. So why should liberals defend communists' right to say the things they did?

Liberals never defended the right of communists to spy on the U.S. government; they supported Truman's Loyalty Act for federal employees, even if they worried about the possibility of overzealous enforcement of the law. And they were often wary of the lies communists told, their deceitfulness and dishonesty. Actions, such as communists' spying at the State Department, mattered the most, whereas ideas—stupid and dangerous as some of them might be—needed to be tolerated in a liberal polity. After making clear how anticommunist he was, Arthur Schlesinger wrote, "The important thing is to preserve the right to free discussion. This right includes the right to hold loathsome ideas."[26] Allow the ideas to go down to defeat in the court of public opinion, Schlesinger suggested, even if we distrust the techniques of persuasion that communists used and even if we are not sure that people will make the right decisions when they encounter communist propaganda. The same could be said for the idea of racism or white supremacy: let it go down to defeat in debate and discussion, but if acted upon, as in Little Rock, racism demanded counteraction. Ideas and actions are not the same thing.

On democracy, the liberal conclusion was that yes, democracy should be preserved, but not to the point of absurdity or national collapse. Liberals could not give up on the idea of entrusting citizens with political decision making. And they believed that educational institutions—funded by tax dollars—had to help improve the status of public judgment and provide social opportunity for all citizens. But, at the same time, liberals remained wary and even slightly distrustful of democracy's perversions. Institutions needed to be strengthened—whether they were representative institutions that filtered out citizens' impulsive desires or civil rights that protected minorities against the domination of majorities (or mobs). Liberals lent their support to democratic processes while remaining on guard; they were always ready to point out potential abuses of power, manipulation of ideas, or signs that democracy might get off track. This stance was a realistic and tempered defense of democracy—one that understood the ideal's weaknesses.

This idea brings us full circle to Little Rock. What eventually won civil rights for minorities was the activism of the courageous parents and children who presented themselves at the doors of white schools and whose actions worked in tandem with the nonviolent direct action of Dr. Martin Luther King and the young students who pioneered sit-ins at segregated lunch counters in 1960. In other words, a movement on the ground—democracy in action—won equality for the black minority. This traditional story of the civil rights movement is convincing and beautiful. But it cannot lead us to forget that civil rights workers often needed the power of a strong government—even, at times, the power of national policing and the ability to point bayonets at fellow citizens—to assert their claims. For liberals, that addition to the story seems to offer a more accurate and sensible interpretation of the civil rights movement and its democratic ideals.

THE LESSONS TODAY: DEMOCRACY, LIBERALISM, AND THE FUTURE

What do the events at Little Rock and the long legacy of liberal distrust of democracy and grassroots action tell us about our contemporary political world? No doubt, we have lived through an important period of American history framed by the attacks of September 11 and the American invasion of Iraq. To turn to this theme in an essay about the civil rights movement and liberalism might seem strange, but not if we consider the connection to the liberal faith in democracy, especially in the realm of public opinion and propaganda.

Numerous Democrats supported America's invasion of Iraq. But liberals generally had misgivings about the decision to invade so quickly and unilaterally. The ambivalence came out in Senator John Kerry's explanation for his shifting positions on the war. Today, the war is much less popular than it was when it began. Nonetheless, a look back on this contemporary history confirms that Americans generally believed that direct links existed between Al Qaeda and Saddam Hussein and that the war against Iraq was a war against the terrorism that struck the country on September 11. This assumption was the rationale for entering the way the United States did, or at least it was the rationale that the president gave.

In September 2003, the *Washington Post* reported that "seven in 10 Americans continue to believe that Iraq's Saddam Hussein had a role in the attacks" of September 11.[27] The president clearly benefited from this connection and often played it up as he moved toward reelection. Throughout stump speeches and even in his debates with Senator Kerry, President Bush spoke of Hussein and Al Qaeda in the same breath. During his campaign—when it was clear that there was no connection—Bush was heard saying, "Do I trust Saddam Hussein? . . . Do I forget the lessons of September 11 or take action to defend this country? Given that choice, I will defend America every time." As a reporter for the *New Statesman* pointed out, such statements assumed that "the 11 September atrocities and Saddam Hussein are connected." Looking at public-opinion polls, the reporter argued that "American voters seem to have swallowed" this line of reasoning, no matter how false it was.[28]

Of course, the rationale for the war has constantly shifted back and forth between the need to fight terrorism and the need to spread the ideal of liberty. This changing rationale makes it harder for liberals to dissent, especially if they believe that the Bush administration is willing to invest the money necessary to support the development of democratic freedoms in Iraq. But it doesn't prevent liberals from asking how the nation reached the point of war in the first place. Liberals are right to ask this question—not because they reject the final rationale of liberty and democracy (which remains to be justified as events develop in Iraq and the Middle East) but because of the disturbing way the administration reached the fateful decision. Leaders misled the public, and public opinion was off base. This situation raises profound questions not just about the policy in Iraq but also about democracy and public opinion today, especially given that an increasing number of Americans get their news from ideologically driven media sources (most famously Fox News).[29] The ghosts of Lippmann and the Federalists haunt the decision to go to war in Iraq. Liberals are right today to ask whether or not the war in Iraq rests upon misleading information and whether it needs to be rethought accordingly.

Whereas liberals annoy conservatives by suggesting that political leaders are misleading the American public, conservatives annoy liberals by their distrust of educational institutions and intellectual virtues—a stance that is popularly termed "anti-intellectualism." During the 1960s, the conservative vice president Spiro Agnew announced that "pointy headed" intellectuals were dangerous for democracy, and thinkers calling themselves "neoconservative" pilloried a "new class" of highly educated people who were adversarial toward mainstream institutions. During the cold war, Senator Joseph McCarthy spent a great deal of his time, as Richard Hofstadter showed, ragging on "eggheads."[30]

Today, conservatives have renewed their attack on higher-education institutions as the bastion of liberal opinion (along with the mass media), and some of them advocate regulating how professors teach in the classroom. They have attacked professors—the thinking classes, if you like—for indoctrinating students, suggesting that they cannot be trusted to educate students responsibly. President Bush himself imbibes an anti-intellectual stance when he's on the campaign trail. The *Chronicle of Higher Education* reports that Bush is "quick with cracks about intellectuals and criticisms of institutions like his own alma mater, Yale University." He has "joked about how little work he did in college, as a history major, and about his mediocre grades."[31] Much of his ridicule of John Kerry's complex thinking about issues was a not-too-veiled attack on intellect. Anti-intellectualism and derision of education—and the cheap populism that fuels such political strategies—threaten the liberal tradition in America.

By defending education and idea-driven debate (and even by defending intellectuals), liberals need not embrace elitism, no matter the recent charges by the Right. Liberals certainly believe in their responsibility to make clear-minded arguments and to persuade their fellow citizens to embrace their ideas. The Federalists took on a similar task when they argued on behalf of the Constitution, as did cold-war intellectuals like Arthur Schlesinger, who wrote for as wide an audience as he could reach and tried to explain the importance of defending civil liberties even while recognizing the threat of communists at high levels of government. Martin Luther King took on this task when he made his famous "I have a dream" speech right before passage of sweeping civil rights legislation. Distrust in self-governance does not grow from elitism but from the idea of fallibility—a self-awareness that our ideas might be wrong, a recognition that we as individuals, when we are most honest, have been wrong in the past. The knowledge that we might be wrong—that our ideas might simply protect our own self-interest and limited perception—and that this ethic must be applied to everyone's behavior is a basic liberal value.

For sure, liberals believe that expertise should inform political decision making. They believe in giving ideas serious treatment and not simply sloughing off ideas that are critical of prevailing public opinion. They believe citizens have a right to pursue education within institutions where they can call into question their own beliefs and values. And they believe that society has an obligation to fund and support those institutions of education. Some of these beliefs might be elitist—in that they suggest that certain people have thought through problems more thoroughly than others and should be given more of a hearing—but some of these beliefs—those in favor of public education and equality of opportunity—are also profoundly democratic. This democratic slant is something that conservative populists purposefully forget when they focus solely on the elitist dimension of liberal ideas.

All of this is why the Little Rock episode is so important to recall today. In the debate that erupted in the late 1950s, the right of citizens to determine who attends their schools clashed with the wider public obligation to offer education to all citizens—in the name of preserving national unity. Today, discussions about education increasingly focus on the issue of "choice," and conservative policies uphold "vouchers" that would allow people to use public funds to attend private institutions. This approach threatens the liberal ideal of mutual obligation among the citizens of a shared national community. Against these policies, liberals must define a more rigorous defense of the conception of *public* schools—as institutions that require shared sacrifice. The idea of choice—the choice to say who will go to your school, black or white, or the choice to determine where your child will attend school—is not sufficient to maintain the health of a liberal society. Liberals believe that we often have to do things that we wouldn't necessarily do voluntarily and thus, in the process, check our own ambition and self-love. Again, liberals, even those who first articulated the principles of liberalism, realize that we all have selfish tendencies. The check that public schooling places on our individual choice is a liberal lesson.

The struggle in Little Rock reminds us of this lesson today. It also opens a window to the question of democratic passion—the passion that typically drives those who demand the right to self-determination—and the importance of law and institutional stability. Passion can be a good thing, but it also needs "restraints."[32] We saw passion in the actions of civil rights protestors throughout the 1950s—in the risks taken by the young people who asserted the principle of equality at Little Rock (and earlier at Montgomery and later in the Birmingham protests). But we also saw passion in the sneering mobs of white parents trying to protect their way of life. Thus, passion is not enough—nor is the principle of democratic self-determination. Liberals believe that a polity needs more than passion and democratic action; it needs to have shared values in place, such as faith in justice and equal opportunity. It needs checks against people's worst impulses. Such is the lesson that Little Rock holds and that liberalism teaches: We need both passion and constraints, passion and order, passion and shared faith in political principles of order and institutional order and the central principle of equality. But sometimes, and this is the challenge of liberal governance, we need to sacrifice one value for another.

The liberal view of democracy does not exactly distrust ordinary people; it's not so easily dismissed as mere elitism. But it does suggest—in large part because of a more pessimistic outlook on human nature—that we cannot *always* trust people (including ourselves). This view sees a plurality of values available in the world, one of which is democracy, which might clash with others. It recognizes that the right thing at a given moment might be unpopular with one's fellow citizens. It supports a disposition that is realistic without giving up hope in the project of education and enlightenment. It is ironic as much as hopeful. And most important, it is a value that we need to remember today.

7

What Liberals Owe to Radicals

MICHAEL KAZIN

M any contemporary tales about the decline of liberalism start by blaming the Far Left. Often, the narrative begins in the 1930s: Alger Hiss and other Communists worm their way into the higher echelons of the New Deal, setting up Democrats for the charge of "twenty years of treason" that gradually undermines the patriotic image liberals triumphantly claimed during World War II.

More frequently, the culprits in such narratives are the new radicals of the 1960s, black and white and, occasionally, Latino. They tear up the campuses and the ghettos, attacking authorities for betraying their own reformist ideals in the service of racism and imperialism. Liberal leaders who can neither squelch nor satisfy the New Left appear guilt ridden, ambivalent, and weak. By the 1990s, rigid advocates of multiculturalism take center stage in the drama of declension. They force liberals to pay tribute to all manner of identities—racial, ethnic, gendered, and sexual—which overshadow talk about the economic concerns that most Americans share.[1]

In each successive story, liberals who are soft on the Left make easy prey for conservatives—from Joe McCarthy to George W. Bush—who know how to stoke the fears and "mainstream values" of the broad majority. As a result, many Americans in the early twenty-first century have difficulty telling liberals apart from their occasional comrades on the Far Left. Of course, conservatives take every opportunity to encourage this confusion. "Here's the reason liberal has become a dirty word," snaps David Horowitz, the onetime radical intellectual who has become an avenging angel of the Right, "because Communists, fellow-travelers, pro-terrorists, terrorist sympathizers have hijacked the word . . . and because organs like the *New York Times* have abetted them."[2]

Such arguments have some merit. American progressives—including a few reporters for the *Times*—did often apologize for tyrants from Stalin to Mao to Castro whose big talk about liberating humanity obscured their despicable deeds. The New Left did assume that the "liberal establishment" was both more established and less authentically liberal than it turned out to be. Most radicals in the 1960s and early 1970s did act as if youthful rage and romantic will could propel the United States toward revolution. And the more strident purveyors of identity politics did spend more time curbing "offensive speech" on campus than attempting to turn back the Right's assault on the welfare of wage earners and the poor. To paraphrase Todd Gitlin, the Left captured the English department, while conservatives were winning the White House.

Such errors—most stupid rather than venal—tarnished the reputation of liberals, even those who tried to distance themselves from the Far Left. After all, most American radicals speak the same language of social equality that liberals do, and both groups routinely find themselves in the same coalitions, supporting the same candidates (albeit with different levels of enthusiasm) and despising the same enemies—from Nazis and Dixiecrats to the Christian Coalition and Karl Rove. So it's hardly a surprise that most Americans, whose interest in politics is quite modest, can easily be persuaded to lump the two groups together—as one party of raging modernists intent on having their way, whatever the big cause of the moment or decade happens to be.

Before contemporary liberals recoil from that image, they should reflect on the history that lies behind it. For all the damage the twentieth-century Left did—to itself as well as to the image of reform—liberalism also owes it a sizable debt. Time and again, activists and intellectuals in too much of a hurry to reach the promised land threw up fresh ideas, challenged entrenched elites, devoted themselves to grassroots organizing, and pushed liberals down paths they might otherwise have shunned or tiptoed along at a craven pace. Though their passion often deluded them about political realities, radicals cannot be separated from the history of American reform. For leftists, politics was the "moral equivalent of war"; it generated extraordinary commitment to end injustice as well as extraordinary loyalty to certain foreign leaders and systems that should have been condemned.

Radicals thus played a vital role in sharpening the contours of successive liberal eras—the early twentieth century, the 1930s and early 1940s, and the 1960s and early 1970s. They catalyzed changes in U.S. society and, at times, in the world—changes that most contemporary Americans applaud, although they know little or nothing about their origins. A strong, visionary Left was essential, although hardly sufficient, for liberals to achieve what they did in the wonderful, dreadful twentieth century.

Exhibit one is the "labor question." In 1919, Woodrow Wilson, in Paris for the conference that settled the scores of World War I, cabled to Congress, "How are the men and women who do the daily labor of the world to obtain progressive improvement in the conditions of their labor, to be made happier, and to be served better by the communities and the industries which their labor sustains and advances?" The Bolshevik revolution and postwar mass strikes in every major industrial nation had made his inquiry impossible to avoid.[3]

But for the genesis of the question, one must look to the preceding half century of workplace conflict. The roots of a more benevolent regime for labor were planted in events that frightened many Americans but also stirred the consciences of others. Most prominent were the national railroad strikes of 1877 and 1894, the eight-hour day uprising of 1886, and revolts in such factory towns as Lawrence, Massachusetts, and Paterson, New Jersey, just before the outbreak of the Great War. At each of these flashpoints, socialists and anarcho-syndicalists did most of the heavy lifting—writing the leaflets, printing the posters, delivering the soapbox diatribes, making strategy, and doing hard time in prison when they lost. During the Gilded Age, radicals created both the Knights of Labor and the American Federation of Labor (AFL)—the first national organizations of workers in U.S. history. Later, Samuel Gompers, the longtime president of the AFL, rejected the socialism of his youth as both impractical and unnecessary. But most of the biggest and most powerful unions in the Progressive Era—clothing workers, miners, machinists— owed their dynamism and ideals to class-conscious radicals who served them as organizers, orators, editors, and sometimes their elected leaders.[4]

The Progressives' revolt against freebooting capitalism was the critical step in their departure from the liberal, individualist faith of paternal figures from Jefferson to Lincoln to Cleveland. Reformers as diverse as

Theodore Roosevelt and Jane Addams had different reasons for making that move, which unleashed the flurry of legislation that marked the Progressive Era. But the working-class revolt—informed and mobilized by Marxists in both Europe and the United States—was the primary event that made change seem so urgent. Repetition of the Paris Commune and the Haymarket bombing loomed as spectral alternatives, whereas the Populist Party vision of a farmer-labor alliance scared such figures as Roosevelt almost as much. Woodrow Wilson proclaimed that his goal was to steer a middle course between socialism and laissez-faire, and he largely succeeded. Thus was born an enduring truism of twentieth-century American politics: the Left's disruptive power yet electoral weakness opened the way for liberals to advance.[5]

On the cultural front, radicals had a more direct and durable influence on their times. Nearly every achievement of liberal modernism—the unchaining of sexual pleasure from procreation, the liberation of art and literature from the didactic imperative, empathy with ethnic and racial outsiders and an identification with the rougher aspects of life, space for women to choose their work and partners, the effective use of wit to skewer all that is pompous and powerful—either originated or first gained prominence in the Left during the early years of the twentieth century. The motto that blazed in 1912 from the masthead of *The Masses*, journal of socialist bohemia, promised a kind of rebellion that would become routine in America half a century later:

> A magazine with a sense of humor and no respect for the respectable: Frank, arrogant, impertinent, searching for the true causes: A magazine directed against rigidity and dogma wherever it is found: Printing what is too naked or true for a money-making press: A magazine whose final policy is to do as it pleases and conciliate nobody, not even its readers.[6]

Some of the heroes and heroines of this movement altered the sensibilities of the larger progressive public without gaining the honors they deserved. Emma Goldman spoke to big audiences from coast to coast, mixing a defense of militant strikers with attacks on obscenity laws and a quasi-Freudian defense of sexual freedom. Margaret Sanger enraged authorities by distributing birth-control literature to working-class women. Beginning in World War I, voices of the "New Negro" such as Langston Hughes, Jean Toomer, and Zora Neale Hurston coupled race-conscious militancy with a talent for seeing black America whole: its arduous history, present condition, and great dreams. These activists were the shock troops of the revolt against Victorianism. Their cultural politics were a fitting expression of the belief that "no more tradition's chains shall bind us. . . . A better world's in birth." But only liberal journalists, intellectuals, and judges could legitimate their mores and domesticate their visions.[7]

The great liberal Woodrow Wilson had no more sympathy for cultural rebels than he did for the leftists whom his administration clapped in jail for protesting the decision to send U.S. troops into the slaughterhouse of World War I. Fortunately, other prominent liberals such as Felix Frankfurter, Jane Addams, and John Dewey found his reasoning repugnant. In 1920, they founded the American Civil Liberties Union to defend people like Eugene Debs, whose only crime was to write and speak against an "imperialist" conflict. In its agony, the wartime Left thus helped turn the First Amendment into a battle cry for every liberal activist during the remainder of the century and beyond.

When liberal Democrats came to power again in the 1930s, they gradually forged a more amicable relationship with the Marxist Left. The affair had a tragic irony. The Communist Party (CP)—the leading radical organization of the era—belonged to a worldwide movement commanded by the USSR under Joseph Stalin. During the period known as the Popular Front, one of the cruelest, most illiberal regimes in human history encouraged its American apostles to work for an expansion of workplace democracy and social equality at home.

In the latter half of the decade, American Communists achieved almost reputable status in parts of the industrial North and West by portraying themselves as uncompromising defenders of union organizers and civil liberties for all races and ethnic groups. Hundreds of party members also proved their antifascist credentials by shedding their blood in the Spanish civil war. It helped that, at the time, a good many nonradical Americans also believed in the myth that the Soviet Union had conquered unemployment, racism, and other allegedly bourgeois evils. Perhaps communists were just a more dogmatic, more disciplined group struggling for the same ends that the most visionary New Dealers were pursuing? Only in the fall of 1939, when the CP jerked into line with Stalin after the Soviet dictator signed a nonaggression pact with Nazi Germany did most liberals shed their innocence. Still, quite a few managed to reclaim it three years later when the Red Army prevented Adolf Hitler and his allies from conquering all of Europe.

The radical critic Irving Howe once labeled the CP's tilt toward reformism during the Popular Front "a brilliant masquerade," pointing out that it coincided with the Great Terror, when the Soviet state murdered millions of Russians for a variety of thought crimes. Yet most rank-and-file Leninists in America were comfortable, even glad, to put their dreams of revolution aside as they devoted themselves to building the industrial unions of the Congress of Industrial Organizations (CIO), defending blacks and Latinos arrested for asserting their constitutional rights, forming antifascist "front groups" like the League of American Writers and the American Student Union, and even boosting their ideas from within the Democratic Parties of such states as New York, Minnesota, Washington, and California.

The Popular Front allowed rank-and-file Communists—most of whom were either immigrants or had grown up in ethnic or racial enclaves separate from the larger society—to embrace Americanism. The new party line gave CP members permission to follow their hearts as well as their minds—to identify and work with a variety of their fellow citizens in big battles for undeniably important and feasible ends. In 1937, the Young Communist League chided the Daughters of the American Revolution for neglecting to celebrate Paul Revere's ride and marched up Broadway with a sign that read, "The DAR Forgets but the YCL remembers." The action didn't seem absurd at the time.[8]

Communists thus put grassroots muscle, and their tightly blinkered idealism, behind the goals of the New Deal and the coalition that kept it in power. "I don't turn my organizers upside down to see what kind of literature they have in their pockets," CIO leader John L. Lewis told critics who doubted the wisdom of allowing radicals to spearhead union drives in auto factories and steel plants. In fact, that literature often promoted causes like interracial unions, progressive taxation, cooperative housing, and national health insurance that many Democrats in Congress opposed. Radicals thus helped give the famously opportunistic FDR reason to believe he might push beyond piecemeal measures and toward the full welfare state suggested in his landmark 1941 speech about the Four Freedoms.[9]

Around a left-wing core grew a sentimental, vigorously democratic culture whose themes endured long after Communists and Socialists had been banished to the crumbling margins of American politics. Major aspects of what historians call "popular front culture" actually predated the Great Depression by decades: Walt Whitman and Mark Twain had celebrated the wisdom and art of working people; Frederick Douglass and Sojourner Truth had preached that "to understand, one must stand under," and Horace Kallen and W. E. B. DuBois had argued that, to realize its promise, the United States had to celebrate its multiethnic character. But CP members wrote "Ballad for Americans," "This Land Is Your Land," and *Mr. Smith Goes to Washington;* and authors who'd spent many evenings in radical circles wrote *Native Son, Citizen Kane, Death of a Salesman,* and *Yertle the Turtle* and popularized the kind of "ethnic pastoral" in novels and films that led directly to *The Godfather*.[10] Liberal intellectuals like Lionel Trilling and James Baldwin later scorned many of these works as bathetic and simplistic. But this creative output helped infuse American culture with an antiauthoritarian, populist tone that rapidly became ubiquitous.

With the coming of the cold war, liberals spurned their erstwhile allies on the Communist Left, amid alarums about espionage, some of which have turned out to be well-founded. But the zero-sum rivalry with the USSR and its ideological allies for the support of the decolonizing Third World also compelled liberals to take a step they had dithered about for decades. In the late 1940s, they finally became open supporters of racial equality. The Democratic Party, galvanized by the oratory of Hubert Humphrey, endorsed a tough civil rights plank for the first time in its history; President Harry Truman desegregated the military; several northern states and metropolises passed equal-housing laws; and black men began playing major-league baseball, beginning with teams in the liberal bastions of New York and Cleveland. These steps were milestones on the way to the national triumph of civil rights laws in the 1960s. But it was no coincidence that they occurred as Henry Wallace, presidential candidate of the communist-controlled Progressive Party, was denouncing Jim Crow and insisting on speaking before integrated audiences—or when millions of Asians and Africans were battling to free themselves from the rule of white Europeans.[11]

Liberals were certainly not wrong to sunder their tacit coalition with the disciples of Stalin. The Soviet empire erected in Eastern Europe may have been an indirect one, willingly staffed by local Communists. But to "choose the West," as Dwight MacDonald wrote in 1952, was to take a stand for both democratic principle and human decency.[12] Yet powerful liberals, especially those at the head of the Democratic Party, came to view politics too much through the prism of the cold war; following the logic of global competition, they sought to manage social problems at home rather than crusade to solve them. This attitude prevented them from giving an array of festering ills—segregation, pollution, urban decay, and poverty—the attention they deserved.

Young activists were quick to point out such flaws from within. The unruly New Left began as a polite, if messianic, new style of liberalism.

Altruists, black and white, left their campuses to register voters in Mississippi, organize welfare mothers in Cleveland, and rally in Madison Square Garden for a ban on nuclear testing. Some joined the Peace Corps or tried to drive segregationists out of the Democratic Party. Red-diaper babies were certainly attracted to groups like Students for a Democratic Society (SDS) and the Student Nonviolent Coordinating Committee (SNCC). But key figures in "the Movement" abandoned their liberalism only when they came to believe that their liberal rulers had abandoned them. President Lyndon Johnson's escalation of the war in Vietnam in the winter and spring of 1965 marked the point of no return, although such events as the 1962 Cuban missile crisis and the humiliation of Mississippi civil rights workers at the 1964 Democratic convention had already made young activists skeptical about the morality of dickering with the powerful.

"Making values explicit," SDS stated in the Port Huron Statement in 1962, should be the purpose of politics: "We regard *men* as infinitely precious and possessed of unfulfilled capacities for reason, freedom, and love."[13] That sentence (its unwitting gender bias aside) remains a fair, if ultraromantic, description of the direction in which the new, mostly young radicals took American liberalism. The tireless, often dangerous organizing of SNCC and its allies thrust black liberation to the front of the liberal agenda. Draft resisters, street protestors, and campus insurrectionaries made sure that an end to the killing in Vietnam would rank alongside the black-liberation agenda, although the conflict split the Democrats apart and helped elect Richard Nixon president in 1968. At the same time, radicals who were female or homosexual or disabled or belonged to a racial minority asserted their precious, unfulfilled right to be respected as such. White men on the left took a while to consider such grievances seriously, and the practitioners of "identity politics" sometimes descended into self-parody. But an expanded and durable meaning of "freedom" did triumph, at least across most of cosmopolitan America.

Leftists were not in the forefront of the environmental movement that mushroomed in the early 1970s. But following the lead of such writers as Barry Commoner and Dave Foreman, a radical counterculture helped popularize a critique of industrialism and consumerism that reversed the gospel of relentless growth that liberal presidents from FDR to LBJ had preached and urged Americans to practice.

None of these achievements mitigated the New Left's general lack of concern for the interests and understandings of the great white majority.

Unlike their predecessors, the radicals of the 1960s and early 1970s looked America straight in the face, confronting its wrenching passions of race, sexuality, violence, and egotism—all displayed on the global stage. But few young rebels, most of whom lived and worked in university towns or in the bohemian neighborhoods of big cities, gave serious thought to building a broad coalition that could change American politics. Neither did they consider how to win over people who loved their country and went to church yet were dissatisfied with their jobs and the war in Indochina.

In most local areas, the movement did not resemble the crazed, druggy image that still flickers from documentaries on late-night cable TV. Thousands of young radicals quietly worked in women's health clinics, edited alternative local newspapers, and took manufacturing jobs in order to organize democratic unions. But hot-faced rascals like H. Rap Brown and Jerry Rubin were the ones who made the cameras roll by shouting that black people should burn down America's cities and white kids should kill their parents. By 1970, for many Americans, radicalism had become synonymous with big trouble. Richard Rorty's ironic judgment is on the mark: "American leftism was revived in the 1960s by calls for revolution which, fortunately, were not successful."[14]

Liberals who embraced a good deal of the radical critique inevitably got tarred by the growing resentment toward its creators. In 1972, most voters probably agreed with Democratic nominee George McGovern, a decorated bomber pilot in World War II, that U.S. troops should withdraw from Vietnam and that they should never have been there in the first place. But they also despised antiwar protestors for rooting against the GIs and for the enemy. McGovern welcomed the support of the peace movement—as well as that of black militants, gay liberationists, and feminists—and was buried in the presidential election by Richard Nixon, under whose command over thirty thousand American soldiers had died in vain. No wonder that when Bill Clinton ran for president twenty years later, he seldom mentioned that he had campaigned for McGovern and tried to avoid answering questions about his own antiwar activism.

Since the mid-1970s, the radical Left has not existed as a coherent movement, although some of its fragments have flashed impressively for short periods. The exceptions include opponents of President Ronald Reagan's interventions in Central America, organizers who aimed to stop U.S. investment in South Africa during the final years of apartheid, and the civil disobeyers of ACT UP and other radicals who demanded a full-scale campaign against AIDS. By the early 1990s, however, each of these campaigns had flared out, having pushed policy makers in humane directions but without leaving behind any group of lasting significance. Meanwhile, the rapid fall of communism in Eastern Europe dealt a blow to the self-image of the Left from which it has yet to recover. Of course, the ugly truth about regimes from the USSR to East Germany had long been available to anyone who cared to read about it, and one of the things that made the New Left new was its rejection of the Soviet model of change. Still, Marxism guided the thought of most American radicals during the cold war, and they hoped that a form of socialism that encouraged democracy and free speech would replace the gray monolith of Kremlin rule. Few imagined that the whole edifice of state welfare, central planning, and Leninist metaphysics could fall to the ground, not with a crash but a whimper.

Back in the USA, the absence of a radical movement hindered the prospects of a liberal revival. Every reform era in the twentieth century had been preceded or propelled by a spurt of left-wing thought and action: the Knights of Labor, the Populists, and Edward Bellamy smoothed the ground for the Progressives; mass strikes led by Marxists pushed the New Deal to embrace workplace justice; and Martin Luther King, Michael Harrington, and SNCC encouraged Lyndon Johnson to envision a Great Society. Yet during his presidency, Bill Clinton felt little pressure from the Left, given that it could neither aid nor hamper his plans. He was thus free to tack cleverly between partisans on both sides of the aisle in Congress and was able to win reelection. But the virtual absence of a Far Left also ensured that the only major domestic accomplishments of the first Democratic president to win reelection since FDR would be measures Republicans had long favored: a free-trade agreement with Mexico and Canada and the end of guaranteed federal payments to poor single women with young children.

Certainly, Clinton could have used a visible, potent Left in 1994 when he proposed to supply every American with health insurance. His plan, drawn up largely by Hillary Rodham Clinton, was overly complex and depended on the support of big corporations, which were vulnerable to the fears of Wall Street investors and their normal allies in the GOP. Opponents were able to destroy the scheme rather easily because no moral argument stood in their way. Back in the 1970s, the Medical Committee for Human Rights, a New Left group, had coined the slogan "Health care is a right, not a privilege." A generation later, that idea—embraced by the governments of nearly every other developed nation on earth—animated no mass protests or lobbying campaigns and was probably familiar only to residents of such villages as Berkeley, Cambridge, and the Upper West Side of Manhattan.

~

To paraphrase the Book of Proverbs, when liberalism has no vision, it withers. The hope for secular transcendence has traditionally been the province of radicals who raise crazy notions that only liberals in and close to power can moderate and legitimate. Without pragmatic liberals, radicals spin into fantasies or eat one another alive from inside their desiccated ideological cocoons. But without radical dreamers, liberals absorb themselves with strategies that lead mostly to defeat. When, in the spring of 2005, I asked a class of intelligent, informed undergraduates to name a contemporary radical, an unplanned minute of silence ensued. Then someone volunteered Louis Farrakhan, head of the separatist Nation of Islam. Two painful minutes later, another student mentioned the filmmaker Michael Moore.

Amid the glittering turmoil of the late 1960s, the Polish philosopher Leszek Kolakowski asked, "Why is utopia a condition of all revolutionary movements?" and then answered his own question: "Because much historical experience, more or less buried in the social consciousness, tells us that goals unattainable now will never be reached unless they are articulated when they are still unattainable."[15]

Deep into the second term of Bush II, one has difficulty recalling the old passion for beginning the world over again. The cold war is history, and where Communists still rule, they usually offer up their citizens as cheap labor to foreign corporations. The once-great social-democratic parties of Europe struggle to keep their welfare states from unraveling amid aging populations and high unemployment. In 2004, thousands of bright-eyed, progressive young Americans threw themselves heart and soul into campaigning for an awkward, cautious Democratic nominee for president—and lost. Liberals in Congress expend much of their energy trying to preserve laws passed during the New Deal and the Great Society.

This nadir of the historic Left calls for a measured defense of utopia. Leon Trotsky once predicted that under socialism "man would become immeasurably stronger, wiser, freer, his body more harmoniously proportioned, his movements more rhythmic, his voice more musical, and the forms of his existence permeated with dramatic dynamism." Quoting this delirious passage in 1951, Daniel Bell added, with splendid insight, that America too "was an unbounded dream"—for the Puritans, for penniless immigrants, even for Marx and Engels.[16]

Today, the big dreamers reside primarily on the right. Capitalism is freedom, they preach from Hong Kong to Chicago, from Washington to Baghdad. In the United States, the Reformation trumps the Enlightenment as conservative politicians boast about how often they pray and as they vow to restore "traditional values" while Fox, their favorite network, feasts on sex talk, near pornography, and comedies that teach cynicism about every manner of authority. The contradictions of capitalist culture have never been more obvious, yet seldom have they had less political weight. Even amid the multiple failures of the Bush administration after the election of 2004, the organized Right's belief in its global mission did not fade.

Meanwhile, some places on earth have regressed to a condition of horrifying disorder. Several states in West and Central Africa have essentially dissolved, as gunmen slaughter one another, and millions of people die of starvation and disease. For male children, the best route to temporary survival is to join a private militia. Russians medicate themselves with endless doses of vodka, as their life expectancies and birthrates tumble and as their leader behaves like an elected czar. For too many young Muslims, resentment of the infidels is without end and without any solution but death. And countless inhabitants of the poor countries, it seems, want to move to America, the land so many others love to hate.[17]

Surely, the time has come to awaken the better angels of our nature and to rescue the virtues of the radical vision from the junk pile of history. Workers who organize themselves could brake the wild ride of the free marketeers; tolerant secularists might form a third force to weaken the armies of intolerant pietists; liberal peaceniks should challenge the disastrous myth that perpetual war can deliver national security or global democracy. In the United States, no less than in the Islamic world, we need a moral equivalent of the passion that drives believers in vengeful fundamentalism. Socialism can no longer be the name of that desire. But, without such a goad on the left, where will liberalism find the will to answer the utopians of the Right, to proclaim, once again, that a system that cannot guarantee a decent life to all its citizens is an obscenity indeed?

8

Liberalism, Science, and the Future of Evolution

MICHAEL RUSE

In the fall of 2005, the American Civil Liberties Union joined in a court case over the issue of what should be taught in biology classes in Pennsylvania. Should the class material on the origins of organisms, including humans, focus only on content that is generally accepted by the scientific community in America today—including evolution—or should teachers be allowed (if not forced) to acknowledge alternative accounts of organic origins, especially intelligent-design theory, a position that supposes that the Creator has intervened in the course of nature. I believe that this case is less about resolving disagreement about the fossil record than about fighting for the intellectual, social, and moral heart of the nation. In particular, those who attack evolution are proposing a very different agenda from that which has been so influential in America in the twentieth century. The proposal for intelligent design reflects the division between the conservative, evangelical religion–sympathetic branch of American thought and power that stresses so-called moral values, the reduction of government, and the use of force to influence and direct events through the world, and the liberal branch of American thought that stresses tolerance and secularism. As always with such conflicts, the story begins back in the past.

In 1859, the English naturalist Charles Robert Darwin published his

On the Origin of Species.[1] Here he argued that all organisms, including humans, are the end results of a long, slow, law-bound process of development and that the cause is natural selection. More organisms are born than can survive and reproduce, and those that succeed are different from those that lose. On average, the differences between organisms make for their success and failure, and thus occurs a natural process of winnowing or selection, leading to overall change. In the eyes of the secular thinkers and liberal Christians of the time, evolution epitomized the belief in progress. Indeed, for many, the very message of evolution reinforced this picture, marking a smooth upward progression from primitive forms to the human species, and ultimately to the civilized nations of the West.[2]

One of the many exceptions to this happy picture, of course, was the American South and then increasingly the West as the nation expanded. The Civil War, occurring just after *Origin* appeared, was a vital factor. The South was beaten and disgruntled. In reaction, many Southerners repudiated the ways of the North, and in the religious realm, sought a return to the Bible, searching for those passages that show that God often inflicts pain, especially on those whom He most favors. For those homesteading out on the vast plains of the West, the Bible was their guide and their comfort, their source of knowledge and support, in the face of backbreaking labor, natural and human threats and pressures, drought, Indian raids, and everything else that made pioneer life so difficult.

Among those disenfranchised from liberal thinking about evolution, literalism became the norm, and evolution (along with Sunday newspapers and the theater) became the touchstone of all that was wrong with the alien North. By the end of the century, the dominant religion in the South (and West) was evangelical Protestantism, which emphasized faith and helplessness and salvation rather than progress and good works and improving one's own lot. Often this strain of religion was rolled in with eschatological views about the imminent coming of Christ, who would lead his troops at Armageddon before ruling over a thousand years of earthly harmony. A farrago of antievolution arguments was produced—arguments about inexplicable gaps in the fossil record, a lack of evidence of the origin of life, the idea that the blind law of processes cannot lead to design, and so forth. But although those who presented these critical points were undoubtedly sincere in their belief, the key factor in their disavowal was hatred of the underlying philosophy of evolution, which they identified with liberalism, and its supporters.

The literalists were not mistaken about their target. Obviously, not every American evolutionist was a liberal in every sense of the term (Henry Fairfield Osborn, the director of the American Museum of Natural History in New York City, was a scion of one of the biggest railroad fortunes in the nation and lived and thought accordingly), but they all, including Osborn, favored gradual, progressive social change, through public education that emphasized the value of science and (for those who were religious) a sophisticated reading of the Bible and understanding of the main tenets of their religion. The background was thus set for the Scopes Monkey Trial.[3]

In a sense, the Scopes trial was sparked by a paradox. Thanks to the progressive thinkers and their allies, by the third decade of the twentieth century, American education had expanded mightily. The number of students enrolled in secondary education (high school), for instance, had jumped from two hundred thousand in 1890 to two million in 1920. The South was affected by this change, and for all that this shift was clearly beneficial overall, it brought tensions in its wake. Not the least of these in science education was the introduction of evolutionary themes. The textbook of the day, *A Civic Biology* by George Hunter, is pretty mild by our standards: it offers lots of good advice about eating good foods and evacuating on a regular basis, strong warnings about the ills of alcohol, and an avoidance of sexual topics as though the main reader were a maiden aunt. It endorses evolution and suggests that humans should direct the course of nature, particularly through eugenics.[4]

Inevitably, some southern states reacted by passing laws banning the teaching of evolution. The best known, of course, became the one that prosecuted John Thomas Scopes in Tennessee. With three-time presidential candidate William Jennings Bryan on the prosecution side and noted agnostic Clarence Darrow on the defense, the proceedings descended to farce when—denied the opportunity of using his own witnesses—Darrow examined Bryan on the witness stand on the veracity of the Bible. "I care not for the age of rocks," claimed Bryan, "I rest my faith on the rock of ages." Clearly, evolution was quick becoming a kind of litmus test for a much broader set of issues and divisions; Bryan himself was no hard-line literalist. He admitted openly that he thought the six days of Creation were six very long periods of time rather than six twenty-four-hour days. But the "Great Commoner" was certainly intent on defending the ways of the little people against the threatening designs of elitist scientists.

Scopes was found guilty, although the fine was overturned on a technicality. More significant was what happened afterward. First, the nation laughed at Tennessee, and the biblical literalists—by this stage known as fundamentalists (after a series of booklets expressing the faith)—retreated from public sight. They attempted no more such trials. Second, and more long lasting, evolution vanished from the textbooks of the nation. No American schoolchild was taught about evolution, at least not from the written word. Why was this? The answer is simple: textbook publishers are businesspeople and want to sell books. If many customers would not accept evolution, the easiest route was to eliminate the topic all around. And many southern states did not want evolution and so their desires prevailed. No one got the word on Darwin.

THE COLD WAR AND SPUTNIK

This state of affairs lasted until the end of the 1950s. Why did no group organize a push to get evolutionary biology into the schools? Franklin Roosevelt was elected in 1932, leading to the New Deal and twenty years of Democratic presidency and, even after this period, Dwight Eisenhower was hardly a hard-line conservative. Surely a nation that was being governed by liberal principles—and that was now making great use, in peace and in war, of science and technology—would endorse and promote one of the major triumphs of empirical inquiry? Einstein was a folk hero. Why not Darwin? Why not give a hearing to Darwinism, especially given its odor of liberalism, hinting at progress in culture as well as in the fossils?

Two major reasons for this omission spring to mind. First, internally, evolution got off to a slow start as a professional, fully established science. In the early years after the publication of *Origin,* people became evolutionists, but no one was much interested in causes, and natural selection was downplayed and ignored. Darwin's main supporters, notably his "bulldog," the morphologist and science educator Thomas Henry Huxley, were less interested in the scientific aspects of evolution than in the adoption of the basic idea as a kind of overall metaphysics, even its use as a sort of secular humanist religion, with which they could battle the conservative established order. Only with the coming of genetics in the twentieth century did people start to consider evolutionary change in a professional mathematics-based fashion, and even then, the process was slow—especially given that the Second World War diverted so much scientific energy to the physical sciences and to their practical use.

For many years, right up through the late 1950s, evolutionary theory had to battle for its place in the sun. Then, after the triumph of the physical sciences, the molecular biological sciences began their dizzying climb and pushed all else aside. Why bother with natural selection with DNA on the horizon? Moreover, the culture of science frowns on the intrusion of external cultural values: Kepler may have accepted the Copernican picture of the universe because he was a sun-worshipping Platonist, but heaven forbid that anyone should mention this fact. Evolution, with its odor of liberalism—and it certainly still had one—was just not the kind of science that many wanted taught in schools. Facts, not theories, please.

Second, an external reason that evolution was not likely to be advanced in the American education marketplace came from the political power of the South. The southern Democrats were a very large tail wagging the American dog. Roosevelt could not and did not fight for civil rights for African Americans. Why should evolution do any better? So the textbooks remained Darwin-silent. And, one should add, at the same time, the literalism of the evangelicals became more dogmatic and narrowly focused. No longer would the moderation of someone like Bryan be tolerated in the movement. "Young-earth creationism"—touting a six-thousand-year earth span and six literal days of Creation—became the norm. The main theoreticians of creationism were drawn from that small sect the Seventh-Day Adventists, one of the millennial groups coming out of the mid–nineteenth century. Their founder, Ellen G. White, had stressed the need to keep sacred the Sabbath, Saturday, and a strongly supporting part of this theology was the need to interpret the days of Creation in an absolutely literal fashion. Adventists, who were a highly organized group with much experience publishing their works and doctrines, slipped in after the Scopes trial and made great inroads into the thinking of people in more mainstream churches.

Why then did the treatment of evolution change? It would be nice to be able to say that evolution came into its own because of the efforts of the liberal establishment, including scientists. Such is not the case, however. Indeed, scientists then and now tend to be the most reluctant of all to defend the products of their efforts in the teaching in schools. The reason is simple. There is no professional gain from such activity. In some respects, science is as ordered and rigid as the Society of Jesus, the Jesuits. It involves rigid training and indoctrination into its ways, and expectations are laid out clearly. For success, scientists are expected to work long and hard on topics of the day and to give evidence of their activity by publishing in major journals. Because science is expensive, they must compete for funds against others. This process is a long and tiresome business, but it is essential, not only to keep working (along with one's increasingly large number of dependents in the form of graduate students, postdoctoral fellows, and technicians) but also to gain the respect of one's peers and to please the administrators of one's organization (usually a university), who judge success as much in terms of hard cash as in discoveries. A scientist who announces that he or she will take time from the lab to promote the place of science in society or of science education will be regarded as foolish—as one who is beyond doing serious research. Certainly such a scientist would not be deserving of grant money. In fact, the culture of science has some similarity to that of a religious or secret society: the person who engages in popular or vulgar activity is downgraded. The most famous science communicator in America in the second half of the twentieth century, Carl Sagan, was denied entry into the National Academy of the Sciences at least as much because he was a television star as because his work was judged of inferior quality.[5]

So, if scientists did not go out into public and battle for evolution, how did things change? As with most developments in the 1950s, the real reason lay in the cold war, and particularly in the Russians' 1957 success launching a satellite. *Sputnik* was put into space on October 4, 1957. At 184 pounds, it was eight times larger than the satellite the Americans hoped to send up. At once, people recognized the implications. Eisenhower immediately gave a press conference to reassure Americans that all was well. His appearance lasted thirty-two minutes, leading the *New York Times* to comment: "As the President began his conference, the Soviet earth satellite was over the Indian Ocean at about the Equator. And when the conference ended at 11:02 A.M. the satellite was flashing over Kodiak, Alaska, on a course that took it 100 miles west of San Francisco five minutes later."[6] The fear was palpable.

America perceived that it was falling behind. Three days after the launch of *Sputnik,* concerned scientists began to speak out. The *New York Times* reported,

> The nation's youth must be taught to appreciate the importance of science or the United States' way of life is "doomed to rapid extinction," the director of the American Institute of Physics said yesterday. "The last few days have given ample evidence that America cannot just sit back and assume that we alone have the world's 'know-how' at our finger-tips," said Dr. Elmer Hutchisson, director of the institute. Through its member societies it represents nearly 20,000 American physicists. He said Soviet scientists and teachers enjoyed a high place in their society and that Soviet policy, in which science is taken almost as a religion, seems to have paid off. Dr. Hutchisson said that the United States must distinguish carefully

between the "highly accumulative" scientific knowledge that can be taught by rigorous discipline and the "namby-pamby kind of learning" that seeks to protect children against inhibition of their individuality "or their laziness." Unless future generations appreciate the role of science in modern society and understand the conditions under which science thrives, he said, "our way of life is, I am certain, doomed to rapid extinction."[7]

An immediate and massive push for science education ensued. The budget for the National Science Foundation went up from around $35 million dollars in 1957 to $135 million dollars in 1958. Within ten years, it was half a billion dollars. Science education also benefited, and because education is a state rather than federal matter, an end run was needed. How could the nation get quality science quickly into its classrooms? The decision was to sponsor the production of high-quality, subsidized textbooks, which then would be taken up and used by the nation's children. School boards would jump at the chance to get these books, especially given that they would be cheap. By now, for all its slow start, evolutionary theory was moving along at a smart pace. Americans particularly were contributing to the field, with studies on animals and plants and interest by a growing numbers of students. Hence, the biology versions of the new textbooks, written anew for the purpose, contained a lot of explicit discussion of evolution, and so finally the topic was being taught openly in America's classes. A classic was the "blue version" of the Biological Science Curriculum Study text *Biological Science, Molecules to Men.*[8]

THE DAWN OF "SCIENTIFIC" CREATIONISM

To every action arises an equal and opposite reaction, and before long, the biblical literalists were up in arms. They posed no small threat. The cold war may not have inspired the liberal establishment to action, but it was a fertile breeding ground for American evangelical Protestantism, which was sympathetic to the literalism of old. Many believers thought the apocalypse approached, especially due to the development of atomic and hydrogen bombs.[9] The bombs' effects seemed very much like the conflagrations predicted in the Bible. The founding of the state of Israel in 1948 was likewise taken as significant, for the Bible forecasts that the Jews must return to their homeland before the end comes. And then, as always in America, effective preachers, like Billy Graham, were on hand to play on and increase such fears.

The spread of evolutionary ideas in the years after *Sputnik,* especially their spread in school textbooks, worried evangelical Christians greatly. They took to their studies to write counterblasts. Particularly influential was *Genesis Flood,* appearing in 1961 and written by two hard-line, young-earth creationists, biblical scholar John C. Whitcomb and hydraulic engineer Henry M. Morris. The book fell on fertile ground.[10] The very fact of the communist empire put many in mind of the forces of evil that are so graphically described in the apocalyptic books of the Bible, Daniel in the Old Testament and Revelation in the New. *Genesis Flood* argued that the fossil record, the evidence of geology, and the theories of physics and chemistry all point to a worldwide deluge some five or so thousand years ago that wiped out all animals, except perhaps a fortunate few who sailed through (or rather above) it all. The Flood, one should add, has a particularly important place in the theology of people like Whitcomb and Morris because they believe it was the first great upheaval in earth history and corresponds to the final, future great upheaval, Armageddon, when God will fight the forces of evil.[11]

With the inspiration of such works as *Genesis Flood,* the 1960s and 1970s saw the rise of an organized opposition to evolution, especially to its teaching in schools. The Supreme Court by this time had decreed that one can teach evolution in schools and that one should not teach the Bible in schools, so biblical literalism was gussied up to look like science—in the form of so-called scientific creationism, which unsurprisingly shows that every claim in Genesis is supported by the empirical evidence. You think that a progressive fossil record proves evolution? Think again. It is an artifact of the Flood. Dinosaurs? They were caught up in the rising waters down the mountain, whereas humans reached the top before drowning.

The stage was therefore set for a showdown between evolutionists and creationists, and this event came at the end of 1981 in the state of Arkansas.[12] The scientific creationists caught the evolutionists flat-footed. The scientists thought that the battles had ended with Scopes long ago. They continued with their science and fought battles between themselves over the fossil record and the extent to which humans are part and parcel of the overall biological picture. They ignored the rising force of creationism to the detriment of their science—especially to the detriment of the teaching of their science. After twenty years' labor, in one state of the union—Arkansas—the literalists won official acceptance of their ideas. Touting a so-called model bill that insisted on the teaching of creationism in state-supported biology classes, the literalists hit pay dirt. Insisting on the "balanced treatment" of evolution and creation science in the biology classes of the state, a bill slipped through the two houses of the legislature with nary a word of comment.

With science thus under threat, at last the liberals rallied around the flag and did their job well. I am speaking somewhat immodestly here, for I was one of the witnesses against creationism—along with such better-known people as the Protestant theologian Langdon Gilkey and the paleontologist Stephen Jay Gould. After a two-week trial, the judge in the case ruled firmly that creationism is religion and has no place in the classroom. He ruled that the "essential characteristics" of science are: "(1) It is guided by natural law; (2) It has to be explanatory by reference to natural law; (3) It is testable against the empirical world; (4) Its conclusions are tentative, i.e. are not necessarily the final word; and (5) It is falsifiable."[13] In the judge's opinion, creation science fails on all counts.

The law mandating balanced treatment of evolution and creationism in biology classrooms was ruled unconstitutional, as was a similar law in Louisiana a year or two later. But the fight didn't end here. Prominent creationists worried that they should not continue this sort of battle. Apart from other considerations, many state officials in Arkansas and elsewhere were pointing out that antievolution laws were bad for business. States in the South, competing desperately for high-tech industries, were hardly going to attract top-quality programmers and engineers and chemists and others if the cost was to be creationism in schools. So other states were unlikely to follow Arkansas. Better to work at the grass roots with sympathizers, the creationists decided. Better to introduce the ideas by stealth, as proves possible.

The 1980s therefore saw a time of truce, or more accurately, a time of exhaustion. Creationists kept a low profile (and some of the more prominent were in fact getting quite old), and evolutionists were happy to go back to more congenial pursuits. But things were merely quiet, not dead or gone. In 1991, Phillip Johnson, a Berkeley law professor, newly converted evangelical Christian, and Darwin hater, published *Darwin on Trial*, a volume that tried and convicted the old evolutionist.[14] In many respects, Johnson's book offered little that was new—he trotted out all the usual criticisms of Darwinism (fossil record and so forth)—but Johnson was not a law professor for nothing. He marshaled his arguments with great rhetorical skill. Again and again, he hammered home the theme that evolution is "only a theory not a fact." The book became a best seller among conservative Christians.

One important theme in *Darwin on Trial,* which Johnson extends considerably and elaborates on in his later books, is that the evolution-creation debate is not simply about science. It is about a whole way of looking at things and of conducting one's life.[15] Johnson makes much of the naturalistic nature of science—of evolution in particular—and he identifies it directly with liberal values and lifestyles. Evolutionists, he asserts, are favorable to things like abortion on demand, sex outside marriage, toleration of homosexual activities and liaisons, and plans for universal health-care coverage. Although he has always been cagey about how he himself regards the future and the coming of Christ, Johnson allies himself firmly with those who think that the proper course of action for Christians is to concentrate on personal purity and proper living according to the Bible.

The big gap in *Darwin on Trial*—one that Johnson himself would not deny—is that he offers no alternative. If evolution (Darwinism especially) is not true, then what is the true story of origins? Is it literally the story in Genesis? Later in the decade, answers came to fill the gap. Two men—Michael Behe, a biochemist, and William Dembski, a philosopher and mathematician—offered what has come to be known as intelligent-design theory. Their books (*Darwin's Black Box* by Behe and *The Design Inference* by Dembski) argue—in a modern version of the traditional argument from design—that the organic world is too complex to explain through blind law and that hence one has to suppose a designer.[16] Although supposedly this designer does not have to be identified with any known deity, in fact these men (as well as Johnson and virtually all others associated with the intelligent-design movement) think that it is the Christian God. And like Johnson, these men and the others think that more is at stake than correcting the fossil record. A whole system of thought and way of life is at issue.

Although some intelligent-design enthusiasts are young-earthers, most think that the earth is very old—as old as evolutionists think it is. Most intelligent-design enthusiasts also accept some form of evolution—but believe that every now and then, God has to get involved. The young-earth creationists think that there was massive evolution after the animals got out of the Ark. But without denying such differences, we can appropriately associate the intelligent-design movement with creationism—creationism lite—because the two groups share an antipathy to progress and liberalism. They share the struggle and aim for the American Way of Life.

EVOLUTION AND LIBERALISM TODAY

As with the fundamentalists at the time of the Scopes trial, the intelligent-design theorists are not mistaken in their target. While the antievolutionists have been busy furthering their cause in the past fifteen to twenty years, evolutionists have not stood still. As a professional field, evolution science has been incredibly vigorous in making new discoveries and proposing new theories.[17] The molecular revolution in biology has begun to make major payoffs, particularly in the study of development and its implications for the processes of change ("evolutionary development," or "evo-devo" for short). In parallel work, scientists are uncovering the fossil record and explaining how today's life forms came into being. Some of the most exciting discoveries relate to the immediate human lineage. One example is the recent discovery of near humans (*Homo floresiensis,* or hobbits) in Indonesia that are only twenty thousand years old; these humans were small and had miniature brains but were apparently capable of advanced thought.

In academe, evolution is the status quo. In tandem with the science's moving forward rapidly and confidently, biology departments are increasingly putting their whole curricula on an evolution-based foundation. Evolution has also entered public dialogue through a number of popular books that make evolution seem interesting and exciting. Particularly noteworthy are the Pulitzer Prize–winning account of work on the Galapagos on Darwin's finches, *The Beak of the Finch,* by science writer Jonathan Weiner; several works, including *The Diversity of Life, Consilience,* and *The Future of Life,* by Harvard ant expert Edward O. Wilson; Richard Dawkins's various books on evolution, including the *Blind Watchmaker,* and most recently, *The Ancestor's Tale;* and many best-selling works by Stephen Jay Gould, including *The Mismeasure of Man* and *Wonderful Life.*[18]

Not all these books extend from the science to ethics and politics and culture generally, but most do, and with few exceptions, the underlying philosophy is a liberal one.[19] For example, Gould's *The Mismeasure of Man* is ostensibly about the history of measuring human intelligence and relating intelligence to biology, but the book also warns against judging one kind of person over another on supposedly hard physical facts, and it discusses how this kind of practice leads to prejudice and hatred. *Wonderful Life* is ostensibly about the five-hundred-million-year-old fossils of the Burgess Shale in Canada, but it's also about the dangers of reading progress into the world of biology and the invariable consequence that some people will be deemed inferior. In turn, Edward Wilson writes about evolution to argue for biodiversity and ecological principles. He cares about the evolutionary story, but in major part, he cares about the underlying moral and social messages that it bears. The same statement applies to Dawkins, who argues for reducing the influence of religious principles in our public life.

So in academia and certain portions of public debate, evolution thrives. Unfortunately, the academy really is an ivory tower. Survey after survey shows that most Americans do not believe in evolution; they opt rather for various biblically based views of origins.[20] Legal or not, 15 percent of American schools today teach creationism in biology classes. This finding is the tip of an iceberg. In 1991, ten years after the Arkansas trial, a Gallup poll reported that 47 percent of Americans were creationists and that another 40 percent believed in some kind of theistic (that is, guided) evolution. These figures have remained constant. A 2001 Gallup poll found that 45 percent of Americans think that God created humans as they are now, 37 percent give the job to some kind of guided evolution, and only 12 percent think that humans evolved through unguided natural forces (this number is up 3 percent from 1982 but chiefly at the expense of the "don't know," which dropped from 9 percent to 6 percent). A 2001 National Science Foundation survey on science literacy found that 47 percent of Americans think that humans were created instantaneously. Amazingly, 52 percent think that humans and dinosaurs coexisted.

Moreover, in various degrees, just about all these people fall at the more conservative end of the political and social spectrum and see opposition to evolution as part of this general world picture. This fact comes through strongly in a recent (spring 2004) survey of four thousand Americans by the Pew Forum on Religion and Public Life. Defining "traditionalist" Christians as those who accept literal readings of the Bible, including nonbelief in evolution, the survey found strong correlations between holders of conservative moral views and conservative theological views (in their language "traditionalists") and, conversely, between holders of liberal moral views and liberal theological views ("modernists")—with acceptance or rejection of evolutionary thinking providing a kind of litmus test of one's position on the spectrum. If one factors in affiliations—especially contrasting people like Southern Baptists who belong to evangelical churches (26.3 percent of the country) with people like Episcopalians who belong to mainline churches (16 percent)—the traditionalist-modernist divide is even more evident.

These findings bring us back to Pennsylvania—and other states like Kansas and Georgia—where people are trying hard to get intelligent-design theory included in biology curricula along with evolution. "Teach the issues," is the cry, meaning that all views should be presented to students as a kind of smorgasbord, from which they can choose. "Evolution is only a theory, not a fact" is the mantra today. I am glad to say that in December 2005, the judge in the Pennsylvania case ruled firmly that intelligent-design theory is not genuine science, that it is rather old-fashioned biblical literalism dressed up to look like science to get around constitutional separations of church and state. He had no intention of letting intelligent-design theory into the classrooms of his state. In fact, the school board that promoted intelligent design has been thrown out and replaced by a group that is strongly proevolution. But liberals should not relax on the basis of one victory. If anything, intelligent-design enthusiasts have the upper hand, for a growing number of school boards are inclined to admit their ideas. Moreover, President Bush is having considerable success in putting conservative (in one case, very conservative) judges on the Supreme Court, and the justices have opined that perhaps the United States has gone too far in separating church and state. In other words, at least the possibility exists that in the next few years, the Supreme Court will allow intelligent design to be taught openly in American schools. Admittedly, intelligent design is not full-blown creationism, but the more conservative creationists are open about seeing the marshalling of intelligent design as a "wedge strategy." By getting a relatively mild form of creationism into schools, they hope to open the way to introduce more literalistic versions.

WHAT IS TO BE DONE?

To isolate evolution from more general issues, particularly the threat to liberalism today, would be a mistake. Rightly, both sides identify evolution with liberalism, and those opposed to evolutionary theory wish to counter liberalism with a more conservative public philosophy and policy.

If the Supreme Court were to become more liberal and science friendly, then the threat of creationism would diminish. But whether the Court is agreeable or not, liberals need to become involved in this crucial fight. Indeed, some liberals are working full time fighting the creationists and their new manifestation, intelligent-design theory. The National Center for Science Education was founded toward the end of the 1980s toward this end, and its first (and thus far only) director, the anthropologist Eugenie Scott, and her associates spend their days recording the moves of creationists, offering advice to those in need and generally promoting the virtues of evolution and the vices of biblical literalism. The center stays away from general political issues and tries to be evenhanded in dealing with issues like religion. Scott has endorsed and promoted several recent books (by scientists and philosophers) critical of intelligent design, but she and those working with her are careful not to take a stand hostile to religion.

But this work is not a strong enough liberal effort on behalf of real scientific values. We are still crippled by the problem that the very people who ought to be staffing the front lines—the professional and academic scientists—are not doing so. An assistant professor in a biology department who announces that he or she is going to spend the summer fighting creationism and promoting evolution in schools will simply not get tenure. Writing a book for students, writing editorials, speaking at local libraries, pacing the halls of state capitols will probably end one's career at the three-year review. This understanding is so firmly part of the mores of science that, together, academics who fear for the culture of their nation must help create a different academic mind-set. Moreover, senior scientists should help lead this change because those whose careers are secure and who have the time and ability to look beyond the bench and computer can be the most helpful. Scientific organizations should also help pry academic scientists from their labs and push them into the newspapers, courts, city commissions, high schools, and other battle-torn areas. In addition, scientific organizations should convince universities that academic professors who work in their communities to strengthen the foundation for a scientific culture could do more to promote the well-being of science than they currently can by writing a few extra articles in remote professional journals. To be fair, organizations like the American Association of Science already do some outreach of this nature, but perhaps action is necessary to involve more associations and more academic scientists.

Liberals, especially liberal scientists, dare not wait for the worst to happen before they take action. With resolve, which has not yet shown itself within the academy, this war can be won. At the risk of being accused of exaggeration, I feel a bit like Winston Churchill in the 1930s begging his nation to rearm. In fact, one cannot overestimate the threat under which science lies at this time in the United States. Unless we scientists do something, we who cherish liberal values will face our Battle of Britain, and this time we might not beat the enemy.

9

Liberalism and Family Values

MONA HARRINGTON

arly in the twenty-first century, liberals are facing deep trouble in the country's social order, complicated problems that they themselves, without recognizing the full significance of their actions, generated and nurtured through the previous century. At the core of the new trouble is radical change in the status of American women. Driven both by economic need and by renewed claims to equality, unprecedented numbers of women began a migration in the 1960s out of the home and into the paid workplace. And liberals were champions of this change—champions of equality and champions of the right of individuals to choose how to live their lives. Liberal writers contributed crucially to the shift in traditional ideas about women's place, undermining the automatic assignment of women to homemaking. Liberal activists struggled to clear away a maze of written and unwritten restrictions that had, for generations, kept women who did work outside the home segregated in domestic, clerical, nursing, or teaching jobs. By the 1980s, the sight of women in medicine, or law, or the military, or politics, or the construction trades was no longer remarkable. In the 1990s, Americans saw a woman attorney general and secretary of state. By the turn of the century, the full-time, lifetime homemaker had become a rarity, and the woman at work—in jobs of all kinds and at all income levels—was an established fact of national life.

But the new work patterns, while opening opportunity for women, also produced disturbing and disorienting effects. Unwarned and unprepared, Americans faced deep disruptions in the country's family structures, its systems of caretaking, its codes of sexual morality, and its conception of sexual equality in the workplace, in public life, and in the home.

The litany of trouble that wound through this social upheaval is all too familiar: high rates of divorce; single-parent households with low incomes, giving rise to the sad pathologies of poverty; two-income households with little parental time for children; schools overwhelmed with the need to become surrogate parents; courts swamped by children and adolescents in trouble; elders without family or community supports; marriages and families across the social scale stressed by long work hours; women torn between the demands of the workplace and the needs of families at home; and, between the sexes, new tensions as words like *discrimination, affirmative action, harassment, abuse, domestic violence,* and *rape* took on new meanings.

Then there is the other piece of the story: women's remaining caretaking responsibilities undermining their equal opportunity in the work world. A still-strong social ethic assigns these responsibilities primarily to women, not to men. And most women, but not most men, compromise their time at work somewhere along the line to spend time at home with their families. In a work world that values employees precisely in terms of time, women then fall behind their male colleagues in all measures of reward and advancement. Women's wages are lower than men's. Women cluster in the lower levels of most workplaces. Top corporate management is 95 percent male. In the professions, only 15 to 20 percent of top positions are filled by women. Middle-class women race between job and home to provide as much of their families' care as possible because they cannot afford to pay for the level of caretaking their families need, or they work part-time or flextime and risk losing opportunities for advancement. Women in low-wage jobs are worse off because even full-time earnings cannot provide for adequate family care. Except where increasingly limited public subsidies are available, the result too often is entrapment of all family members in a downward spiral that makes the promise of equal opportunity a cruel joke.

Sadly, care workers themselves generally fall into this last category. Pressing need for child care and elder care at all income levels creates a huge market demand for care. But because most families have limited resources to pay for it, wage levels for caretaking remain low, and the supply of care workers depends on people who have no choice but to take low-paid jobs. The result in the new century is a hardening of inequality as we create a new, low-wage servant class to do our caretaking for us.

Further, because the pool of workers for low-wage service labor consists heavily of immigrants—both legal and illegal and largely non-white—we are creating not just a servant class but one made up of racial and ethnic minorities who, in large part, lack the economic or political power to improve their employment conditions.

This is the juncture—or disjuncture—where the liberal imagination that shaped the reforms of the 1930s and the 1960s falls short of its challenge. In the past, mainstream liberal programs focused on threats or injustices stemming from two sources of danger to ordinary Americans: business, which holds the power to exploit economic weakness; and government, which holds the power to override individual freedoms. In the New Deal, liberals used government to restrain and regulate business. In Lyndon Johnson's War on Poverty, they tried to subsidize enough education, and housing, and health care, and small-business start-ups to boost the poor into the middle class. And throughout, liberal lawyers have kept vigilant watch for abuses of civil rights.

But, intensely absorbed with questions of economic justice and individual rights, liberals have never formed a clear social theory that connects individuals, economics, and families. Nor have they looked squarely at the tortuous implications of moving women from the separate sphere of the home to a position of full, meaningful equality.

Specifically, there is no mainstream liberal program that measures the economics of caretaking for the whole country, that charts the distribution of caretaking work, that assigns weight to care as a value defining national goals, that takes a stand on the importance of family as a source of care, that speaks to the moral dimension of families as a social unit, or that even begins to recognize the ways in which women's equality is bound up with the organization of families and care. There is, in short, no mainstream liberal politics of the family. Therefore, the liberal task is to change the conversation, to confront and name the fundamental pieces of the family problem for liberals, and to construct principles to guide policies for decades to come.

~

At the root of the family-care dilemma for liberals is a broader American problem: We don't "see" the contours of what we are looking at. We don't see a collapsing care system because we don't see care as a system to begin with. We see individuals making private decisions about who takes care of the children or helps an arthritis-plagued elderly parent. We see families using the private market for services they don't have time to provide themselves: day care, housecleaning, fast food. We don't add all of this up and call it a system that is working well or badly.

When things go wrong, when a mother leaves children alone because she cannot afford day care while she works, when marriages fail under the stress of job and family demands, when unsupervised teenagers in cities *and* suburbs turn to sex and drugs, we generally see specific problems—moral or economic—but not an entire care system in trouble. If we did see systemic collapse, we would have to start thinking about care as it affects the workings of the whole society. We would have to start seeing it as a matter of "the general Welfare," which we are charged by the Constitution to promote. We would have to start thinking about a social responsibility for family care in ways that we have never previously imagined. We would have to think about care as a public value.

Long tradition defines the national values for which the United States stands as freedom and equality. As I have argued in *Care and Equality,* to that bedrock of human decency, liberals should insist on adding care. Starting with the value of care as a national priority, liberals need next to break away from the idea that care consists only of ministering to people who for some reason—age, illness, disaster, poverty—are helpless and cannot take care of themselves. A liberal conception of care would include all the caring—and the thought and work that goes into it—that supports everyone's everyday life.

Six-month-old babies obviously need attentive care, but so do sixteen-year-old high schoolers. These teens need to be listened to. They need the kind of guidance that can take a parent hours to think through carefully before saying a word. Families need time for adults to read to children and to talk with each other about the day. They need time for the inevitable emergencies—from strep throat, to heart attack, to depression, to a broken hip. And they need time for the dailiness of laundry, shopping, cleaning—and eating. In other words, a system that values care would be organized to allow time for the full range of family activities that support well-being.

Related to this is the essential idea that the need for socially supported care, broadly understood, runs across all income levels. And this idea is one that liberals especially need to confront, because traditionally they have tended to focus heavily on the family problems of the poor. Of course, the poor do need particular attention, but we need to widen the context of liberal concern, because by focusing on poverty as a special circumstance, we leave untouched the idea that family care is solely a private responsibility. Implicitly, we ratify the assumption that all is well for everyone else, that all other families can take care of themselves out of their own resources. And in doing so, we create problems across the board.

One such problem is the difficulty of defending against conservative arguments that the poor too could take care of themselves if they tried hard enough—a winning argument in the welfare debate and one enshrined in the title of the 1996 antiwelfare law, the Personal Responsibility and Work Opportunity Act, enacted by the Republican majority that was swept into office in the congressional election of 1994. But a further problem is even more serious, if less immediately obvious. To act as if only the poor need protection leaves families in all income brackets dealing with market forces that are generally blind to family needs. Whether the market demands too much time from workers or returns too little money, or both, caretaking suffers throughout the society, not just below the poverty line. The liberal vision has to extend to the whole picture, the whole system. As political theorist Joan Tronto has written, "Care is not a parochial concern of women, a type of secondary moral question, or the work of the least well off in society. Care is a central concern of human life. It is time that we began to change our political and social institutions to reflect this truth."[1]

This issue poses a philosophical challenge for liberals because it calls for taking families seriously while maintaining a strong, moral commitment to the freedom of individuals. In the older family tradition, this was a difficult dilemma. Legal rules—on sexual relations, on abortion, on divorce—imposed heavy restrictions on individuals; and social rules, particularly on the division of labor, severely restricted the freedom of women. That is, the price for all the good work of families seemed to be a chronic compromise of freedom and equality for individuals. So liberals, putting individuals first, fell into their defensive silence on the nature, the value, and the importance of the family as an institution.

But now in the twenty-first century, with greatly changed social and legal rules, the dilemma is solvable. The key is to recognize that the problem for the individual is not the family, as such, but conservative tradition, as such. If freed from conservative codes that make care a private responsibility and assign it to women, the family holds potential—which exists nowhere else—to further liberal values by nurturing individuality and sustaining it.

First of all, families serve individuals by creating a veritable cocoon of privacy. They provide protected private spaces where individual values, tastes, and customs can flourish, where the pressures of the prevailing culture are relieved, and where people can feel comfortable with their singularity.

Historically, liberals have been uneasy about the claims of family privacy because of the conservative tradition that made everything that went on in families a private matter, including terrible domestic violence and abuse. But a liberal principle that recognizes the value of families as a shield for individuality clearly distinguishes between privacy that protects and privacy that endangers the individual. That is, the potential for abuse should not discourage liberals from offering open and enthusiastic support for families as zones of privacy that make space for the flourishing of personal identities.

Further, the very nature of a family's functions allows the individual to express an important dimension of personality, and that is a desire for meaningful connection to others. But liberal thinking about families gets stymied on this point as well. A desire for connection seems to contradict a desire for freedom, and a position that supports both seems hard to imagine. Certainly, neither liberals nor conservatives have imagined it in any coherent way. Again, however, resolution is possible.

The contradiction between freedom and connection is not absolute. The desire for both and the need for both coexist in human beings. And a fully developed, fully humane politics—a new liberal politics—must encompass this complicated state of affairs. The challenge for liberals, as Martha Minow and Mary Lyndon Shanley argue, is to imagine the family constructed by individuals as social beings, individuals seeking relation.[2]

In a new liberal lexicon, the individual would appear not only as a self-defined, self-directed, self-sufficient person encased in the body armor of private rights but also as a real-life woman or man who values autonomy and rights *and* wants and needs committed, responsible relations with others.

For the relational individual, the family provides a needed base for sociability, a place to practice intimate interdependence, an exchange of caregiving and care receiving. It's a place for connecting, cooperating, reaching for understanding, expressing the need not to be alone in the universe. It is a place where constant, dependable care contributes to the strengths an individual needs for the fullest development of personality and talent as well as respect and concern for others.

For liberals, this idea means that their traditional support for individuals requires *simultaneous* support for families. And it also requires something of individuals. The "individual in relation" is not the individual whom conservatives depict as engaging in virtually any kind of sexual or marital behavior without regard to its effects on others. Relation implies responsibility. In making the individual in relation the moral basis for family policy, liberals would support a family system that requires clear obligations. It would be a system that individuals enter with the serious intent of engaging in sympathetic, understanding, supportive, caring, mutual responsibility for others over the long term. It would be a system that allows and supports the value of responsible individual relation.

Finally, as a base for a new liberal family politics, is recognition of the combined moral values of care and equality. How can we organize good care for everyone who needs it without constructing a class of caretakers who are excluded from the pursuit of equality? Political philosopher Eva Kittay calls for clear recognition of this problem, particularly with respect to "dependency," the need of some individuals for extensive or permanent care, the desire of families to provide such care, and the extreme difficulty of doing so without support.[3] Robin West, contributing to the growing field of feminist jurisprudence, makes support for caregiving an essential element of a just society. Her concern is the obliteration of a strong sense of self in caregivers when lack of support creates exhausted "giving selves" rather than "genuinely compassionate and giving individuals."[4]

A new liberal politics calls for redrawing the boundary between private and public responsibility. It calls for shifting some responsibility for care to the society at large, some different allocation of caretaking costs, some new division of paid and unpaid labor, and serious attention to the connection between care and women's equality.

~

One needed step, designing and promoting public policies that provide security for families at the low end of the income scale, requires no great leap of imagination for liberals. Architects of the New Deal laid a broad base for such policies—in the Social Security, Fair Labor Standards, and National Labor Relations Acts and the Aid to Families with Dependent Children program—and for a continuum of commitment to them. They even laid the basis for the struggle to promote social policies against the efforts of conservatives fighting government spending, fighting taxes, and extolling the social efficiency and political morality of the free market. Claims for the virtues of the market and the evils of tampering with it have scarcely changed.

The element that has changed and that requires new thinking and new political effort by liberals is a fearsome alignment of new blockages to continuing the New Deal tradition. At the forefront are the new power of market forces now extending globally and the related new levels of control over markets by megacorporations. With greatly unbalanced power between employers and employees, families face, almost as a commonplace, sudden layoffs, just-in-time hiring, contingent work, outsourced work, and the disappearing connection between work and health-care coverage and pensions. And complicating the problem of responding to the new insecurities for families in the global market are multiple new forms of communication, which create a cacophony overriding attention to social issues, and the new consolidation of control over the major media by producers of entertainment, which debases political discussion generally. Developing and sustaining a politics of protecting families against the combined effects of greatly enlarged corporate power and popular distraction cannot be easy, and liberals need to recognize the implications of these changed conditions.

But one part of the agenda has not changed for much of the past century: asserting a public need to ensure the necessary bases of security and opportunity for families with limited incomes. This agenda, of course, has never been fully achieved but should remain the liberal definition of the essentials for a just society: minimum family incomes secured by minimum wages and the earned income tax credit; access to health care of high quality for children, parents, and elders; child care for working parents with quality assured by salary supports for the care-providing staff; family housing made possible by supports for affordability; secure pensions; effective education, prekindergarten to twelfth grade, adequately funded; education for workforce development; paid family and medical leave for all workers with parallel supports for small-business employers; strengthening and retention of laws that protect processes of union organization and collective bargaining; and family supports given high priority in union contracts.

Another needed direction in public policy, however, is less firmly established in the liberal tradition: workplace policies that protect time for family care. Along with wage levels, hours and schedules of work have the most direct effect on the way families—at all income levels—can organize their lives, and liberals need to direct new, clear, specific attention to the question of work time. This means attention to the particularities of work hours and pressures for people in all types and levels of work and with widely varying incomes, but with the aim, in each case, of assessing the costs to workers of attempts to reconcile work time and family time.

For low-income workers, the time crunch may result from the need to hold several jobs; or to work shifts at odds with family mealtimes, childcare availability, and school hours; or to manage long commutes on inconvenient schedules of public transportation. Middle-class workers have incomes that give them somewhat greater control over their lives but may still be under time pressures because of conflicts between work hours and family needs, such as children's complicated school and sports schedules, the usual or unusual illnesses afflicting families, or the need to care for an elderly parent or relative. Furthermore, incomes for families in the middle, while not high enough to cover extensive time-saving services such as home help or daily home care for elders, are generally too high to qualify for publicly subsidized services that could reduce the time squeeze.

For managerial and professional workers, the time problem is different. At these levels, workers are generally salaried, and though there may be a usual practice that defines work hours, there is often no certain limit on hours and no clearly defined overtime; rather, there may be an assumption that workers will stay as late as necessary to finish the work to be done. For them, and for women especially, the problem is not income but the tyranny of time at work that most severely compromises time for family care.

Lawyers in law firms and legal-aid agencies, managers in manufacturing and financial-service companies, doctors in teaching hospitals and private practice, researchers in high-tech companies, and assistant professors in universities all work in systems that generate fierce pressures to demonstrate value with commitments of unlimited time.

An additional difficulty for professional workers, again especially for women professionals, is that the world at large—employers, relatives, neighbors, policy makers, often even women professionals themselves—see their work-family conflicts not as a problem but as a freely made choice. Unlike middle-class workers, professional women have sufficiently high incomes to pay for help with home care, child care, elder care, and other services. And if they have a second high income in the household and are unhappy with their work-imposed time squeeze, they can cut back hours, move to a less pressured job, or leave the workforce entirely. The public's lack of concern for the work-hour problems of women in this privileged class means that the problem receives little public attention, other than episodic news or feature stories that focus sympathetically on professional women who quit jobs to be with their children.

In the context of such stories, the connection between professional women's time crunch and equal opportunity for women is rarely made. And this is a place for clear liberal intervention. Professional work systems that operate without serious concern for the families of employees effectively reduce the ranks of women in them. They effectively and consistently limit the possibilities of promotion and advancement for women. And they effectively limit women's access to positions of professional or political leadership.

This limitation on equal opportunity for women, so blatant in visible venues—such as the U.S. Congress, not to mention the executive and judicial branches of government—makes workplace experience a matter of public concern. But making that connection and seeking effective change calls for confronting the considerable remaining strength of the traditional divide between public and private business.

Take the now much-cited case of Joanna Upton decided by the Massachusetts Supreme Judicial Court in 1997. Upton, the single mother of a young son, sued her former employer for wrongful dismissal from her job when she was fired for refusing to work overtime—until nine or ten o'clock at night—because of family responsibilities. She had been told when she was hired that her hours would be 8:15 to 5:30, but she found that her duties as a manager kept her at work until six or seven o'clock every evening, even before her employer demanded that she work overtime.

The firing, she claimed, violated Massachusetts public policy favoring the care and protection of children. But the court dismissed her claim on the grounds that an at-will employee may be fired "for any reason or for no reason at all" unless the firing violates a "clearly established" public policy. And it concluded that Massachusetts had "no public policy which mandates that an employer must adjust its expectation, based on a case-by-case analysis of an at-will employee's domestic circumstances."[5]

There is the care/equality/time problem for managers and professionals in a nutshell. Even without "overtime," Upton was working ten-hour days, and with commuting time added in, scarcely seeing her son. Her choice was to accept that situation or to suffer a career setback because no public-policy system was in place that made her family situation relevant to her employer. The question is *how* to make it relevant, *how* to construct public policy that makes family time a legitimate, broadly recognized part of an employer's concern.

~

The best precedent for a family-oriented policy is the Family and Medical Leave Act, and expanding its coverage is obviously a strong starting point. By doing so, the United States would join most European countries in providing paid leave, extending the application of the act from companies with fifty or more employees to those with twenty-five or more, and defending it against persistent pressure for restriction.

Other liberal additions to a family-supporting work-time agenda would be the extension of antidiscrimination laws to cover negative employment decisions based on a person's caregiving responsibilities and establishment of an employee's right to submit proposals for flexible work hours and to have them accepted if demonstrably feasible. To move such issues forward, however, given the strength of the cultural barrier against public intrusions in the private domain, the liberal voice needs to be loud and firm and sustained.

An ancillary approach is to press for workplace change from within, engaging business leaders in efforts to develop supportive workplace practices, including family-focused programs that promise mutual benefits for an enterprise and its workers. Various types of flexible work systems, combined with redesigned bases for promotion, can be made compatible with workers' needs for time at home *and* with women's needs for equal opportunity at work without losses—and sometimes with gains—in productivity and profit for employers.

Of course, by now, most large employers and many smaller ones already offer employees an array of flexibilities—maternity leave, emergency day care, part-time, flextime, job sharing—but their effective support for families and for women's opportunity at work is often undermined by unchanged workplace practices that value the "ideal worker." This is a person who is available to work regular or longer hours over a typical career span, someone whose work is not subject to interruption to attend to the needs of others except for the occasional disruptions of illness or death.

This ideal, of course, cannot apply to women whose work lives are interrupted by childbirth or to women and men whose responsibility for families takes them out of the workforce for periods of time or requires irregular work hours. Therefore, instead of defining patterns of work that include periods of time devoted to families as normal, natural, and logical, reigning attitudes define such functions as nonideal, a deviation from the norm. And those workers—mostly women—who do not accept the prevailing workplace ethic, and instead opt for flextime or part-time or family leave, demonstrate that they are not committed to work first. As a result, they are unlikely to be valued highly and promoted, and unequal opportunity for women stays in place.

The typical story, however, borne out by statistics showing low usage of flexibility options because of their negative consequences, is that employees work the expected hours and strain to find family time. The liberal task, then, is to contest the old assumptions about ideal workers and open space for new thought—including the ideas that family-supportive flexibilities and high productivity are not necessarily inconsistent and that methods of achieving the dual goals are worth trying.

A corollary strategy, which the MIT Workplace Center has initiated in Massachusetts, is to promote the establishment of state work-family councils to promote work practices beneficial to families, women, and employers.[6] The center chose to seek the establishment of the Massachusetts Work-Family Council by an act of the state legislature to emphasize that work-family issues are of public concern.

The proposed council is not designed to be a regulatory agency with powers to impose mandates on employers. Rather, in the language of the bill, its charge is "to develop broadly shared understandings of critical work-family issues in the Commonwealth" and "to promote through privately funded research, experimentation, and education both responsive public policies and innovative private sector practices."

To promote the development of policies beneficial to both employers and employees, the bill specifies that the council will include all major groups with stakes in such policies: employers, unions, professional associations, women's organizations, advocates for low-income workers, community-based service organizations, and government.

The specified duties of the council make the dual focus on employers and workers' families clear. Council members would be directed to hold hearings to identify major work-family issues in the commonwealth, and to devise processes for engaging stakeholders with differing interests in work-family conflicts and in constructing solutions that support both workplace productivity and family care. Other duties would include designing and implementing pilot projects as requested in workplaces, proposing public-policy solutions to work-family issues, and providing public education on the need for policies and practices that support the well-being of both employers and families. The widespread establishment of such councils could put the connections between work hours, family strength, and women's equal opportunity in clear relief—as well as advance attention to the benefits to business of workplace policies that take the connections seriously.[7]

~

In developing and promoting a liberal politics of family care that preserves women's equal opportunity, it is important to use, accurately and forthrightly, the word *women*. The problem here is the virtual disappearance of "women" in present discussions of work-family issues, which tend to use *gender* in its place—just as they replace *equal opportunity* with *gender equity*. This linguistic convention softens the hard edges of the different experiences of women and men in the workplace and blurs the consequences of that difference.

The term *equity,* of course, implies that inequity or unfairness is an issue—that some people are being treated differently than others and that the differences are unfair. The term *gender* conveys the fact that the people in question are men and women—so *gender equity* as a whole means that unfairness is a problem in the treatment of men and women. And because *gender* does not reveal which group is being treated unfairly, the term suggests that both are. In fact, that is the thinking behind the term. Men who take significant time for families risk the tag of lack of commitment, just as women do, and many who would like to take the time do not do so because they want to avoid this perception.

But the fact is that the question of equity in the workplace has to do mainly with inequity for women, and this fact becomes muffled in the gender-equity conversation, which usually reduces the matter to parenthetical phrases such as "those who assume responsibility for family care (for the most part women)."

The language of work-family issues needs to reflect the reality that, as things stand, women are the primary providers of care to families, suffer the greatest disadvantages in workplaces by doing so, and stand in the greatest need of new arrangements that are carefully designed to be fair to them. They need arrangements that do not penalize them for extending a maternity leave, or cutting back to half time until a child is in kindergarten, or refusing night and weekend work while teenagers are still at home, or responding to the emergencies of a parent with Alzheimer's disease. Flexibilities need to be fair to men who make such decisions also, but given the present reality, the ultimate fairness test for family flexibilities in the workplace will be their on-the-ground benefit for women. So the conversation needs to be about women.

Clearly, this usage has its dangers. Many feminists are wary of publicly linking women and caring roles for fear of encouraging essentialist thinking. To many of them, images of women as the mainstays of families, the caregivers, the builders and sustainers of relations in networks of relatives, friends, and neighbors come too close to connecting these roles to capacities natural to women and not to men—and to confining women within their traditional places. As conservatives do.

The strategy also has immediate, practical political implications. In arguing for a change in any kind of policy or practice—whether in the public or private sector—there are reasons not to link the change to women. Women-focused politics are typecast as not serious and of low priority. In the conventional wisdom, the safest approach for seeking advances for women is to use a generalized vocabulary in which they appear on the political stage as parents, workers, caregivers, part-timers, or members of other non-sex-specific categories. But when real issues are not named clearly, responses to them do not clearly apply.

~

If liberal values are to have meaning, liberals need to construct new moral ground on which they link explicit support for families and care with explicit support for individual rights and equal opportunity for women. A liberal family politics must recognize care as a national value, along with liberty and equality. It must recognize that giving and receiving care are goods, that they are indispensable elements of individual wholeness and social connectedness. The principles of this politics must be clear. Taking care of children well is important. Giving care to elders and others who need it is important. Caring relationships of intimacy, love, trust, and loyalty are important. Ordinary, daily, nonemergency feeding, cleaning, listening, helping, and remembering are important. So are thoughtful contributions of time to community institutions of care. Liberals must declare that a decent society places value on and provides a sustaining base for what is important.

To move these values into practice, liberals must recognize that workplace policies that encourage, if not require, long work hours and the paucity of public supports for families in the United States compared with those of less-wealthy countries, testify to the lurking, lingering assumption that families and those who take care of them are outside the realm of public responsibility. Liberals must explicitly and forcefully contest this assumption with language placing family care at the center of public as well as private values and making it a public as well as private responsibility—and they must promote policies putting these beliefs into practice.

10

Liberalism and Religion

AMY SULLIVAN

On the morning of November 1, 2004—the day before a highly competitive presidential election—the National Council of Churches (NCC) issued a press statement. As the umbrella organization for most mainline denominations in the United States, the NCC had been a moral force to be reckoned with, in both the cultural and the political spheres, for a good part of the twentieth century. But it has been overshadowed during the past few decades by its counterparts on the right. In the 2004 election season, various conservative Christian organizations mobilized to root out an extra four million evangelical voters to help reelect President George W. Bush. The Christian Coalition, though a shadow of its former self in membership and financial strength, managed to distribute approximately thirty million voter guides. The Denver-based Focus on the Family got into the political game as well, mailing voter "kits" to its members. And at the grassroots level, conservative church members organized into teams to lobby their friends and neighbors.

Now, the NCC appeared ready to weigh in. Religious organizations—like other nonprofits—are subject to all manner of complicated rules governing their political involvement, particularly in the weeks before an election. Even so, given the intense efforts on the right, one might expect a preelection press release from the premier institution of the religious Left to have some bearing on the decision facing the country. This expectation would be wrong.

"NCC Urges U.S. to Accept Responsibility for Uighur Chinese Refugees at Guantanamo," read the headline of the NCC's press statement, followed by nearly six hundred words detailing the dilemma of Chinese prisoners held in an American facility.[1] The issue may indeed be a worthy cause. On the eve of the election, however, as millions of conservative evangelicals prepared to go to the polls, the NCC's press release confirmed and underscored the total irrelevance of the once-powerful religious Left.

Everyone knows about the religious Right, a movement of conservative—mostly Christian—religious communities that has become increasingly involved in American politics over the past three decades. The idea that there might be a countervailing religious force, whether defined as the religious Left or simply as everyone who is not part of the religious Right, has long since been dismissed from public consciousness.

And yet there was a time—not so long ago—when liberalism was fed and informed by religion, when the term *religious* was not immediately assumed to connote "conservative." Moral giants with names like Reinhold Niebuhr and Dorothy Day and Martin Luther King Jr. and William Sloane Coffin led intellectual and social-justice movements and provided the spiritual underpinnings for liberal politics. One cannot page through American history without coming across political causes that were driven either partly or entirely by progressive people of faith: abolition, women's suffrage, labor reforms of the Progressive Era, peace movements, and civil rights. Just a few decades ago, the pronouncements of liberal religious voices—not conservative ones—carried weight in the political world. In short, the likes of Pat Robertson, James Dobson, and Ralph Reed have not always dominated American politics; indeed, in the span of American history, the past three decades are an anomaly.

The decline and fall of the religious Left has been so complete that news organizations, exit polls, and conventional wisdom regularly conflate terms like "religious voters" and "moral values" with "right wing." When *Time* magazine ran an article about Democratic religious outreach efforts in the winter of 2005, the piece concluded that "religious voters might like the music, but they're unlikely to be seduced by it so long as Democrats stick to their core positions," as if religious Americans could support liberal politics only by putting their faith aside, not by acting on their faith.[2]

How did we arrive at this point? The religious Left had a hand in its own demise, withdrawing from the political sphere at the exact moment that religious conservatives strode onto the scene. When conservatives insisted that religion and morality are inherently conservative concepts, and no one stood up to dispute the claim, political liberals developed an overnight allergy to all things religious. The result was twofold. First, liberalism was decoupled from the religious traditions and communities that had always translated political goals into moral imperatives for religious liberals, leading to an ineffective religious Left and a spiritually weak political Left. Second, and perhaps more troubling, liberalism acquired a reputation for being generally hostile to religion. In a country in which 87 percent of Americans say that religion is an important part of their lives, that perception is a recipe for disaster.[3]

~

From behind his pulpit in Columbus, Ohio, the Reverend Washington Gladden wove together politics and religion. Week after week, he inveighed against pervasive immorality. Christians, he argued, had a responsibility to act to change the world. Gladden's words were welcomed by Americans concerned and frightened by the changes around them. By giving voice to previously unnamed social and political fears—and by providing a religious solution to them—Gladden gave Christians permission to flex their muscle in the public square.[4]

We should perhaps not be surprised that the national movement Gladden led started in Ohio, the state that became associated with phrases like "moral values" and "culture war" in the aftermath of the 2004 elections. But Gladden preached in the nineteenth century, and he was no denizen of the Christian Right. His sermons weren't about sexual politics or gay marriage or abortion. Instead, Gladden arose from a strong tradition of religious liberalism in America. What outraged him were the slums and poverty that began to take over cities during the late 1800s, the often subhuman working conditions that accompanied industrialization, and the morally suspect activities to which disconnected urban dwellers often turned to deal with the massive changes taking place. His preaching focused on moral values, "social-gospel" style. And it is part of a long tradition of liberal religious activism that stretches back to John Winthrop and the first Puritans who fled to America.

For much of American history, religious involvement in public affairs and political causes was dominated by leaders of a distinctly liberal flavor, while conservative evangelicals—focused primarily on saving souls—made a principled decision to stay out of the realm of politics, entering mostly when they saw their beliefs threatened (as in the Scopes trial during the 1920s). "Preachers are not called upon to be politicians," the Reverend Jerry Falwell explained in 1965, a decade before he formed the Moral Majority, "but soul winners. Nowhere are we commissioned to reform externals."[5] At a crucial point in the latter half of the twentieth century, however, a perfect storm developed that changed the political landscape forever, catapulting religious conservatives into political activism.

In the late 1960s and early 1970s, a series of Supreme Court decisions that took prayer and Bible reading out of schools—and culminated in *Roe v. Wade*—angered conservative evangelicals, and convinced them that they needed to engage with the political world. Similarly, Catholics had generally steered clear of political involvement (they supported John Kennedy in 1960, but his election wasn't the result of an organized Catholic effort), focusing instead on assimilating amid anti-Catholicism. They were outraged by the *Roe* decision, however, and developed into a politically active force, forming pro-life groups and organizing them not by diocese but by congressional district. Both these groups were embraced by Republican strategists desperate to form a political majority, who recognized that they could find common ground in the belief that government should stay out of their lives. It was a match made in heaven.

Within a few years, evangelical activists were credited with defeating several liberal U.S. senators, blocking passage of the Equal Rights Amendment, and disrupting the Carter White House's Conference on the Family.[6] The popular televangelists Jerry Falwell and Pat Robertson (fundamentalist and charismatic, respectively) launched the politically oriented Moral Majority and Christian Coalition.

At the same time, religious liberalism, instead of sticking around to check this budding conservative movement, effectively disappeared, allowing the rise of the religious Right to take place unabated. The folks on the left had considered their work done. The civil rights movement had been their crowning achievement, establishing once and for all the power of moral arguments to bring about political and social change. In addition, the same Supreme Court decisions that had outraged conservatives convinced many religious liberals that they had won the debate: Religion and politics were both best served when religious leaders and communities were independent from the state, when the state did not appear to be sponsoring and controlling religion. One other factor contributed to their disengagement. Some political liberals turned the ire of their growing anti-institutionalism on organized religion. And so the religious Left, not wanting to enter that fight, took a much-planned and oft-postponed vacation.

The debate, however, was not over. It was simply shifting to a different arena, out of the court of law and into the court of public opinion. Moreover, liberals' reliance on the courts to establish the role of religion in public life had set up a grievance that conservatives would nurse and exploit for decades. During George W. Bush's administration, even religious conservatives have found it difficult to persist with the argument that they are shut out of positions of power: conservative evangelicals, after all, run the White House, the House of Representatives, the Senate, and a number of federal agencies. But they have simply shifted their focus to the judiciary branch, accusing "activist" (read "secular") judges of waging a "war on faith." Even the nomination of Harriet Miers—though ultimately unsuccessful—was calculated to play on this sense of grievance. The selection was peddled to James Dobson and other conservative evangelical leaders as a chance to fill an "evangelical" seat on the U.S. Supreme Court.

Once liberals realized the speed and fury of the religious Right's ascent, they could have acted to reassert their own religious tradition, fighting back against the assumption that concepts like morality and values and faith were, by their nature, conservative. But they did not. Only a few years had passed since the high point of the civil rights movement, when liberalism—buoyed by the cultural power of leaders like Martin Luther King Jr. and Abraham Joshua Heschel—occupied the moral high ground. Even so, by the late 1970s, the religious Left was already significantly weakened, and the political Left was developing a dangerous aversion to religion. If anything, the religious Left and Right seemed to have switched roles: conservatives were now the ones lending their moral force to political questions, whereas liberals largely withdrew to focus on other matters, in the process losing their influence and institutional strength.

The first problem for liberals was that without the guiding cause of civil rights, they no longer had a unifying goal. While their conservative counterparts were setting aside differences to focus on a single mission, members of the religious Left lost their way, dispersing their attention over myriad policy issues (the rights of Uighur prisoners just one of them), and busying themselves with internal denominational battles over female ordination and other debates. Religious communities had not escaped the social turmoil of the 1960s; with newly empowered women now seeking to serve as clergy in greater numbers, many denominations hunkered down for battles over the ordination of females and, later, homosexuals. Outside their communities, meanwhile, growing economic problems called out for attention. When Amy Waldman of the *Washington Monthly* set out in 1995 to discover what had become of the religious Left, she found that many religious leaders had spent the preceding decades organizing their congregations around service, not political activism. "I am consumed with binding up wounds, caring for people," one such minister told her. "How much time do I have left [for political activism]? How much energy?"[7]

Not all religious liberals disengaged from politics. But many of them, not wanting to be associated with the nascent Christian Right, filtered religion out of their rhetoric and secularized some of their appeals. In doing so, they handed Christian conservatives an uncontested public square. Years before the religious Right had the membership numbers to match its boasts of political influence, it won debates simply by controlling the agenda and cornering the market on religious authority. Richard Parker, who teaches religion and politics at the Kennedy School of Government, believes that the religious Left simply forgot about a crucial part of its mission. "The Catholic Church believed it needed to learn how to articulate for its members faith-based reasons for action, and to frame arguments in the public square in ways that did not directly derive from church teaching," he explains. "Mainline Protestants [who form the bulk of the religious Left] lost the first habit, and only carried out the second."[8]

As a result, those members of the religious Left who did remain politically active often seemed like caricatures of left-wing activists, agitating to save baby seals and third-world orphans and marshaling only the faintest of biblical appeals on their behalf. By setting aside the elements that made them unique, the religious traditions that gave them moral power, religious liberals became indistinguishable from members of the Sierra Club or Amnesty International.

The sustained focus on internal issues and dissolution into secular political efforts caused the skills and resources of the religious Left to atrophy. Financial and other scandals weakened some existing organizations—such as the once-powerful NCC—which are now so hamstrung that they lack the ability to offer much guidance to their congregants in the pews. With partisans of the religious Right currently defining the media world, liberal religious leaders are often loath to "spin" their beliefs and positions, taking principled stands that nonetheless leave television producers underwhelmed and frustrated. And a few ego-driven leaders, concerned that someone else might become the movement's visible spokesperson, have insisted on coalition efforts and joint statements that, while demonstrating the breadth of support, make decision making virtually impossible and ensure that no one emerges as a reliable voice for the movement.

When the Center for American Progress—a then-new liberal think tank—held a conference in the summer of 2004 on faith and progressive policy, it provided an unintended lesson about the contemporary religious Left. Every speaker referred to and quoted famous leaders on the religious left, making the day something of a history lesson: All of the leaders they mentioned came from the civil rights movement or earlier.

The exception was Jim Wallis, an ordained minister and founder of *Sojourners* magazine and the Call to Renewal movement. At the time of the conference, Wallis was organizing a bus tour to hit key campaign states and remind voters that religion exists on the left as well as the right. Since then, he has published a best-selling book, *God's Politics,* and chatted with the likes of Tim Russert, Charlie Rose, and Jon Stewart on television. As a longtime advocate for the poor who led faith-based organizations decades before George W. Bush ever heard the phrase, Wallis has the street cred and moral authority to make his case.

But one reason that Wallis has attracted notice after more than thirty years of religious activism on the left is that he is hard to categorize. In today's media world, which thinks in terms of conflict and neat, tidy boxes, he doesn't quite fit. Wallis is pro-life but antiwar. He challenges the role of Hollywood in promoting "coarse entertainment" and the role of Enron in violating a basic compact with its workers. On balance—particularly given his primary commitment to the elimination of poverty—Wallis's sympathies are more in line with Democratic policies and values than with Republican ones. But he does not, he stresses, want to become the liberal equivalent of Pat Robertson. "The media like to say, 'Oh, then you must be the religious Left,'" he writes in *God's Politics.* "No, not at all, and the very question is the problem. Just because a religious Right has fashioned itself for political power in one utterly predictable ideological guise does not mean that those who question this political seduction must be their opposite political counterpart. The best public contribution of religion is precisely not to be ideologically predictable or a loyal partisan."[9]

Wallis is right. Both politics and religion are best served when religious leaders and communities maintain their prophetic independence. One cannot easily speak truth to power if one's fondest wish is to rub shoulders with power at the negotiating table or cocktail parties. Moreover, history—including that of just the past few decades—is replete with examples of how a too-close relationship between the worlds of religion and politics can bring out the worst in both. But the reality of American politics today is that religious conservatives have inextricably aligned themselves with one political party. If religious liberals are not at the negotiating table, it's not as if their absence is palpable—it's just that much easier to ignore their concerns.

~

If the religious Left sees no use for the political Left, the feeling—at least until very recently—has been mutual. This disconnect started, in many ways, when, in 1976, Americans elected their first evangelical president: the Democrat Jimmy Carter. Though presidents from Lincoln to Wilson to FDR used religious rhetoric and referred naturally to religious beliefs, Carter was the first to discuss his own religiosity, to share the fact that he was "born-again." The northeastern and midwestern Catholics, mainline Protestants, and reform Jews who made up the Democratic establishment listened to Carter and pronounced his open discussion of faith gauche and inappropriate for politics. After all, if Emily Post said that one should never discuss politics or religion in polite company, one should *certainly* not talk about the two topics together.

Unfortunately for Democrats, the cultural trend was in the other direction. Over the next three decades, evangelical characteristics of worship and language and culture began to flavor many American religious traditions, as well as American politics. The development that started with Carter could not be stopped. In addition, Carter was elected in part because post-Watergate voters decided that knowing about a candidate's character was just as important as knowing about his policy positions. This decision marked a lasting shift in the way American voters evaluate their political candidates.

Presidents must make momentous, life-and-death decisions while in office, and voters want that person to have something bucking him up other than his pollster—something he or she can turn to for guidance and strength. Knowing that our leaders feel the pull of a greater interest is re-assuring. Judging whether a candidate has this intangible attribute can be difficult, but for many people, religion serves as an acceptable proxy. Voters naturally interpret professed faith as an indication that a candidate at least thinks about the morality of things and tries to make decisions based on a cause or power higher than himself or herself.

With the memory of Richard Nixon's misdeeds still fresh in their minds, millions of American voters responded favorably to Carter's pledge "I'll never lie to you" and took his evangelical faith as proof of that conviction. Again, though many liberals were uncomfortable with these allusions to Carter's faith, they could have proposed other ways of talking about and communicating personal morality to reassure voters. But they did not, leaving the field wide open for Republicans and conservative evangelicals to dominate.

Political liberals made the calculation that they had only two options: they could talk about and relate to religion the way that conservatives did, or they could remain silent and stay away from religious matters. As it happens, they had a handy role model and political justification for choosing the second option. In 1960, hounded by accusations that he would answer to the Vatican on matters of policy, John F. Kennedy went before the Houston Ministerial Association to declare that he would make presidential decisions "without regard to outside religious pressure or dictate."[10] There was, Kennedy assured his audience, very little connection between his personal religious identity and his public political responsibilities. Using the rationalization that "if it's good enough for JFK, it's good enough for me," countless Democrats (most recently, John Kerry in the early spring of 2004) have pointed to Kennedy's campaign as proof that religion has no place in Democratic politics.

But Kennedy was in a unique position: he was a Catholic running in a predominantly Protestant country that still had an undercurrent of anti-Catholicism. (Although Kennedy captured the support of 80 percent of Catholic voters that year, he received less than one-third of the Protestant vote.) To win, Kennedy had to downplay—or set aside—the issue of his religion. By contrast, a full 70 percent of voters in 2000, according to a survey by the Pew Research Center for the People and the Press, reported that they want their president to be a man of faith.[11] Candidates today who don't engage in conversations about their faith—or, alternatively, about their moral worldviews—have no chance of winning these voters' support.

This fact should be obvious. Both Carter and Bill Clinton, the only

Democratic nominees to have won the White House in the past forty years, went out of their way to discuss issues of faith and to speak before congregations early in their respective campaigns. Yet most liberal politicians lack not just the facility for religious language—which, for many, is a means of communicating to voters that they have been formed with a specific moral framework—but also the willingness to make moral appeals.

The result has been devastating for liberalism. Over the past few national elections, liberals have watched in disbelief and frustration as many voters have continued to side with social conservatism rather than with economic populism. But they miss the fact that these voters are not choosing one moral view over another. They are choosing the political party that talks about morality and religion over the party that doesn't. By default, they end up with the party that offers them something in the way of answers for their concerns about the direction of the culture and changes in society around them. Just as Washington Gladden provided a way for anxious religious citizens to grapple with the turmoil wrought by the Industrial Revolution, the religious Right and the Republican Party have responded to worries brought about by the cultural and sexual revolutions. Liberals, instead, have insisted that Americans really have nothing to worry about.

In his book *What's the Matter with Kansas,* Thomas Frank disputes the idea that liberals don't take the concerns of social conservatives seriously, and he cites a passage by University of Chicago professor Mark Lilla as an example of an unjustified conservative complaint:

> It is not that anyone thinks that incivility, promiscuity, drug use, and irresponsibility are good things. But we have become embarrassed to criticize them unless we can couch our objections in the legalistic terms of rights, the therapeutic language of self-realization, or the economic jargon of efficiency. . . . Our new explicitness about sex in television and film . . . scares the wits out of responsible parents, who see sexual confusion and fear in their children's eyes. But ever since the sixties they risk ridicule for raising objections that earlier would have seemed perfectly obvious to everyone.[12]

If Frank hadn't been so busy mocking this statement, he might have seen the truth in it. Liberals all too often act like teenagers, afraid of appearing uncool if they raise questions about the type of entertainment their children are exposed to. Tipper Gore is ridiculed when she suggests that music should come with warning labels about explicit lyrics. Hillary Clinton is charged with advocating censorship when she suggests that thirteen-year-olds should not be allowed to purchase video games rated for adults.

And the problem goes beyond children and culture. The language of "privacy" and "choice" has made it difficult for liberalism to accommodate questions about the morality of abortion. The fury when Tom DeLay and his congressional colleagues decided to butt into the Schiavo case in Florida drowned out discussions about whether one family member should be able to end the life of someone whom other family members are willing to care for. For so long, liberals have been proudly—and rightly—economic communitarians, reminding us that we have a responsibility to alleviate poverty and ensure that everyone who is able can work to support his or her family. But while liberals excoriate conservatives for economic libertarianism, they refuse to recognize the value of being social communitarians as well.

Writing in the *Boston Review* in April 2005, organizer Mike Gecan put his finger on the essential moral problem for liberals. They have failed, he says, "to realize that multiplying programs or policies designed to meet people's needs is doomed to fail unless and until those people sense a fundamental level of recognition of *who they are, not just what they need.*"[13] Liberals are appalled that socially conservative voters do not act in their economic self-interest. Setting aside the fact that many wealthy liberals vote against their economic self-interest in acting on their values, this response suggests a very illiberal idea: that individuals are wrong to place the needs of others above their own. It is hard to believe that this is what liberalism has become, an appeal to paycheck politics.

The Democratic Party hasn't helped matters. To begin, many Democratic operatives still think of religion mostly as a constituency problem— that is, they want to know how many Catholic votes in the Rust Belt they can "get" by employing a certain strategy and how many endorsements they can squeeze out of religious leaders; they have yet to be convinced that religious Americans are "their" voters. One immediate problem with this mind-set is that faith leaders are under special restrictions— whether legal or self-imposed—that don't bind the leaders of other constituencies. Ministers may come out in support of a particular candidate in their role as individual citizens, but only if they have the support of their congregations. If a pastor appears to be leveraging his position for political influence, he can quickly find himself in hot water with parishioners. Thus, assembling a "who's who" list of religious leaders who support Democratic candidates is a bit harder than finding key labor or African American or environmental-group leaders to lend their endorsement.

In addition, this attitude treats religion as a purely functional tool, boiling it down to "If we do X, we will get Y million religious votes." Religion doesn't generally work this way. Millions of Americans look to the faith of their political candidates as a proxy for a general moral worldview. Many voters understand that one can be a good and moral person without necessarily having religious faith. But in the midst of a campaign, voters may have difficulty getting a good sense of a candidate's moral compass.

The Democratic Party has also traditionally ghettoized religion, flooding into black churches on the Sundays before elections but treating religion as a quaint ethnic characteristic. In 2004, the Kerry campaign ran just one television ad that mentioned its candidate's background as an altar boy: The ad was in Spanish and appeared only on a Spanish-language network. And when the candidate spoke about faith (which he often did, charging that Bush was a "man [who] claims to have faith, but has no deeds"), he almost always did so in front of an African American audience, fueling charges that his faith was insincere and brought out only for political purposes. No one has argued that Democratic politicians should suffuse their rhetoric with hymn lyrics and claim God's endorsement. But by backing away from each other like opposing magnets, the religious Left and the Democratic Party have ceded the language of faith and values and morality to conservatives.

Today, the religious Right and the Republican Party are clasped in a mutually beneficial relationship, whereas the religious Left and the Democratic Party are barely on speaking terms. During the 2004 presidential election, the two liberal camps cooperated more closely than they have in recent memory, and yet relations clearly were still dangerously strained. Though the Kerry campaign hired several individuals to coordinate religious outreach—marking the first time a Democratic presidential campaign has branched beyond outreach to black churches—these operatives were not held in high regard; the campaign's director of community outreach often mockingly referred to her religious colleagues as "the Romper Room." The candidate's advisors furiously debated whether or not he should describe himself as a former altar boy in a presidential debate. And until one month before the election, the campaign had not one person who was authorized to talk to reporters about religious questions. Compared to the Bush/Cheney campaign, which could fairly be described as a religious outreach effort unto itself, the Democratic efforts were feeble, and the results were commensurate.

~

Following the dispiriting results of the 2004 election, some desperate Democratic leaders tried to resurrect the relationship between religion and liberalism. They hired religious-outreach advisors, sent faith consultants to key campaigns, and gathered sympathetic leaders of religious organizations to say "we believe in values, too!" For their efforts, they saw the percentage of American voters who think Democrats are religion friendly drop by double digits from just a year earlier.[14]

These circumstances are enough to make liberals throw up their hands and become unrepentant secularists. But things aren't as dire as they seem. Liberals just need to remember that the book of Hebrews describes faith as "being sure of what we hope for and certain of what we do not see." They may not be able to see the outlines of a new religious liberalism just yet, but they have reason to hope nonetheless. The campaigns of Bob Casey in Pennsylvania and Tim Kaine in Virginia have shown that Democratic candidates who explain how their faith has shaped them can neutralize the religion issue, taking away a traditional advantage of Republican politicians. Senators Barack Obama (D-IL) and Hillary Clinton (D-NY) have emerged as powerful moral voices for their party, proving that liberals can take on social and cultural problems without sacrificing their principles or becoming conservative Mini-Me's. (Clinton's proposed solution to the abortion issue—policies that make unwanted pregnancies less prevalent—may finally provide a way for her party to gain support on this controversial topic.) And liberal religious leaders—realizing that "moral issues" are not just what Republicans say they are—have spoken out against the Bush administration's funding priorities, calling the budget an "immoral document." Their statement marks the first time that the community has come together to protest a federal budget "since the early Reagan years," said one of the leaders.

Certainly, in the realm of religion, conservatives hold all the advantages of organization, outreach, rhetoric, and strategy. One thing they don't have, however, is political substance that reflects their religious commitment. This lack gives liberals an important opportunity. The liberal agenda—issues they have advocated passionately for decades—reflects the values of many religious moderates and progressives; yet many of the voters in these camps have been siding with Republicans simply because they feel more welcome in that party. The dirty little secret is that conservatives rely on religious rhetoric and strategy because they have to. If they don't, Americans might notice that they're not walking the walk in policy. They're not caring for the sick, the poor, the widowed, the orphaned. They're not acting as stewards of God's green earth. They are suffering the little children, but not in the way that Jesus meant.

Throughout the 2004 campaign, John Kerry challenged his listeners to remember the warning in the New Testament book of James: "What good is it, my brothers, if a man claims to have faith but has no deeds?" Liberals have claim to deeds that have defined them throughout American history—whether they have fought to give voice to racial minorities or workers or women, to promote peaceful solutions to international conflict, or to care for the most vulnerable in society. Now liberalism must reclaim its faith.

11

Liberalism, Environmentalism, and the Promise of National Greatness

ALAN WOLFE

In the age of Bush, Americans are less likely to identify themselves as liberals than ever. Such seems the clear conclusion from the presidential campaign of 2004. Liberals, conservatives charged during the campaign, are flip-floppers, inconsistent, woolly-headed idealists whose dreams for a better society are wildly out of touch with Americans' need to protect themselves from the evil of terrorism. The charges, to much liberal dismay, stuck. Despite advocating policies such as tax cutting, which has remarkably little public support, and despite his determination to further reward the already rewarded, President Bush was reelected, in no small part because he persuaded Americans that his toughness is right for the times.

Things were not always this way. Not so long ago, Harry Truman took dramatic steps to protect American security, often against fierce conservative resistance; John F. Kennedy stressed his energetic dynamism as a contrast to Eisenhower-like complacency; and Democrats in general fought for an active government capable both of strengthening Americans through domestic policies and of strengthening America by devoting greater resources to national security. The American public has frequently viewed Republicans as the party of toughness, but in fact, Republicans have a long tradition of isolationism and small-government conservatism that has prevented them from putting into practice the strong-America policies they advocate.

We hear echoes of this history today. For all their enthusiasm for the wars in Iraq and Afghanistan, Republicans were more likely to revert to isolationism when Bill Clinton was president and could do so again if a Democrat were to win in 2008. By cutting taxes, conservatives inevitably weaken America's defenses. The outcome of the war against Saddam Hussein is increasingly bleak, and American forces are stretched thin. The administration's failure to win a decisive victory in Iraq, furthermore, has undermined its tough talk about the nuclear ambitions of Iran and North Korea. Nor is the administration interested in reforms that would improve in any serious way America's intelligence gathering. The country has heard no significant talk of reducing America's dependence on oil through conservation. And if one believes that America can be strong internationally only if Americans have adequate health care and make decent livings, an idea associated with previous Republican presidents such as Teddy Roosevelt, the administration's domestic policies are unlikely to take advantage of all the resources that a great country ought to be able to mobilize.

If ever liberals needed a reminder of the importance of insisting on strong and ambitious programs to ensure American security, the realities of contemporary politics offer one. Yet the painful truth of the 2004 election is that liberals are partly responsible for their vulnerability to conservative attacks. Stunned by the failures of the Great Society and the war in Vietnam, liberal intellectuals and policy makers in recent decades had turned their backs on the strong programs that won them the public trust of Americans. They began to advocate a politics of smallness rather than to appeal to American greatness, as if the energy that John F. Kennedy tried to muster would push the United States into dangerous directions. If they are ever to win Americans' trust again, they need to restore the ambitions they have been avoiding.

~

One indication of liberals' loss of energy is their attitude toward environmental issues. Published in 1973 by the British economist E. F. Schumacher, *Small Is Beautiful* was an immediate sensation.[1] Although the book was wordy and often unpersuasive, the title was brilliantly chosen. In three words, Schumacher captured the spirit of his age. He understood that for the kinds of well-meaning liberals who would likely turn to his analysis, bigness had become bad. And nowhere was that belief more evident than in the arena of primary concern to Schumacher: the way human beings interact with the natural environment.

Preoccupations with the environment are anything but a recent phenomenon in American political thought. So much have attitudes toward nature been intertwined with the meaning of America that we have had not one strain of environmentalist thinking but at least two. Henry David Thoreau was an early exponent of one of them, a tradition that also includes naturalists like John Muir and contemporary advocates of deep ecology. This strain, which is often called pastoral, sees nature as pure and defenseless and in need of considerable protection against human onslaught. The pastoral view can take many forms, from worries about population growth or resource depletion to the pursuit in nature of an alternative to civilization's artificiality. Their common feature is the sense that ecology, not economics, is the true dismal science. Pastoralists, in the spirit of Christopher Lasch, can never celebrate "progress." For them, the earth's ability to replenish itself is problematic. Pessimistic toward the future, suspicious of human intention, protective by instinct, the pastoral tradition in ecology shares considerable intellectual turf with the antifederalist tradition in politics, which also looks with a wary eye at anyone proclaiming that big might be better. Environmentalism is a global movement, but it finds specific resonance in an American intellectual tradition that contrasts the natural innocence and purity of this side of the Atlantic with the corruption and decadence of the other.

The other environmental tradition, aptly labeled progressive, dates back to Gifford Pinchot, the first head of America's Forest Service and a Bull Moose activist. The progressive environmentalist does not view nature and civilization as inherently antagonistic; each can improve the other so long as one finds the right tools for maximizing their utility. Management of resources is crucial for progressives, and this emphasis on problem solving leaves little place for a neo-Malthusian pessimism that would distract from the immediate tasks at hand. Nor do progressives share the romantic naturalism of Thoreau and his twentieth-century epigones; on the contrary, progressives view themselves as hard-nosed realists, willing to consider the trade-offs involved when society has to make difficult choices between equally compelling objectives. The language of progressivism is one of trusteeship and stewardship; the land is not meant to sit unused or to be treated as an object of spiritual worship; it has been placed under collective authority for the benefit of everyone.

As the political scientist Bob Pepperman Taylor argues, these two approaches, which hold to very different conceptions of nature, correspond to differing conceptions of politics.[2] The pastoral tradition is contemptuous of power and politics and dismissive of the do-good intentions of reformers. Religion, especially prophetic religion, is the model for the pastoral style; its basic text is the jeremiad, and its basic stance is uncompromising. Progressives, by contrast, are administrative, utilitarian, and technocratic in outlook, and they respect power and want to obtain their share of it. In their view, forces that would destroy the environment by using it for exploitative purposes, such as big industrial and mining concerns, are already well organized and motivated, and the only hope to curtail their influence is to organize a force against them, inevitably by harnessing the power of the government. The prophetic style of protest is not part of their arsenal; Pinchot, labeling the ecological extremists of his day with a word of his own choosing, wrote that "I could not join the denudactics, because they were marching up a blind alley. . . . The job was not to stop the ax, but to regulate its use."[3]

Because the two traditions of environmental thought differ so much in their underlying assumptions about politics, they have sharply contrasting perspectives on the question of American greatness. When Thoreau called himself a "true patriot," he was not dissembling; his writings are filled with love of his country, especially as it contrasts with Europe. "If the heavens of America appear infinitely higher, and the stars brighter, I trust that these facts are symbolical of the height to which the philosophy and poetry and religion of her inhabitants may one day soar," he wrote in "Walking."[4] But the greatness to which America aspired did not, and could not, originate in Washington. In "Civil Disobedience," Thoreau had much to say about one of the figures who stands tall in any treatment of American greatness: Daniel Webster. Thoreau liked him. "Compared with the cheap professions of most reformers and the still cheaper wisdom and eloquence of politicians in general," he wrote, "his are almost the only sensible and valuable words."[5] But Webster's quest for a great country was, in Thoreau's opinion, futile because it put its faith in civilized, and therefore transient, things; in any case, Thoreau lost his appreciation for Webster after the latter supported the Compromise of 1850. Politics was simply not in Thoreau's blood. "Hope and the future for me are not lawns and cultivated fields, not in towns and cities, but in the impervious and quaking swamps."[6]

Pinchot, by comparison, was not only a political activist closely identified with the prime advocate of American greatness, Theodore Roosevelt, he also linked his concern about land management to the future strength of his country. "The conservation of natural resources is the basis, and the only permanent basis, of national success," he wrote. For Pinchot, natural resources were not sacred and otherworldly but indispensable for human happiness; in his exuberantly optimistic outlook on the world, the application of scientific management to the land is a precondition of democratic equality. As he put the matter in his manifesto, "I stand for the Roosevelt politics because they set the common good of all of us above the private gain of some of us; because they recognize the livelihood of the small man as more important to the Nation than the profit of the big man." Pinchot's vision may well have been too optimistic; corporate interests had little trouble dominating the agencies established by Progressives to regulate them. But clearly, for him, "the great fundamental problem" is one with which Hamilton and Marshall would feel a sense of kinship: "Shall we continue, as a Nation, to exist in well-being?" Nor can we doubt that his answer is that we could continue, so long as we applied principles of rational planning and allocation as much to the natural world as to the industrial one.[7]

Although Pinchot must surely have thought that his approach to the environment, tied as it was to modern techniques of scientific management, would prevail, the pastoral tradition is the more influential among contemporary writers concerned with the environment. Like Thoreau, Wendell Berry is an American patriot; a recent collection of his essays is dedicated to the signers of the Declaration of Independence. This patriotic bent may explain why the America he evokes has such an eighteenth-century feel about it; the independence he desires for his nation "can be maintained only by the most practical economic self-reliance. At the least, a nation should be able sustainably to feed, clothe, and shelter its citizens, using its own sources and by its own work." Many of the Declaration's signatories, moreover, considered themselves to be citizens of their states, as does Berry, who has strong loyalties to Kentucky and the South of which it is part; he admires the Southern manifesto *I'll Take My Stand* for "its astute and uncompromising regionalism" and finds himself relatively untroubled by its segregationist origins. Berry's agrarianism fits into no existing political camp, which is clearly how he likes it. Distrustful of movements, even those dear to his own heart, he writes not as a citizen endeavoring to shape elections and policies but as an elegiac essayist and poet.[8]

Bill McKibben also writes in the shadow of Thoreau, even if he finds Thoreau "intensely anthropocentric." We should not make Thoreau's mistake of valuing nature because nature is valuable to human beings, McKibben insists; instead we need a "humble philosophy" that appreciates that "the rest of creation mattered for its own sake and that man didn't matter all that much."[9] Progressive environmentalists want to conserve nature to further human happiness, but human happiness is not all that important to McKibben: who are we, he frequently asks, to think that nature owes us anything? In his more recent work, McKibben extends the same reasoning to contemporary genetic engineering and to research into robotics and artificial intelligence. Society should have an "enough point," he argues, that enables us to draw a line in the sand and to say that beyond this point, we will not go. McKibben himself will not go so far as therapeutic cloning, for if we take that step, he believes, we will be unable to stop the rush toward human cloning. And if his concerns might make him seem an ally of the Christian Right, McKibben responds, correctly, that a number of people on the left—Judy Norsigian, one of the feminist authors of *Our Bodies, Ourselves,* and former New Leftists Tom Hayden and Todd Gitlin—have expressed similar reservations.[10] Though compelling moral reasons exist to raise alarms about the prospect of human cloning—therapeutic cloning is another matter entirely—one can find, on the left perhaps even more than on the right, a fear that in the face of the unknown gains and losses that go along with scientific advances, the most prudential course is one of wariness rather than enthusiasm.

The pastoral tradition may have strong appeal among writers with a prophetic sensibility, but we would expect, given its antipolitical character, that it would have little attraction for politicians, who, as seekers after power, ought to be more sympathetic to the progressive inclination. However, matters have not worked themselves out in this way. As Taylor correctly observes, the contemporary political figure who comes closest to embodying Pinchot's progressive scientific management is actually one of the more forgotten recent minority-party candidates for president, Barry Commoner.[11] Commoner, unlike Pinchot, was a socialist, yet like the earlier man, both his science and his politics were devoted to securing natural resources for improved human use and to furthering the quest for social justice. Commoner rejected neo-Malthusian formulations of the environmental problem and their dour pessimism, barely concealed misanthropy, and attacks on economic growth in any form. If citizens were more willing to confront private industry than Pinchot was, Commoner argued, they could begin to make progress on the environment front.

By contrast, pastoral visions of the environment have featured prominently in the thoughts of a number of prominent officeholders, including William O. Douglas, Stewart Udall, and, not surprisingly given his taste for eighteenth-century republican virtue, Gary Hart. In more recent times, the pastoral tradition has, if anything, gained saliency for liberal politicians; in sharp contrast to Commoner's relative obscurity, two of the candidates in the 2000 election were closer to the pastoral tradition than to the progressive one. One of them, Ralph Nader, has been both a critic of corporate capitalism and an advocate for the environment, and despite his running, at least the first time around, on the Green Party ticket, Nader has focused his recent speeches and activities more on economic populism than on ecological awareness. Still, Nader has much in common with the Thoreauvian strain in American political thought.

Ralph Nader grew fascinated by "outsiders," as he called them, prophets such as John Muir, Ida Tarbell, and Jeanette Rankin who were willing to denounce the machinations of Washington insiders. Nader believes in a political process he calls "authentic" democracy, in which, as in the classic film *Mr. Smith Goes to Washington*, the voices of ordinary people drive the corrupt from the halls of power.[12] This vision of politics has its roots in both the progressive and the pastoral traditions in environmental thought, but if there are any doubts that Nader belongs primarily in the American-greatness camp, he dispelled them when he chose to run for president in 2000 and then, remarkably, chose to run again in 2004, even though his argument that the two parties are indistinguishable had lost so much credibility that even he had abandoned it. Third-party candidates are spoilers, and what they spoil is the possibility of majority government. Though Nader fills his speeches and writings with appeals to social justice, his commitments to purifying what he views as an evil system of politics clearly take priority over his outrage at the unjust policies of either of the two dominant parties. Like so many previous adherents to a politics of goodness, Ralph Nader prefers abstractions and principles to real-life dilemmas, as if the only point of politics is to make a point. A world in which the evils he identifies are reduced because leaders are willing to make pragmatic compromises for the sake of social improvement holds little interest for him.

The other candidate in the 2000 campaign with an interest in ecology was, of course, Al Gore. *Earth in the Balance,* his ecological manifesto, was, as Republicans were quick to point out, a most unusual book for a major party's presidential candidate to have written. The book does not lack for ambition; Gore calls for an international campaign rivaling the Marshall Plan to address the environmental crisis. Yet the most striking aspect of Gore's approach is its relentless pessimism. The environmental crisis, he writes, "serves as a kind of mirror in which we are able to see ourselves more clearly if we are willing to question more deeply who we are and who we want to be, both as individuals and as a civilization." Neither the people nor the society he holds up to that mirror have flattering images. Turning to some of the most depressing modern authors one can find—among them R. D. Laing, Gregory Bateson, and Alice Miller—Gore compares contemporary civilization to a dysfunctional family committed to endless cycles of addiction. No addiction is more powerful, in Gore's view, than the one "to the consumption of the earth itself. This addictive relationship distracts us from the pain of what we have lost: a direct experience of our connection to the vividness, vibrancy, and aliveness of the rest of the natural world."[13]

As concerned as it is with climate, waste, food, forests, and oceans, *Earth in the Balance* has relatively little to say about human beings. The book therefore shares more of Bill McKibben's hostility toward progress than it shares Gifford Pinchot's sense that progress can serve the cause of human equality. Indeed, social justice never registers as a theme in *Earth in the Balance,* as if matters so this-worldly as taxation or the welfare state should not interrupt deep thinking about Heiddegerian preoccupations with the nature of Being. Gore does deal with one earthly matter that has allowed the less well off to participate in some of life's satisfactions: consumption. But, as one might expect, he treats the phenomenon with heavy-handed disdain. *Earth in the Balance* strives for spiritual truth, not political reform. At least thinkers like Lani Guinier who reach back to the eighteenth century are still within the purview of the Enlightenment; Albert Gore harks back to a much earlier period, when people, or so we are to believe, lived in a more organic relationship with the natural world around them.

Some of the claims Gore makes in his book, like those of Berry and McKibben, rest on scientific evidence that politicians and polemicists are not well equipped to address. (I count myself among those so ill equipped.) If indeed energy resources will soon be depleted, food supplies will be exhausted, and global warming will unleash flooding not seen since Noah, all earthly matters, including the question of whether one country can ever reclaim its greatness, do come to seem trivial. Alas for the cause of certainty, the scientific data are far from definitive; skeptical accounts of the earth's environmental crisis have appeared, and at least some predictions of doom, including those of progressive environmentalists such as Barry Commoner, have not yet borne fruit.[14] But even

if one grants claims of an impending crisis that warrants immediate attention, the question is still open about the most effective way to respond. Because that question is political rather than scientific, we might
well ponder why a politician of the stature of Al Gore would reach, as if
instinctively, for a tradition that has historically rejected politics, skip-
ping almost entirely over another one that ties the question of environmental preservation to questions of American power and success.

The answer, I believe, lies in the turn against progress that has led so
many on the left to take a second look at the antifederalists and the tradition of civic republicanism. At least since the time of Edmund Burke,
conservatives have questioned the notion that bigger and newer implies
better, but this essentially reactive temperament now seems to characterize the way the American Left approaches nearly all the issues it confronts; one could not imagine a Republican conservative writing a book
as filled with doomsday scenarios as Al Gore's. Fear of the future has
seemingly shifted from one political party to the other; Democrats today
are as unlikely to call for Kennedy-like ventures into space—George W.
Bush has in any case preempted them on that front, even if his fiscal policy, allowing no room to finance such activities, led him to drop the idea
within weeks after it was proposed—as they are to manifest Pinchot-like
confidence in government. In this mood of retreat from big government
and economic growth, environmentalism, especially in its antipolitical
form, seems the inevitable outcome. If small is beautiful, American greatness, a big project if there ever was one, must be especially ugly.

From the perspective of American greatness, the slogan of the environmental movement—"think globally, act locally"—is particularly revealing because the one thing that the global and the local have in common
is that neither represents the national. With our thoughts directed to the
rest of the world, indeed to the universe of which it is a part, and with
our actions confined to families and friends at home, we don't have to
think about the political community in between, the one that requires as
much care and cultivation as the natural environment to flourish and survive. Suspect on the left for its complicity with imperialism since at least
the time of the Vietnam War, the American nation is now viewed by a
significant number of left-leaning intellectuals as a hegemonic force
whose expansionist tendencies must be resisted.

When David W. Noble titled his 2002 book *Death of a Nation,* he did not frame the title as a lament.[15] To him, *the nation* is a value-laden term, an ideological construct designed to make Americans believe that their society is different from and better than any other society. Noble equates the nation with the efforts of capitalist elites to impose their imperialistic designs on the rest of the world, as well as with the efforts of white Anglo-Saxon Protestants to impose their values on Americans who are different from them. In choosing his title, Noble did not mean to imply that the American nation has lost its power; on the contrary, its tentacles, he believes, reach everywhere. But knowing what we now know about America's awful racism at home and global designs abroad, scholars such as Noble have begun to suggest that the nation should indeed rest in peace.

Noble, writes George Lipsitz in his introduction to *Death of a Nation,* is "one of the few people in his generational cohort to remain intellectually and politically alert to the new possibilities emerging from contemporary contradictions and conflicts."[16] In that statement, he is correct: Noble's attack on the idea of the American nation resonates strongly with contemporary scholars in American studies, who have turned their professional association and scholarly activities into a strikingly vehement attack on the United States.[17] The founders of the discipline of American studies—Perry Miller, Vernon L. Parrington, Henry Nash Smith, Leo Marx—were, academically speaking, the progressives of their day, similar in their outlook to James MacGregor Burns and Cecelia Kenyon. Not only did they attempt to provide a coherent narrative about the emergence of the American nation, but they conveyed a sense of discovery in their work; they found greatness in American literature—Hawthorne, Twain, Fitzgerald—that was typically dismissed by the guardians of high culture who had their eyes on Great Britain. The American studies of earlier generations did not ignore social problems—class stratification featured in their work, and Marx's *The Machine in the Garden* anticipated environmental preoccupations—but it was an optimistic field because the America it studied was an optimistic society. To be sure, much of this literature emphasized consensus, and thus avoidance of conflict. But that stance, too, was progressive for its time; by developing a national narrative, early exemplars of American studies extended the concern of nineteenth-century political reformers to fashion a society in which everyone has a place.

Contemporary students of American studies, by contrast, want, as one of the leading scholars in the field, Jan Radway, says, "to complicate and fracture the very idea of an American nation."[18] For Radway and her colleagues, the term *America* is, on the one hand, an imperialist pretension—other nations also have a claim to the name, writers in this camp are fond of noting—and, on the other, an empty shell, signifying a futile effort to put boundaries of space and time around a fluid global reality. Creating and sustaining the American nation are as dangerous to the world as fashioning a coherent political majority, spending on consumer goods, or using the environment to advance human purpose. Nations, especially the American nation, are big things; fracturing them is a way of trying to make them smaller.

One of the more interesting aspects of the Left's attack on the idea of the nation is how smoothly it intersects with a similar attack by the Right not that long ago. From Lincoln through the two Roosevelts and into the era of Kennedy and Johnson, the idea of the nation has traditionally been resisted by the Right and embraced by those who believe in progressive ideas such as equality. Nowadays, the roles are reversed.

One cannot exaggerate the fear and loathing of the nation that conservatives have expressed throughout American history. "There is," as Kentucky Senator James B. Beck said in 1875, "that contemptible word *Nation*—a word which no good Democrat uses, when he can find any other, and when forced to use it, utters in disgust."[19] For men such as Beck, the idea of the nation implied equality for all those guaranteed citizenship within it; standing firm against the principle of nationhood was a price worth paying to keep the races apart. In the years after Beck expressed his views, moreover, conservatives kept up the attack; Southerners like M. E. Bradford, although he was a Republican rather than a Democrat, were as hostile to the nation as James Beck was. When economics replaced race as the major issue in the United States, conservatives had an additional reason to oppose the principle of American nationality, for as the national government was increasingly called upon to regulate the extremes of the market, protecting private interest required attacking national power. Conservatives, in other words, have been second to none in their assertions of patriotism, but they have also been typically last in their commitment to nationalism.

Those speaking in defense of equality, in contrast, came to view the nation as an indispensable ally. "When a group of abolitionists established a postwar magazine designed to carry on in the spirit of Garrison's *Liberator*," historian Morton Keller points out, "*The Nation* seemed an eminently appropriate name."[20] (One wonders whether today's editors of the magazine, who are firmly committed to frequent attacks on American power, ponder changing its name.) Former abolitionists, of course, generally believed that the most pressing form of inequality was the one between the races that seemed so curiously persistent even after so much blood had been shed to eliminate it. But the link between equality and the idea of the nation could extend to arenas other than race. Theodore Roosevelt's New Nationalism illustrates one such link. "As a New Yorker," historian Gary Gerstle writes of TR, "he understood how large a proportion of the working class comprised immigrants and their children. His New Nationalist program was meant to bring them into the nation, not just politically and culturally, but economically as well."[21] As Roosevelt's life and career demonstrated, nationalism could indeed have its racist and imperialist sides, yet without it, assuring citizenship for all was impossible.

This history ought to give pause to contemporary scholars of American studies who contemplate fracturing the nation they are studying. Their hostility toward the idea is clear: In an especially unpleasant episode, the literary theorist Barbara Hernnstein Smith responded with over-the-top sarcasm to E. D. Hirsch's suggestion that schools make students more aware of the history and culture of their nation: "Wild applause; fireworks, music—*America the Beautiful*; all together now: *Calvin Coolidge, Gunga Din, Peter Pan, spontaneous combustion.* Hurrah for America and the national culture! Hurrah."[22] Leftist intellectuals apparently can be as contemptuous of the idea of the nation as Kentucky's Senator Beck was in 1875. Properly speaking, we cannot place these intellectuals in the same camp as adherents to American goodness; they are the kind of thinkers who would attack a term like *good* as hopelessly impossible to define with precision and as dangerous if it somehow could be realized. But even though they lack a vision of what America should stand for—it is one thing to argue that the nation stands for the wrong things and another thing entirely to argue that there is not, nor should there be, any such thing as the nation—they have taken the American Left's characteristic fear of American greatness to its extreme position. So long as politics remains the only method of achieving common objectives, and so long as politics takes place within nation-states, calling for the death of the American nation is an effective formula for irrelevance, which is perhaps fortunate if intellectuals of this persuasion have so little positive to offer in the first place.

~

Something happened to the Democratic Party in the 1960s as its leaders, John F. Kennedy and Lyndon Johnson, became embroiled in Vietnam.

Although Democrats had achieved power in postwar America by emphasizing their commitment to a strong national defense, the cold-war consensus within the party was frail; some on the left, admirers of one sort or another of the Soviet Union, distrusted the cold war from the start, and others began to question nuclear brinkmanship as practiced during the Kennedy administration. In any case, Vietnam split the party in two, sending the hawks in the direction of neoconservatism and Republicanism while convincing the doves that ambitious foreign policy undertakings ought to be avoided at all cost. Although historically Republicans and conservatives were America's true isolationists, by the time Jimmy Carter and Bill Clinton managed to get themselves elected president, the tendency to withdraw from the world's problems had shifted parties and ideological coloration.

Domestic and foreign ambitions, as much as liberals these days like to separate them, are inevitably linked; the more the Democratic Party viewed itself as fighting the cold war, the stronger was its commitment to domestic reform, and, conversely, the turn against international intervention abroad seemed to match the mood of resignation so prevalent at home. The "Vietnam syndrome"—the foreign policy paralysis that took over the Democratic Party, and to some degree the nation as well, as the United States was unable to win the war—reinforced all the themes that had led the American Left in the past fifty years to question its once-strong sympathies toward centralized government, economic growth, environmental management, the idea of the nation, and increased immigration. The greater the Vietnam War grew in intensity, the further back in history liberals looked to oppose it. Prominent critics of the war, such as Arkansas Senator J. William Fulbright, held positions on domestic issues that were more reminiscent of John C. Calhoun than of John Marshall (a pattern that would be repeated when another southern senator not known as a friend of racial equality, Robert Byrd of West Virginia, took the lead in opposing the war in Iraq). Many people who were farther to the left than Fulbright took an even longer view; speaking at a 1965 rally against the war, the then president of Students for a Democratic Society, Carl Oglesby, described Thomas Jefferson and Thomas Paine as "heroes" and wondered what they would have to say to Lyndon Johnson and McGeorge Bundy.[23] The eighteenth century hovered over the spirit of the antiwar movement; historian Howard Zinn, for example, described the North Vietnamese as eighteenth-century Jeffersonians committed to our Declaration of Independence, not as twentieth-century communists with a soft spot for Joseph Stalin.[24]

By looking longingly on a time when goodness so clearly triumphed over greatness, opponents of the war in Vietnam began to question nearly all their assumptions about the need for centralized power to achieve liberal objectives. With an even a far more moderate voice than Zinn's, Arthur Schlesinger Jr., a strong advocate for liberal ambition in the 1950s and 1960s, wrote about an "imperial presidency" in ways that, in its invocation of the founders and their commitments to the separation of powers, seemed to have more in common with Lani Guinier's later fears than with the earlier hopes of James MacGregor Burns.[25] In this sense, the Vietnam syndrome long outlasted the Vietnam War. No one should doubt that the rise of conservatism since the 1980s is primarily attributable to the political skills and determination of conservative activists.[26] But nor can it be denied that the Right flourished because the Left, having begun to question ambition in Southeast Asia, began to lose its taste for great ventures in all spheres of political life.

September 11 might have led to a change of heart among many on the left, but it was followed so quickly by the war in Iraq, and the war in Iraq in turn transformed itself with such speed into a quagmire resembling Vietnam, that leftist critics' opposition to this war took up where their opposition to the earlier one left off. Once again, the eighteenth century, with its implication of unspoiled goodness, became the alternative against which to compare the imperialistic pretensions of the Bush foreign policy makers. "All those who really love this country are obliged to resurrect the legacy of Jefferson and Madison, so that the antidemocratic legacy does not prevail," wrote media critic Mark Crispin Miller.[27] For T. D. Allman, another critic of the Bush policies, Jefferson and the Founding Fathers adhered to the twin principles of separation of powers at home and noninvolvement abroad because they "did not pretend that Americans were somehow exempt from the temptations that corrupt people of other nationalities."[28] War in Iraq undermined both principles; not only did we search for devils overseas, which John Quincy Adams warned us not to do, but we put all the power to do so in the hands of one man. Thomas Paine "wouldn't have had much trouble recognizing the Bush administration as Federalist in sentiment, 'monarchical' and 'aristocratic' in its actions, royalist in its mistrust of freedom, imperialist in the bluster of its military pretensions, evangelical in its worship of property," added Lewis H. Lapham.[29]

Antifederalist and republican at heart, the Iraqi war's leftist critics not only had little sympathy for the rebuilding of Iraq, but their polemics offered few suggestions for constructing a political system at home for the twenty-first century if their models of political wisdom are Jefferson and Paine. No wonder that some of them began to use language indistinguishable from that of conservatives such as Robert Bork. "The regime's goal," as Mark Crispin Miller wrote, using the kind of vocabulary one associates with those writing for *First Things,* "is to abort American democracy, and to impose on the United States another kind of government entirely."[30] Apparently, all friends of the eighteenth century have to hang together, whatever the ideological differences that divide them.

So unexpected was the resistance in Iraq and so vulnerable was the Bush administration to criticism because of its failure to anticipate it, that leftists were free to attack the war without specifying how and why they would have done things differently. But these questions cannot be ducked forever, especially because America's misadventures in Iraq brought the Democratic Party back to influence and respectability. The question facing liberals and leftists is whether their criticisms of Mr. Bush's intervention abroad will be sustained when and if a Democrat decides to deploy troops somewhere in the world to respond to a threat to American values.

Providing an interesting indication of the future, some writers on the left were not willing to suppress their doubts about the militarism and aggressive intentions of the Democratic candidate in their haste to remove the Republican one from office. John F. Kerry, from their point of view, is not unlike the president who shares his initials. Kerry, after all, voted for the initial resolution to go to war in Iraq, even if he changed his mind subsequently. Like any successful politician, he has ties to wealthy campaign contributors, including military contractors, and can be expected to do their bidding. Nothing in Kerry's record indicates that he shares the suspicion of military intervention that still drives those who protest against globalism and believe that imperialism is America's destiny; on the contrary, as one leftist critic of Kerry and his foreign policy advisors said, the Kerry plan for the world "diverges from that of the Republicans. But it also endorses many of the administration's hard-line policies and in some cases is prepared to go further."[31] We cannot know whether such attitudes will shape the choices of future presidential candidates, but if they do, Americans may continue to find the Republicans more trustworthy than the Democrats.

If the age of Bush suggests the difficulties liberals face in reclaiming appeals to American greatness, it also suggests the opportunities. Mr.

Bush's attempts to privatize Social Security, for example, have met with considerable public skepticism, which suggests that the American public is fully aware of the need for domestic programs that give Americans a sense of security in the face of market-driven uncertainties. Though tax cuts have not permitted talk of new public programs, the issue of health care could emerge in the future, and the American public consistently trusts Democrats more than Republicans on that matter. Politics goes in cycles, and if the cycle returns to issues of domestic reform, Democrats ought to be ready with ambitious proposals.

The same conclusion holds for foreign policy. It remains to be seen whether unilateral instincts, small-government proclivities, and an inability to talk about national sacrifice are the best ways to protect Americans against threats such as terrorism. When a threat is unprecedented, so must be the response. The 9/11 Commission, former intelligence tsar Richard Clark, Zbegniew Brzezinski—all have raised questions about the need for new approaches to national security in an age of terrorism. The Bush administration is uninterested in national conversations about this subject, but such discussions are necessary if the United States is ever to become stronger in today's uncertain world.

As Democrats and liberals think about questions of national purpose, they have much to learn from earlier attempts to define the meaning of the American experience. Like Gifford Pinchot and other advocates of the progressive approach to the natural environment, they will need to recognize that American civilization is what Americans make it. The natural world is a cause for wonder, but we ought not stand powerless before its majesty. The forces of nature that result in breathtaking forests and magnificent canyons also cause events such as Hurricane Katrina. The rebuilding necessary in the wake of natural disasters reminds us of both the preciousness of our social order and the need to take action to protect and sustain it. America's greatness is contingent on the willingness of its citizens to use their collective powers for collective goals, efforts for which government is essential.

The same reasoning applies to U.S. foreign policies. The failure of the Bush administration to call on Americans to join together in the face of external enemies is a scandal of monumental proportions. No country can fight a war abroad while pretending that no war exists at home. War in defense of the nation's security is from time to time essential, but when it is fought, the energy of all Americans is required. Summoning up this energy requires full participation by all American citizens in the life of their nation, a goal incompatible either with the tax-cutting inclinations of conservative Republicans or with the eighteenth-century longings of contemporary leftists. There are ways for liberals to return to power in the United States, but these paths require a defense of the idea of a strong America that is currently missing from so many liberal ideologies.

PART THREE

LIBERALISM AND AMERICAN POWER

12

Liberalism, Internationalism, and Iran Today

DANNY POSTEL

n her 2003 memoir, *Reading Lolita in Tehran,* the Iranian literary
scholar Azar Nafisi tells the story of a group of her female students who
surreptitiously gathered in her living room once a week to discuss
works of Western literature deemed unfit for classroom instruction by
the Islamic Republic's censors. Every Thursday morning for almost two
years in the mid-1990s, the women snuck into their teacher's home, removed the veils they are legally required to wear in public, and mixed it
up over Nabokov, Fitzgerald, Flaubert, Jane Austen, Henry James, and
Saul Bellow.[1]

Reading Lolita is about how these women experienced internal freedom amid external repression—about a struggle to carve out a space for
the imagination under the crushing weight of a regime committed to
dominating both public and private life. It's a story about the transformative power of great literature, its ability to connect and transport its
readers to an outside world—in this case, a world that is prohibited,
closed, off-limits. It's an attempt to contravene, however momentarily
and precariously, what Andrei Codrescu calls "the disappearance of the
outside."[2]

As Nafisi shows, the encounter with books under such conditions has
a transformative effect not only on those who read them but on the

works themselves. The women in Nafisi's clandestine book club see things in these novels that people on the outside are unlikely to see. *Invitation to a Beheading* resonates differently for readers in the Islamic Republic of Iran than it does for readers, say, in North America or Western Europe.

Indeed, a confidant of Nafisi's, a reclusive intellectual she calls her "magician," tells her that she "will not be able to write about Austen without writing about us, about this place where you rediscovered Austen. . . . The Austen you know is so irretrievably linked to this place, this land and these trees," he professes, that Nafisi can't think this is the same Austen she read in graduate school in the West. "This is the Austen you read here, in a place where the film censor is nearly blind and where they hang people in the streets and put a curtain across the sea to segregate men and women."[3]

In turn, we in the West can discover a great deal about our own literature by seeing it reflected back through the prism of an outsider's perspective or interpretation. We can gain new insights and discover fresh angles on the works read in Nafisi's group by seeing the novels refracted through the prism of the Iranians whose imaginations were kindled and whose lives were transformed by them.

In reviews and informal discussions of *Reading Lolita in Tehran,* people almost invariably note that the book makes them think anew about novels they'd previously thought about in quite those ways and that the discussions in Nafisi's group cast new light on canonical European and American authors they'd grown bored with. (Many have resolved to finally read some of these novels for the first time in their lives.) In an interview, Nafisi poignantly captured this two-way street—this process of give-and-take. The West's "gifts to us," she explains, "have been *Lolita* and *Gatsby,*" whereas Iran's gift to the West "has been reasserting those values that they now take for granted." This gift, she says, is a form of "reminding."[4] I believe we can apply this insight to international politics.

To go where people are reading Hannah Arendt and Karl Popper, Nafisi has admonished, "go to Iran."[5] Go to Iran, I would add, if you want to go where people are reading Jürgen Habermas, Isaiah Berlin, Leszek Kolakowski, and Immanuel Kant.[6] Indeed, one can often find "more vibrant resonances of 'Continental' thought" in places like Iran, notes the political philosopher Fred Dallmayr, "than can be found in Europe today." In a rich elaboration on this point, he observes, "This does not mean that European perspectives are simply disseminated across the world without reciprocity or reciprocal learning. Nor does it mean that local origins are simply erased in favor of a bland universalism. . . . What it does mean is that landscapes and localities undergo symbolic metamorphoses, and that experiences once localized at a given place increasingly find echoes or resonance chambers among distant societies and peoples."[7]

One would be hard pressed to find a more luminous illustration of Dallmayr's point than contemporary Iran. In the words of the Iranian scholar Farideh Farhi, an "elaborate and extremely rich conversation . . . has taken shape in Iran in the past few years concerning the requirements of a democratic and transparent political system and the relationship between faith and freedom."[8] The Iranian political scientist Mehrdad Mashayekhi describes "an epoch-making renaissance in [Iran's] political culture and discourse."[9] The Tehran-based philosopher Ramin Jahanbegloo argues that nothing less than "a renaissance of liberalism" is taking place in Iran today.[10]

Why is there such intense interest in these authors in Iran today? How do books like *The Open Society and Its Enemies* and *The Origins of Totalitarianism* speak to contemporary Iranians? Do the ideas of Habermas and Berlin look the same to Iranian intellectuals and dissidents as they do to us? And of the many intellectual-political currents emanating from the West today—Marxism, poststructuralism, postcolonialism, subaltern studies, and various blends thereof—why is liberalism the most popular school of thought among Iranian intellectuals and students at this historical moment?

First, let me state exactly what I mean by liberalism. Of course, a robust and complex theoretical debate is under way among philosophers, political theorists, and intellectual historians about the precise contours and varieties of liberal thought, its historical evolution, its tensions and contradictions, and the like.[11] Many of the arguments being advanced in that debate are important and useful. But in this essay, I aim to provide a concrete description of what liberalism means in Iran today. Broadly speaking, liberalism finds expression in the struggle for human rights, women's rights, civil liberties, pluralism, religious toleration, freedom of expression, and multiparty democracy.[12]

The struggle for these things defines the upheaval in Iran today. And the reason is quite straightforward: Iran is a theocratic police state. The so-called Islamic Republic, established after the 1979 Iranian Revolution, defines itself largely in opposition to these things. Its human rights record is atrocious.[13] Newspapers and magazines that criticize the regime are routinely shut down. Dissident journalists and intellectuals are jailed and tortured, in many cases killed. Article 4 of Iran's constitution prohibits the establishment of any law or policy not in keeping with Islam. Without the official permission of the Ministry of Islamic Culture and Guidance, writes Naghmeh Zarbafian, "no books or magazines are published, no audiotapes are distributed, no movies are shown, and no cultural organization is established."[14] The unelected Guardian Council—a body of six clerics appointed by the unelected Supreme Leader—has the authority to veto any legislation passed by Iran's parliament and decides who may or may not stand for office. Women are required to follow a strict dress code, covering their heads in public. A sixteen-year-old girl was recently sentenced to death and hung for having sex outside of marriage. That she claimed to have been raped did not matter.[15]

Under conditions like these, liberalism is a radical political project. A triumphant Iranian liberalism would involve dismantling the entire apparatus of the reigning political order and constructing a dramatically different one. In the Iranian context, liberalism is a matter of life and death: people are literally putting their lives on the line when they write articles for opposition newspapers calling for an end to theocratic rule; when they take to the streets to participate in student demonstrations for democracy; when they publish a blog at an Internet café that dares to criticize the regime's human rights record.

Most of us in Western liberal democracies, for all their faults, are at liberty to do these things without worrying about hearing a knock at the door in the middle of the night; without fearing that one of our relatives will suddenly disappear; without fearing that much of anything will happen to us, let alone that we will be tortured or killed. We can largely take these freedoms for granted, and we largely do.

Iranians don't, because they can't. For them, liberalism is a fighting faith. They have to struggle, at great personal risk, to realize the "bourgeois liberties" we take for granted.[16] "Human rights and freedom are luxuries for us," says Akbar Ganji, Iran's leading dissident. "In order to get them, we have to pay. We have to fight, actively resist, go to jail."[17]

As the French political philosopher Pierre Manent has argued, most of us who live in liberal democracies have forgotten what it means to be political. We are tempted, he writes, "to forget that [we] are political animals."[18] We're largely incognizant of the struggles that had to be waged to achieve the rights and arrangements that liberal societies enjoy today: the sacrifices that were made, the blood that was spilled, the lives that were lost, indeed, the world-altering convulsions that were endured.

Many, if not most, of us inhabit a liberal landscape whose provenance is invisible. We exercise rights and liberties more or less the way we drink water: as things that simply are rather than as things that we have to fight for.

Sometimes it takes an outsider to bring things into focus and give us perspective on ourselves, someone who can see things in us that we can't. The Canadian political theorist Bonnie Honig meditates on this theme in her fascinating book *Democracy and the Foreigner.*[19] Immigrants, she points out, "enact" the rituals of citizenship in a way native-born Americans never have to. First, in voyaging here—often at great peril—they've voted "with their feet" to live in America, whereas those born here are American by default, not by choice. Immigrants who decide to become citizens lift their hands and take the oath of citizenship—another act that native-born Americans never undertake—and in so doing, they proclaim or affirm an identity that is automatically conferred on those born here. Foreigners thus play an indispensable function, Honig argues, in nourishing a democratic community and an active, as opposed to a passive, "performance" of citizenship. They can't take for granted the benefits of citizenship the way we can.

Some of that tendency to take things for granted seems to have ebbed since September 11. Outrage has erupted over the PATRIOT Act, the machinations of the Justice Department under John Ashcroft and Alberto Gonzalez, the National Security Agency's phone-surveillance program, the Bush administration's assault on habeas corpus, and related developments. Thousands of Americans have mobilized in defense of civil liberties. The American Civil Liberties Union has robust new gusts of wind in its sails. Everywhere one turns there are new books and articles on the subject. One can debate whether some of the rhetoric emanating from the post–September 11 mobilization overstates the threats that Bush and Gonzalez (and Ashcroft before him) pose to civil liberties and the Constitution—some of it is recklessly hyperbolic—but however grave the threats are, they have renewed the dialogue about rights and liberties and triggered passionate affirmation of things that have, for many years, been more in the background than in the foreground of American political debate. In reminding liberals that we have to fight to defend civil liberties, the age of Ashcroft has thus—unintentionally, of course—had a salutary effect on American political life.

Left-wing critiques of liberalism, which seemed in many ways to have lost their sting and appeal amid the revolutions of 1989, have been making something of a comeback in the age of Bush. Whereas in the imme-

diate aftermath of communism's collapse, radicals argued that "the future of socialism seems now to hang in the balance of its reorientation
towards the liberal tradition,"[20] liberalism now finds itself, if anything,
on the defensive. Liberals are saddled with the burden of disentangling
the liberal project from *neo*liberalism, from the Iraq war, and from U.S.
imperialism.[21] We're busy responding, in other words, to the radical critique of liberalism.

Marxists thus talk about liberalism's "*essential* links with racism and
Eurocentrism"; radicals describe human rights as nothing more than
"the rhetoric of empire" and characterize liberalism as a global "virus";
or, as a friend of mine said recently, "liberalism is the *National Security
Strategy of the United States of America.*"[22] Thanks in large part to Bush
and company, this kind of talk is gaining a hearing. A receptive and
growing audience is gathering for claims like Immanuel Wallerstein's that
we are witnessing "the collapse of liberalism and our definitive entry into
the world 'after liberalism.'"[23]

Thus, as we teeter between boredom and suspicion about what I'll call
Actually Existing Liberalism, we can benefit from thinking about the upheaval in Iran today. By reasserting the values that we now take for
granted, the Iranian struggle for liberalism can breathe new life into our
own liberalism by reminding us, among other things, of how profoundly
radical a force it is.

Habermas himself has made this point. He was invited to lecture at
the University of Tehran in 2002. The event drew an enormous crowd;
the auditorium was overwhelmed. His visit left Iranian intellectual circles abuzz. Study groups have since formed in Tehran to read his works,
notably *The Philosophical Discourse of Modernity.*[24] Reflecting on the
experience, Habermas has spoken of his "encounters with intellectuals
and citizens of an uninhibited, spontaneous and self-confident urban
population" laboring under the weight of authoritarian rule. A young
political scientist he met told Habermas that he "likes to return home [to
Tehran] from Chicago, where he occasionally teaches, despite all the difficulties that await him," because in Iran, he told Habermas, "there is at
least a political public realm with passionate debates."[25]

And those passionate debates have high stakes. They carry deadly serious consequences for those engaged in them: first, because merely being
a participant in political discourse in a closed society and having the
"wrong" views can land one in jail or in a grave; second, because the outcome of those debates could determine the future of one's society. These
discussions are not merely debating clubs or equivalents of CNN's

Crossfire (now fortunately in the grave itself). Iranians are trying to fig-- ure out what kind of society and political system they want. They're thinking through the essential questions of political life, and doing so at great personal risk—holding clandestine meetings in dormitories, read- ing Habermas and Berlin and Arendt and Kolakowski, pondering what role religion might play in a pluralistic, posttheocratic system, and brainstorming about how to get from here to there.[26]

In a context such as this, ideas take on vital, burning relevance: Pop- per's open society; Arendt's emphasis on the primacy of the political and her anatomy of totalitarianism; Berlin's distinction between positive and negative liberty; Habermas's notion of a legitimation crisis and his re- construction of how the public sphere took shape in modern European coffeehouses; and Kolakowski's insistence that there is "one freedom on which all other liberties depend—and that is freedom of expression, free- dom of speech, of print. If this is taken away, no other freedom can exist, or at least it would be soon suppressed."[27] These ideas take on an im- mediacy in Iran today that they simply don't have in the West. But what if we were to reconsider them through a Persian prism?

"Our dilemma," the Iranian political theorist Javad Tabataba'i has said, "is how to understand the gap that has developed between us and the West since the Renaissance. . . . We need to re-link to this part of our tradition that also inspired the West. . . . We can reread [the great me- dieval Islamic philosopher-scientist] ibn-Sina [Avrceina]," for example, "with a Western horizon in mind."[28] What I propose is the mirror image of Tabataba'i's suggestion: that we in the West should "relink" to the thinkers in *our* tradition who have inspired Iran and thus reread Haber- mas and Berlin with a *Persian* horizon in mind. To do so, we have to ex- amine why Habermas and Berlin inspire Iranians today and why their ideas have become the intellectual raw materials of a revolution in the making, a *liberal* revolution.[29]

The great theorist of liberal revolution, the early twentieth-century Italian writer and agitator Piero Gobetti, believed that precisely the mar- ginality of liberal movements—their being on the outside rather than the inside of political power—makes them radical in nature. The Italian lib- eralism of Gobetti's age, of course, had to labor under the creeping weight of Mussolini's Fascism, which came to power while Gobetti was editing the journal *Liberal Revolution,* furiously writing essays, and being beaten and arrested (eventually dying from wounds inflicted in one attack by Fascists). This sense of battling uphill, living with the precari- ousness of the liberal project, and eventually seeing it thwarted convinced Gobetti that liberalism is, at its best, a militant and revolutionary force. His writings are, in the words of the political theorist Nadia Urbinati, "witness to a liberalism conscious of its imminent and perhaps long-lasting twilight."[30] But precisely for that reason, they are a fog light in the historical sea of liberalism, illuminating the militant liberating power of the credo—a self-conception that we liberals would do well to recover today.

I should be clear, however, that the parlance of "revolution" is far from the lips of Iranians today. Iranians are understandably turned off by revolutionspeak, given the "revolutionary" regime they've been living under since 1979, but also—and this point is critical—because of the general failure of the revolutionary Left in Iran. "The leftist, anti-imperialist ideas of the 1970s have given way to a more pragmatic discourse about economic and political dignity based on Western models of secular democracy," observes the Iranian journalist Afshin Molavi. "Iranian youth largely dismiss the radical ideas of their parents' generation, full of half-baked leftism, Marxist economics, Third World anti-imperialism, Islamist radicalism and varying shades of utopian totalitarianism. 'We just want to be normal,' is typical of what hundreds of students have told me. 'We're tired of radicalism.'"[31]

Some sectors of the Iranian Left, moreover, forged outright alliances with Khomeini's forces—with disastrous results, both for themselves (upon fully consolidating power, the Islamic Republic decimated the Left, murdering thousands of its members and scattering the survivors into exile), and, crucially, for the Left's reputation and legacy among Iranians. As the dissident Iranian writer Faraj Sarkohi has written, "the left wing's co-operation with the despotic government and their rejection of democracy is firmly engraved on the memory of the Iranian people."[32] Their many differences aside, the Islamist and ultraleft wings of the Iranian Revolution shared a virulent antipathy toward liberalism. "Death to America!" may have been the more famous slogan of 1979, but "Death to liberalism!" was shouted along with it on the streets of Tehran. As many Iranian commentators have pointed out, the Iranian Left—not unlike its counterparts elsewhere in the world—lashed out at liberalism with a ferocious zeal and in doing so contributed to the Islamist ascendancy. This antiliberalism was especially misplaced and ironic, given that the greatest anti-imperialist leader of twentieth-century Iran, Mohammad Mosaddeq, was nothing if not a liberal democrat![33]

A painfully salient illustration of Western leftism's irrelevance to contemporary Iran is Antonio Negri's visit to the country in January 2005 to deliver a series of lectures. Given the intellectually omnivorous climate in Iran today, it's no surprise that Negri was invited to lecture in Iran and that his talks were well attended. But most of his audience found the radical theorist's comments "oddly tangential to [Iran's] most pressing concerns," according to Nina Power. With the country's "widespread suspicion of classical Marxist or revolutionary solutions," she asks, "What exactly does Antonio Negri have to say to Iran?"[34]

Most of the audience saw "little of relevance in his 'communicative, productive' model of mass political agency to what is, in many ways, a society constrained, at virtually all levels, by a ubiquitous, if internally riven, state." Negri's "concept of radicalism," Power wrote, appeared to possess "no frontal relation to the constraints of the existing order" in Iran. If anything, Negri's message appealed more to the religious hard Right and to Iran's conservatives. "If there is to be a new Iranian revolution from below," according to Power, "it is unlikely to take the form of a plebeian carnival or quasi-Biblical 'exodus.'"

Liberalism is not only the political tendency of choice in Iranian opposition circles today; it is the most *radical* force on the Iranian political landscape (and in the contemporary Islamic world more broadly, though I will limit my discussion to Iran).[35] Contemporary Western radicalism simply doesn't speak to Iranian progressives. Why would it? The issues atop its agenda—anti-imperialism, antiglobalization, and (in a few remaining outposts) anticapitalism—are not the central concerns of the Iranian opposition, which is fighting for democracy, pluralism, human rights, women's rights, freedom of expression, and freedom from theocracy. It's not that radical leftism is opposed to these things, but these ideals don't form the *core* of the radical-leftist project.[36] They do form the core of the liberal project, however, which is why Iranian progressives naturally gravitate to liberal thinkers. Ultimately, Kolakowski once poignantly remarked, "there are more important arguments for freedom and democratic values than the fact that Marx, if one looks closely, was not so hostile to those values as might at first sight appear."[37]

Conversely, the Western Left has been largely silent about—and flummoxed by—the liberal upheaval in Iran. One would have hoped to see the Iranian struggle figure prominently in the world of solidarity activism, or at least get some play in the left-wing press—especially at the high tide of unrest, during the student-led demonstrations in the streets of Tehran in June 2003, which the regime crushed in a paroxysm of repression. Compared to the attention the Western Left typically pays to student revolts in the third world, the Iranian struggle has been virtually invisible on the radar screens of most leftists.[38] In short, the tunnel-vision anti-imperialism of much of the Left (which has intensified considerably under Bush) leads down a dead-end road to myopia and confusion about cases like Iran, in which the people's struggle is not against the American empire or its proxies.

This silence has not gone unnoticed by Iranian dissidents. In hundreds of conversations I've had with Iranian intellectuals, journalists, and human rights activists in recent years, I've invariably encountered exasperation: Why, they ask, is the American Left so seemingly indifferent to the struggle taking place in Iran? Why can't the Iranian movement get the attention of so-called progressives and solidarity activists in the United States? Why do neoconservatives seem to be the ones who express the most interest in the Iranian struggle? Afshin Molavi captured this situation all too well recently: "I know far too many Iranian leftists who have gone neo-con as a result of their feeling of abandonment by the American and European left. I wish they had not gone that route."[39]

We need a *radical* liberalism to fill this vacuum. Leftists have largely ceded involvement in Iran because the Iranian situation doesn't conform to the all-consuming anti-imperialist paradigm; they're letting the imperialists, in other words, set the terms of the debate and thus do their thinking for them. Liberals have the right intellectual sympathies in their insistence on the primacy of human rights, liberty, and democracy. But far too few liberals are willing to roll up their sleeves and engage in the kind of solidarity politics that the Left, to its credit, made a centerpiece of its activism in Central America and East Timor, for example, during the 1980s and 1990s. That kind of activism requires a degree of militancy and intensity that liberalism isn't exactly known for. But it should be. We liberals need to make our creed *radical* again—to infuse it with a spirit of internationalism and solidarity.

Radical leftists have no monopoly on that spirit. In fact, they've dropped the ball in that area repeatedly, formerly in Bosnia and Kosovo and now in Iran. When the Balkans were engulfed in a frenzy of murderous nationalism and death-squad terror in the 1990s, human rights groups, feminists, and liberal internationalists took action while the radical Left either sat on the sidelines in silence or came to the defense of the "demonized" Milosevic. As mass graves were being filled and hundreds of thousands of people being dislocated, the likes of *Z Magazine* and *New Left Review* disgracefully turned their scorn not on the murderers but on the West; hell-bent on squeezing the Balkan nightmare into preconceived Marxian categories, they claimed that the Western powers were intent on dismantling the last outpost of socialism in Europe—as if Milosevic ran anything other than the most vulgar form of gangster capitalism. Some even became outright apologists for the Milosevic regime and denied its atrocities.[40]

Meanwhile, thousands of humanitarian workers, international lawyers, and human rights activists went to the Balkans and did something; the putatively "tepid" liberals at the *New York Review of Books* featured the Balkan cataclysm front and center in its pages, providing vital reportage and analysis that stand in marked contrast to the muted, convoluted, and morally disfigured record of the radical intelligentsia. The Balkan episode should be remembered as one of liberal internationalism's finest moments.

Of course, the geopolitical constellation that created that liberal-internationalist moment and opened the intellectual space for the humanitarian-interventionist paradigm to take shape seems to have been torn asunder by subsequent developments, rendered obsolete by the rampages of Bush, Cheney, and Rumsfeld.[41] To be sure, the geopolitical equation and the terms of the debate have been dramatically refashioned. The principles of liberal internationalism may now be on the defensive, but they remain as vital as ever to struggles taking place around the world, and we liberal internationalists need to be *avant la lettre* in advancing their cause—from standing in solidarity with struggles like the one in Iran today to asserting the continued need for humanitarian intervention in places like Sudan.

In this period of widespread withdrawal from internationalist thinking—in which many self-styled leftists share the traditionally conservative suspicion that liberalism and democracy are somehow foreign to non-Western societies and pose an imperializing threat to their "traditions"—we should note that Iran has had a robust and long-standing *internal* struggle for democracy. Indeed, as Ali Gheissari and Vali Nasr point out, Iran's is a "culturally indigenous and popular demand for democratization." "In Iran," they argue, "the democracy debate is neither a Western import nor a concession to the West, nor is it a project of the state or the elite foisted on the masses. Here the debate is now a popular idea that has developed from within the society."[42]

The imperative to reach out to liberals struggling around the world is not simply a matter of internationalist principle. We certainly should reach out, but the fact is that liberals around the world *seek* our support and recognition. Iranian liberals, for example, have said in no uncertain terms that they want the active support of liberals around the world. When I interviewed the Iranian human rights lawyer and Nobel Peace laureate Shirin Ebadi in the spring of 2004, I asked her what she thinks of the view, widely held on the Left, that Iran's issues are internal and that Western "outsiders" should stay out of them.[43] She firmly rejected this position and expressed a desire for "human rights defenders . . . university professors . . . international NGOs [nongovernmental organizations]" to support the struggle for human rights in Iran. "All defenders of human rights," she said, "are members of a single family." "When we help one another we're stronger." It is important, she said, "to give aid to democratic institutions inside despotic countries."[44]

Echoing this view, Akbar Ganji has said, "We don't want anything from governments. We are looking to the NGOs. And we want people to know what the Iranian reality is, for people to know what's going on in Iran. The intellectuals, the media and NGOs in the world have to draw attention to the human rights abuses in Iran. We need moral support. I emphasize: we don't want intervention, we only want the moral support of the global community for our fight."[45]

Both Ebadi and Ganji are keen to distinguish this kind of international solidarity from the sort of "help" neoconservatives would like to visit upon Iran. Indeed, not only are they against military intervention in their country, preferring instead a nonviolent transformation from within, but they don't even want *assistance* from the U.S. government. Thus, the Bush administration's announcement that it was earmarking $75 million to support Iran's democratic forces met with a resounding thud among those very forces, an unambiguous "thanks but no thanks."

Ebadi, Ganji, and other Iranian activists thus reject both the radical Left's phlegmatic isolationism and the neoconservatives' dubious, itchy-trigger-finger imperialism. This gaping political void is screaming out for liberal internationalists to fill it. We liberals can't leave our fellow liberals in places like Iran out to dry. Nor can we allow the impression that the neocons are the only ones in the West paying attention to them. Our counterparts are seeking our solidarity. Our internationalism demands that we listen and find ways to help them.

I'm calling for a liberal third worldism, if you like, to take the place of the failed and moribund third worldism of the New Left and its inheritors. Rather than cede the turf of the third world to the revolutionary Left (as many liberals and social democrats have done since the 1960s), we should proactively claim that turf as our own, advancing liberalism as a superior framework for addressing the dilemmas facing the third world today—parts of it in particular.

Fred Halliday identifies the defining properties of Actually Existing

Third Worldism, if you will, as follows: "a ritual incantation of 'no war' that avoids any substantive engagement with problems of international peace and security, or reflection on how positively to help peoples in zones of conflict; a set of vague, un-thought-out, uncosted and often dangerous utopian ideas about an alternative world; a pleasing but vapid invocation of global human values and internationalism that blithely ignores the misuses to which that term was put in the 20th century."[46] To be fair, this description doesn't apply to everyone in the antiglobalization or global-justice movement, many of whom possess a more sophisticated understanding of the world and apply more intellectual rigor than Halliday's polemic would suggest.[47] Nonetheless, his portrait has a great deal of truth. Anyone even casually familiar with the political scene Halliday describes knows that large swaths of it are guilty as charged.

But pointing out the inadequacies of Actually Existing Radicalism isn't enough. It's necessary, but insufficient, to demonstrate the third-worldist Left's limitations and oversimplifications: to criticize and emphatically reject its political monism, its tunnel-vision obsession with U.S. imperialism, and the resulting myopic picture of the world. We liberal internationalists have to go beyond critique and propose alternative visions. Where, for example, do we stand on the current architecture of global capitalism (that is, neoliberalism)? What is our position on the Free Trade Area of the Americas and on the Central American Free Trade Agreement? What is our contribution to the debate about international economic institutions like the World Trade Organization, the International Monetary Fund, and the World Bank and their impact on the third world?

We can take the antiglobalization movement to task for failing to provide realistic solutions to these problems, but what solutions do *we* have to offer? And how do we respond to the radical argument that liberalism is complicit both in the neoliberal economic order and in the American imperial enterprise—that it functions as intellectual fuel for the machinery of Global Pax Americana? Again, we can—and should—spurn the vulgarity of such assertions. But we need substantive responses to them. What exactly is our critique of neoliberalism and U.S. imperialism? And how do we make sense of liberalism's complex historical entanglement with imperialism?[48]

I don't propose one set of answers to these questions in the limited space of this essay. But I do want to emphasize that we liberals must confront and work through these questions if we are to speak to the international arena and engage the third world—which I believe we must.

We're in our element in the Iranian and Bosnian fronts, in which the preeminent issues are, in the case of Iran, freedom of expression, human rights, democracy, pluralism, and secularism; and in the case of Bosnia, human rights, international law, and humanitarian intervention. That's the stuff of liberalism and internationalism; it's our home court.

But we have to be able to operate effectively away from our home court, too. Some struggles in the world today are tailor-made for a liberal-internationalist analysis, but many are not. In places where the core principles of liberalism are at stake, our role is crystal clear. But where the core issues are poverty, development, trade policy, capital flows, financial markets, sweat shops, structural adjustment, landless workers, transnational corporations, ecological destruction, genetically engineered crops, and the like, we find ourselves on the home court of Marxists, anarchists, third worldists, and other radicals in the antiglobalization movement. They, not we, are usually the ones who organize the forums and the demonstrations, who publish the magazines and the websites, and who write the books and the working papers on these issues.

This situation needs to change. If we fail to engage the third world ourselves, we will be seen precisely as "oddly tangential" to its most pressing concerns. We need to formulate liberal-internationalist and social-democratic perspectives on the most pressing concerns of the global South—constructing alternatives to both Actually Existing Neoliberalism and its radical third-worldist critics. We need to bring our collective intellectual energies and political sensibilities to bear on the global struggle for justice—on the economic and political fronts alike. To be sure, some liberal internationalists and social democrats are already doing vital work in this area.[49] But a much more aggressive and concerted effort is required.

The approach I'm suggesting requires concrete, piecemeal, reformist organizing around, on the one hand, direct solidarity with workers in the third world and, on the other, efforts to tinker with the institutional architecture of the global economy (international trade negotiations, World Bank policies, U.N. Development Program projects, and the like). We need to insinuate ourselves pragmatically into these institutions and processes, bending the ears of green and labor-friendly bureaucrats to push for tougher environmental and labor agreements and the like.[50]

Such steps are, of course, already under way, in the form of myriad NGOs, civil-society organizations, and social movements around the globe.[51] For example, to be provincial for a moment, an organization in my neighborhood of Chicago, the U.S./Labor Education in the Americas

Project (www.usleap.org) organizes highly specific campaigns in solidarity with workers in specific industries in Latin America—banana and coffee workers, for example. The organization has no "revolutionary" pretensions; it favors hands-on pragmatism, working within the existing framework of the global economy but with the *spirit* (too lacking in liberalism, I think) of internationalism and solidarity—of rolling up one's sleeves and doing something concrete to support struggles abroad.

It's this spirit that distinguishes social-democratic internationalism or liberal third worldism from official liberal internationalism. The radical dimension of this vision stems from the principle of solidarity: We liberal internationalists need to incorporate this principle into our approach to international politics, taking lessons from the leftist Central America solidarity movement of the 1980s and 1990s. Solidarity on the political front means supporting struggles for democracy and pluralism in places like Iran and advocating humanitarian intervention in places like Darfur; on the economic front, it means supporting the struggles of workers and others in the third world/global South.

Liberal internationalism tends to focus on the state, as well as on global bodies, as the nerve center of political action. National and transnational measures are desperately needed, especially humanitarian interventions to stop genocide and crimes against humanity, but liberal internationalists tend to focus too heavily on this realm. We need to engage in direct solidarity with opposition movements and workers in the third world, building active, on-the-ground relationships with dissidents and human rights activists in other countries. We can bring them to North America for speaking tours; organize (to the extent possible) delegations of Western liberals to travel to the third world (and make individual trips); write about the struggles of our third-world counterparts in our magazines; spread the word about what activists are doing; have the work of dissidents and liberal intellectuals in the third world translated into English and disseminated. In these ways, we can make their struggle ours—and thereby help radicalize liberalism.

In doing so, we should draw strength both from our own accomplishments, like those in the Balkans, and from the people with whom we stand in solidarity, like those in Iran. We can derive much inspiration from the dissidents and bloggers and human rights activists struggling against authoritarianism and repression in Iran today. The militancy with which they assert the values of liberalism stand as a reminder of the vibrancy and enduring relevance of those values, not only in Iran but globally.

I close where I began, with Nafisi's *Reading Lolita.* Her book, she says, is about "how Tehran helped redefine Nabokov's novel, turning it into this *Lolita,* our *Lolita.*"[52] I would like to suggest that by looking closely at the struggle of Iranians today—for human rights, an open society, freedom of expression, freedom to believe or not believe as one wishes, pluralism, democracy, the freedom to read whatever books one wants to read, without restriction—and by taking that upheaval seriously and seeing ourselves in it, we enter into a dialectical space, a short circuit in which the Iranians waging that struggle redefine liberalism, turning it into this liberalism, *their* liberalism.

13

Beyond Iraq: Toward a New Liberal Internationalism

MICHAEL TOMASKY

t is often observed that the Iraq War has created a crisis for conservatism, particularly for conservatism's more aggressive striation, neoconservatism. It is obvious now—or should be—that the neoconservatives' fantastical notion that the United States could invade a country and completely remake its government and society at little cost to Americans and the invaded country (even winning the world's gratitude at no cost!) was madness and that the cocksure manner in which the neoconservatives insisted on this notion was delusional. One recalls the photographs of young communists rolling a model of Vladimir Tatlin's Monument to the Third International through the streets of Moscow in the early 1920s—the bold new future incarnated in a utopian, but utterly unbuildable, building (there was not enough steel in all of Russia for this single structure). Such was the besotted exuberance with which the neocons paraded their equally impossible idea through the streets of Washington in the spring of 2003.

To the extent that the war's failures have undermined neoconservatives' credibility, all to the good. One might think, then, that the neocons' failures should lead to some sort of triumph for liberals. But we look around, and we do not see this outcome at all. If anything, liberal foreign policy thinking is as unsettled as usual. And something worse than unsettled: Beginning with the presidential election of 2004 and intensifying in the spring of 2005, an element of bitterness crept in, and distrust, between liberals who supported the Iraq War and those—including my-self—who opposed it.

The liberal hawks say the doves have given up on a future of human-itarian invention; that we have become, or risk becoming, amoral Kissin-gerian realists, able to recognize only American national interest, willing to leave the suffering peoples of the world to their fates at the hands of tyrants toward whom we maintain indifference.[1] The liberal doves say the hawks may have thought—more likely, fooled themselves into think-ing—they were supporting a war of "humanitarian intervention" in Iraq, but they in fact were dupes or stooges.[2] Whether they like it or not, they supported a war of neoconservatism, with all the malign particulars that entails, and they need to admit this fact and apologize for it.

This argument among liberal intellectuals and pundits is largely hidden from the view of the larger public (admittedly, on the list of bad things to result from the Iraq War, this argument is fairly far down the list for the average American). The public might see a version of this argument among Democrats; Wisconsin Senator Russ Feingold announces, as he did in August 2005, that troops should be withdrawn by the end of 2007, and the more hawkish senators like Joe Biden and Hillary Clinton step forward to slap him down. But elected Democrats are not the center of the action on this matter. Politicians follow public and elite opinion rather than lead it on questions as large as war and withdrawal—as the Dem-ocrats demonstrate virtually every day. Thinkers and writers, who don't have to seek votes, must lead, staking out the points of view and ideas about the future that politicians might eventually adopt.

So the schism between the liberal hawks and doves is serious, and it has serious consequences for the past and the future of liberalism. The temp-tation, given the nature of intellectual life and the demands of the egos in-volved, is to keep the focus on Iraq eternal: to keep debating Iraq long after such a debate has any use. In fact, we have already, as I write these words in October 2005, reached that point. There is no profit in arguing further about it. The question for the future is: Can we draw the right lessons from the experience and move beyond the categories of hawks and doves to agree on a set of foreign policy principles that both sides can accept?

THESIS: THE HAWKS' ERRORS AND LAMENT

The hawks' starting lineup is well-known. *New York Times* columnist Thomas L. Friedman has been an important figure, possibly the most important; his arguments, on the op-ed page of the newspaper of record, undoubtedly persuaded many more moderates and liberals to support the war than could have been convinced by William Kristol or Robert Kagan. Another notable in this camp is Paul Berman, a man in the mold of his New York intellectual predecessors, whose support for the war was an important signpost for the cultural elite. Michael Ignatieff of Harvard lent a liberal academic imprimatur to the attack. George Packer of the *New Yorker* was not a prewar, prowar polemicist per se, instead making his support for the war clear in certain forums after the war was under way (in *Slate,* for example). Packer was joined at the *New Yorker* by its editor, David Remnick, who wrote an editorial arguing for the war shortly before it started. (Remnick wrote only the one piece, so it would be quite unfair to say that he agitated for the war at any length.) Jeffrey Goldberg, another writer at the *New Yorker,* went farther—again, in *Slate*—writing in October 2002 that in five years' time, "the coming invasion of Iraq will be remembered as an act of profound morality."[3] *Slate* editor Jacob Weisberg declared himself prowar a few days before Goldberg wrote those words. The editors of the *New Republic* carried the liberal prowar case into George W. Bush's Washington. Beyond these writers were several Democratic hawks one rung farther up the food chain, the foreign policy gurus: Madeleine Albright, Richard Holbrooke, Sandy Berger, a few other former Clinton officials (and Bill Clinton himself, of course), and a small number of liberal policy intellectuals who backed the war as well.[4]

Each hawk had his or her own reasons for supporting the war. Friedman simply saw a need to break some eggs to make the new omelet of Arab democracy: "I am for invading Iraq," he wrote in the fall of 2002, "only if we think that doing so can bring about regime change and democratization. Because what the Arab world needs desperately is a model that works."[5] Berman saw Saddam Hussein's Ba'athism as a continuation of the European totalitarianisms of the previous century, evils that Muslim totalitarianism followed "in all important particulars," he wrote.[6] Berman didn't so much care whether specific evidence of a Saddam–Al Qaeda link was unearthed; fascism, communism, and Ba'athism were of a piece, a dangerous and evil piece, and the twentieth century had taught us what happens when liberals in the West fail to recognize danger and evil early enough. Packer saw the invasion in the context and tradition of the humanitarian interventions in Bosnia and Kosovo in the 1990s. Goldberg believed—as did many observers both pro and con—that Iraq possessed weapons that made the country a genuine threat to regional and world (and thus American) security.

So we cannot say that the liberal hawks agreed on one reason, or set of reasons, for war. But I do think that, in general, they or many of them collectively succumbed to two temptations, which bear mentioning if hawks and doves are to move forward to liberal common ground.

First, the hawks rationalized away the fact that they were lying down with an administration that they professed to loathe in nearly every other way. "In their blindness," Berman wrote of liberal war opponents in *Dissent* in the winter of 2004, "they cannot identify the main contours of reality right now. They peer at Iraq and see the smirking face of George W. Bush. They even feel a kind of Schadenfreude or satisfaction at his errors and failures. This is a modern, television-age example of what used to be called 'false consciousness.'"[7] Berman, as has been his wont since September 11, put the matter more alarmingly than other liberal hawks did, but many made a similar point: Liberal war opponents simply could not see past their contempt for Bush. Meanwhile, for the liberal hawks, their ability to see around that contempt became a point of pride; it made them better, smarter, more open to complexity, aware of the dialectical contradictions and able to grapple with them as any honest intellectual should. And—by the way—it won them limitless panegyrics in the mainstream media.

A second temptation to which I think several liberal hawks succumbed was what I call the "City College cafeteria" temptation—the natural yearning of intellectuals to be participants in important conversations at an important point in history and to make the right decision in history's eyes. The young radicals of the 1930s had done so, when the cafeteria at the City College of New York, which many of them attended—Daniel Bell, Nathan Glazer, Irving Howe, Irving Kristol—teemed with arguments about the great questions of the day (and there were many great questions, in those days) among Stalinists, Trotskyites, Lovestoneites, and socialists. Contemporary intellectuals (especially on the left) have a well-known wistfulness for the 1930s, because in the 1930s, that golden age of horrors, intellectuals had to make choices that mattered. But in late twentieth-century America, what *really* mattered? Fascism was barely a memory, and communism had collapsed; the -isms really *had* become -wasms. Liberals were left bickering over a stained blue dress. But then came September 11: Here, at last, was something to argue about! For liberal hawks, 9/11 was their September 1939.[8] History had grabbed all intellectuals by the lapels and screamed, "Choose!" And the liberal hawks saw one governing imperative in making their choice: At all costs, do not be on the side of the Left of "abject pacifism," as *New*

Republic editor Peter Beinart said to the *Washington Post*'s Howard Kurtz a month before the war.[9]

These temptations were political in nature (although I believe the second temptation contained an emotional element as well). They are worth remarking upon now, as we try to settle accounts, because if hawks and doves are to go forward and if a stronger vision of liberal internationalism is to emerge, both sides need to acknowledge their shortcomings (I'll get to the doves' shortcomings anon).

But now, having cataloged the hawks' errors, let's look at their lament. To my mind, the case was put most powerfully by Richard Just, a young editor at the *New Republic*, in an essay he contributed to a book published in summer 2005 called *A Matter of Principle: Humanitarian Arguments for the War in Iraq*. Just called his essay "Liberal Realism or Liberal Idealism: The Iraq War and the Limits of Tolerance." Surveying liberal opposition to the various arguments for war offered by both the administration and the liberal hawks, Just concluded that liberals "seemed less concerned with moral costs and more concerned with what would serve U.S. interests, narrowly conceived." Noting, with dripping irony, that leftish Democrats like Dennis Kucinich had suddenly discovered the wonders of cold-war containment (in arguing that Saddam had been and could be contained), Just took issue with the idea that containment—the epitome of foreign policy realism—had contained Saddam at a low cost. Leaving Hussein in power for twelve years, he wrote, did not come at a low cost to Iraqis: "No, the costs of containment were only low if understood within a realist framework. If understood within a framework that took into account interests *and* moral considerations, containment became a much more complex proposition."[10]

Just directed these comments primarily to Democrats (he even went counterintuitive on Barack Obama's much admired keynote address at the Democratic convention, noting with disappointment that Obama's passages on foreign policy contained none of the moral urgency that came so naturally to Obama when discussing domestic affairs). But I think, in fairness, much of what he wrote applies to many war opponents. And his point raises disturbing questions about the future, questions that I and other war opponents I know have wrestled with: Had liberalism given up on morality in foreign policy? Would we miss the next Bosnia, the next Kosovo, and just sit out turmoil in other countries, letting people die because no national-security imperative was at stake? Jose Ramos-Horta, a courageous leader of the East Timorese fight against the Indonesian occupation (and a deserving Nobel Prize winner for his efforts), wrote an essay in the same volume called "Sometimes, a War Saves People." Ramos-Horta wrote that he didn't remember any hubbub when French paratroopers, without U.N. approval, landed in the then Central African Republic and deposed Jean Bedel Bokassa, a tyrant known for cannibalism. Why is Iraq different? Just's and Ramos-Horta's questions are important ones, and hawks are justified in demanding an answer.

ANTITHESIS: THE DOVES' CASE AND ANGER

The liberal doves of my side constituted, of course, a much larger group than did the liberal hawks. Some opponents of the war were, like Zbigniew Brzezinski, genuine realists and not just realists of convenience. At least, Brzezinski is historically known as realist, but in his 2002 book, *The Choice,* one finds someone who accepts arguments about the need to protect human rights and who asserts that the previous generation's politicization of the peoples of the third world is the most important change in world politics, and one that must be addressed in a variety of ways. Also among the doves were many liberal interventionists—people who backed the 1990s interventions in Haiti, Bosnia, and Kosovo and who supported America's attack on Afghanistan after the attacks of September 11 but who saw Iraq as qualitatively different. I put myself in this camp, along with writers like Todd Gitlin, Eric Alterman, and Arthur M. Schlesinger Jr.

On our left was a third camp: the American Left, which takes the general position that American use of force is illegitimate, and many of whose members opposed the Afghan invasion (or found a way to give a grudging endorsement to "limited military action in self-defense," as the *Nation* said in an editorial called "The Limits of War" in October 2001).[11] This view was not the mainstream liberal view; virtually every mainstream liberal I know supported the Afghan war without qualification. The liberal interventionists had also parted company with the Left, for the most part, throughout the 1990s on Kosovo and other interventions. (The *Nation*'s editorials on Kosovo had headlines like "Destroying Kosovo," "Stop the War Now," "Protest the War," "Oppose a Wider War," and "Dark Victory.")

So, though the idea may seem paradoxical given the intensity of the argument between the liberal hawks and the liberal, non-Left doves, these two groups have more in common with each other than either group does with the Left. Liberal hawks and liberal (non-Left) doves share a presumption that the Left does not share: that the United States is not chiefly bent on establishing world hegemony but is still, even after its catastrophic misconduct during the cold war (especially in Vietnam), for the most part interested in leading the world to a better future and is more capable of doing so than is any other nation. These distinctions aren't evident in most mainstream press accounts, in which reporters who covered demonstrations came away thinking that everyone who opposed the Iraq War is a Noam Chomsky acolyte. And certain liberal hawks, like Beinart, who took aim at "abject pacifism," sought to blur the distinction between the liberals who were against this war and the leftists, who are against practically all wars. For many doves, opposing the Iraq War was a close call. And even those of us for whom it wasn't a terribly close call had to admit, with some appreciation, that President Bush was right to make the United Nations come to terms with the fact that Saddam was flouting its resolutions.

The liberal doves' opposition to war was, like the liberal hawks' support of it, varied, but I think it came down to three main bases. The first—a tactical point of opposition rather than a principled one—was the suspicion that the war would be more costly than its proponents admitted. The second argument contained elements of both tactic and principle: that the war on terror had to be waged against, well, the actual terrorists and not against a tyrant who, however perfidious, was not, as far as we knew, allied with Al Qaeda. The third main argument was entirely one of principle: opposition to the nonhumanitarian goals of the neoconservatives. These goals, hidden in plain sight in various documents produced over the course of the 1990s, dealt with how best to establish American unilateral superiority in the post–cold-war era—plans the neocons began drawing up right after the collapse of the Soviet Union, when Dick Cheney was still secretary of defense under George H. W. Bush.

This basis of opposition was strictly ideological, and Brzezinski was its highest-profile expostulator. Brzezinski galvanized antiwar opinion with a dramatic speech at a foreign policy conference in the fall of 2003 organized by the Center for American Progress, the Century Foundation, and my magazine, the *American Prospect*. Invoking Gillo Pontecorvo's chilling film *The Battle of Algiers* (which a quick-thinking distributor rereleased to select American theaters in 2004), Brzezinski struck deep into the heart of neoconservative darkness. His critique was not about unilateralism or weapons of mass destruction or Bush's intemperate rhetoric, although it mentioned these elements. It was instead aimed at the precepts of the neoconservative agenda, first sketched out in a 1992 Defense Planning Guidance document, incubated through the 1990s by the Project for a New American Century, and finally given life when George W. Bush came to power. The Bush administration, Brzezinski said, had defined the war on terrorism in "vague, abstract, and quasi-theological terms"—exactly the terms that neoconservatives pressed upon the president.[12]

Events have proven Brzezinski, and the liberal doves in general, essentially correct. But we doves are not, or should not be, especially happy about having been proven correct; we are right only because tragedy has occurred. Moreover, to be essentially correct is not to be right about everything. So, in the spirit of accommodation in which I write this essay, let me acknowledge two missteps by liberal doves. First, I would be less than honest if I failed to acknowledge that, at least in my case, my opposition contained a dose of emotional anger at Bush and the neocons along with the principle. If the liberal hawks were guilty of being too cavalier in putting aside their other disagreements with Bush, then many liberal doves were guilty of seeing everything a little too relentlessly through the Bush prism. Berman overstates the case when he calls this flaw "false consciousness"; that phrase, as Berman knows, has a particular historic meaning, and if anyone was misleading the proletariat, it surely wasn't liberal war opponents. But certainly, anger at Bush—about the way he came to office, his invention of a mandate for himself that he did not win from the people, and most of all, his and his appointees' use of 9/11 as an excuse to launch a war they'd long desired for reasons having nothing to do with terrorism—colored our reasoning.

The second mistake of some war opponents has been to embrace realism just a little more enthusiastically than they should have. If many of the liberal hawks bought into some neoconservative arguments, then too many liberal war opponents probably went a bit too far toward the other extreme of arguing that the United States can't solve the world's problems. The laws of physics apply to intellectual combat no less than they do to gravity, and the action of the liberal-hawk–neoconservative alliance provoked the reaction of a liberal-dove–realist alliance. Liberal hawks are within their rights to note a mordant irony in this development; for decades, liberal internationalists were the realists' greatest foes, so it is odd that they have become allies. Thus, when the liberal hawks worry that we'll shrink from taking action in future Bosnias and Kosovos, they mean that Iraq will have taught ex–liberal internationalists to flinch in the face of future challenges like those in the Balkans.

The liberal-internationalist answer to this challenge is simple: The hawks may be correct that the United States will flinch from acting during future humanitarian actions. But that stance will not be the fault of the war opponents. It will be the fault of the people who prosecuted the Iraq War, because that disaster is the event that has made the American people resistant to backing future actions like it. As for the next Bosnia, we already missed it: It was called Darfur, and we missed it not because I or Eric Alterman and Todd Gitlin may have adopted some realist positions. We missed it because the neoconservatives' obsession with Iraq left the United States without the troops or popular will to save the non-Arab Sudanese population destroyed by the Janjaweed: about 300,000 dead, and 1.8 million displaced from their homes.

Nevertheless, liberal opponents of the Iraq War need to be alert to the pitfalls of adopting a realist mind-set. Liberals spent decades arguing to realists that American foreign policy needs a moral element that takes into consideration human rights and the plight of people not fortunate enough by accident of birth to live in a country in which rights are protected and the law is respected. Such was our pursuit, and our rhetoric. We can't abandon that pursuit just because some people we don't like took up the rhetoric in behalf of a war we don't like.

In evaluating where we are today, I repeat the question for the future that I asked toward the beginning of this essay: Can we draw the right lessons from the experience and move beyond the categories of hawks and doves to agree on a set of foreign policy principles that both sides can accept?

SYNTHESIS: BEYOND HAWKS AND DOVES

Here, then, I offer a six-point plan around which liberal intellectuals can rally to create a foreign policy for the future.

1. We agree to quit fighting about the Iraq War and agree further on a joint assessment of it. That assessment includes these points: The war has been a disaster. But it may yet, someday, produce beneficial results for the region and the world, and we all hope without reservation that it does. But we all also recognize that, even if it does, it can never be seen as an act of "profound morality," in Jeffrey Goldberg's words. At some point in the future, it may be seen at best as a risky notion that was sold to the public with falsehoods, executed with scandalous incompetence that somehow ended well (that is, with a multiethnic democracy in Iraq) despite America's irresponsibility and error.

2. The liberal hawks need to acknowledge that they were wrong in thinking and arguing that Iraq was just a bigger, bolder Kosovo and that they bought into a neoconservative concept that, upon scrutiny, may have a liberal-internationalist heart but is guided by its hegemonic brain. Putting one hundred fifty thousand soldiers on the ground and nation building are very different from commencing some air strikes (with modest ground support) and trying to stop bloodshed or to give an ethnic minority a degree of regional autonomy. Regime change and nation building, the hawks need to acknowledge, are much messier affairs than they thought. We may not—and should not—categorically rule out these options for the United States in the future. But we need to agree that they are expensive, difficult, tragic; that they take years; and, crucially, that the American people need to be told the truth about their costs and that no liberal intellectual will ever support such an action by an American administration that does not tell the truth.

3. In return for these admissions, the liberal doves acknowledge that our feelings about the Bush administration colored our thinking about this war. More importantly, we affirm that we are not realists. We take seriously foreign totalitarianisms, and we take especially seriously fundamentalism and terrorism. We will never say that an oppressed people are not our concern. We believe the United States and the West have a responsibility to confront those totalitarianisms. But we believe that, in accordance with our best traditions, we should first seek to confront them in concert with our allies and to confront them realistically (we also believe that there are forms of confrontation other than military force). We don't a priori rule out regime change and nation building in some future case—provided that the above-stipulated conditions are met.

4. Both sides affirm that the United States and the West should continue to undertake smaller-scale humanitarian interventions along the lines of the Kosovo action. We understand that these interventions will have to pursue rather limited aims; that is, we may not be able to transform a political culture, but we can try to end a genocide, protect an ethnic minority, and so on. These interventions will be brief and will not place inordinate burdens on American soldiers and our military.

5. Both sides acknowledge that, in the ongoing battle against fundamentalism and terrorism, a situation is likely to emerge in the coming

years that occupies a more difficult middle ground between small-bore interventions and regime-change interventions on the huge scale of Iraq. For example, moral and strategic concerns about the dangers of extremism in the Arab-Muslim world might call for toppling a tyrant who is not at a given moment slaughtering hundreds of thousands of people, not just for humanitarian reasons but for national-interest reasons, too. We'll have to assess these instances as they arise, and we may not agree on what the United States should do about them. Such disagreement is fine; all we need to do now is to agree that a conflict might arise that will require new thinking.

6. Finally, we agree that there is much the United States can do to change the world short of invading countries. We look here to the generation of leaders—those midcentury liberals—who carried us out of World War II and who established bodies on world monetary policy and global aid as models for the kind of creative thinking we will need to defeat terrorism. We recognize that, all over the world but in the Arab world in particular, the mass of the population doesn't support fundamentalism and terrorism and wants the benefits of an open society. The United States and the West can work on many fronts, most of which have been ignored or slighted by the Bush administration, to help those societies. Our job as liberal writers and intellectuals is to help create the space in which politicians might act with courage and vision to convince the American people that the United States has to do more to enfranchise, politically and economically, the world's poor and suffering people and to convince Americans that we have to do this not only for the sake of those people but for our own sake. We writers and intellectuals have a responsibility to help locate and fortify the moral intersection of mutual action and benefit.

I don't know exactly how to label these six items: do they represent pragmatic idealism, internationalist realism? I place no label on them. Labels are insidious. Principles are what matters, and these are good ones: The debate is no longer about Iraq; both sides give, both sides get; to the extent that the people I'm talking about have any influence at all, the country and the world will be better off. Let the post-Iraq era begin.

Notes

INTRODUCTION

1. George Packer, *Blood of the Liberals* (New York: Farrar, Straus, and Giroux, 2000), 333.

2. Richard H. Tawney, *Religion and the Rise of Capitalism* (Gloucester, MA: P. Smith, 1962); Max Weber, *The Protestant Ethic and the Spirit of Capitalism,* trans. Talcott Parsons and Anthony Giddens (Boston: Unwin Hyman, 1930); Harold J. Laski, *The Rise of European Liberalism* (London: Allen & Unwin, 1936).

3. Immanuel Kant, "An Answer to the Question: 'What Is Enlightenment?' " in *Kant: Political Writings,* ed. Hans Reiss and H. B. Nisbet (Cambridge: Cambridge University Press, 1991), p. 54.

4. Lionel Trilling, *The Liberal Imagination* (New York: Doubleday, 1953), vii; John Kenneth Galbraith, *Economics and Public Controversy* (New Brunswick, NJ: Rutgers University Press, 1955), 81.

5. Hartz quoted in James Kloppenberg, "In Retrospect: Louis Hartz's *The Liberal Tradition in America,*" *Reviews in American History* 29 (2001): 461.

6. Arthur Schlesinger Jr., *The Vital Center* (1949; New York: Da Capo Press, 1988).

2. THE CONTEMPORARY CRITIQUE OF THE ENLIGHTENMENT

1. Jean M. Goulemot, *Adieu les philosophes: Que reste-t-il des Lumières?* (Paris: Le Seuil, 2001).

2. Jean-Claude Guillebaud, *La Trahison des Lumières: enquête sur le désarroi contemporain* (Paris: Le Seuil, 1995).

3. Alain Finkielkraut, *In the Name of Humanity: Reflection on the Twentieth Century* (New York: Columbia University Press, 2000), 3.

4. John Patrick Diggins, *Max Weber: Politics and the Spirit of Tragedy* (New York: Basic, 1996), 69.

5. Jean Erhard, ed., *Images de Robespierre* (Naples: Vivarius, 1996).

6. Robert Kaplan, *The Ends of the Earth: A Journey to the Frontiers of Anarchy* (New York: Vintage, 1996), 401–20.

7. Gabrielle Bonnot de Mably, *Observations sur le gouvernement et loix des États-Unis d'Amérique* (1784), *Oeuvres complètes*, vol. 8 (London: 1789), 301, 408. On the French response to America's moving toward the idea of a "mixed government," see the valuable study by Denis Lacorne, *L'invention de la république: Le modèle américain* (Paris: Hachette, 1991).

8. Quoted in Keith Michael Baker, "Souveraineté," in *Idées: Dictionnaire Critique de la Revolution Française,* ed. Francois Furet and Mona Ozouf (Paris: Flammarion, 1992), 483–506; Alexander Hamilton, *The Federalist,* No. 85.

9. On Adams and Rousseau, see Zoltan Harasztzi, *John Adams and the Prophets of Progress* (Cambridge, MA: Harvard University Press, 1952).

10. Max Horkheimer, "The End of Reason," in *The Essential Frankfurt School Readers,* ed. Andrew Arato and Eike Gebhart (New York: Continuum, 1982), 26–48; see also the recent valuable anthology edited by Daniel Gordon, *Postmodernism and the Enlightenment* (New York: Routledge, 2001).

11. Quoted in John Adams, *Discourses on Davila: Series of Papers on Political History by an American Citizen (1790),* 266.

12. Ibid., 403.

13. Hamilton, *The Federalist,* No. 85

14. John Adams, *A Defence of the Constitutions of the Government of the United States of America* (1787–88; New York: Da Capo Press, 1971).

15. Isaiah Berlin, "The Question of Machiavelli," *New York Review of Books,* November 4, 1971, posted at www.nybooks.com/articles/10391. Berlin once pointed out to Conor Cruise O'Brien that there are at least twenty-six ways to interpret Machiavelli; see O'Brien, *The Suspecting Glance* (London: Faber and Faber, 1972).

16. Mona Ozouf, "Regeneration," in *Idées,* 373–89; see also David A. Bell, *The Cult of the Nation in France* (Cambridge, MA: Harvard University Press, 2001).

17. *Journal and Correspondence of Miss Adams* (New York: Wiley and Putnam, 1841), 21–47.

18. Quoted in Harastzi, *John Adams,* 201–28.

19. I am indebted to the valuable essays in Vere Chappell, ed., *The Cambridge Companion to Locke* (New York: Cambridge University Press, 1994).

20. Adams, *Discourses,* 232–52; Denis Diderot, *Le Neveu de Rameau,* ed. Jean-Claude Bonnet (Paris: Flammarion, 1983); Bonnet offers a comprehensive introduction to the text together with a dossier of comments by other writers, from Goethe to Hegel to Foucault.

21. George Santayana, *The Life of Reason* (New York: Scribner's Sons, 1953), 152.

3. LIBERALISM AND THE CONSERVATIVE IMAGINATION

1. Dwight Macdonald, "Back to Metternich," *New Republic*, November 14, 1949, 35.

2. Arthur Schlesinger Jr., "Terror versus Decorum," *New York Times Book Review*, October 23, 1949, 49.

3. Clinton Rossiter, *Conservatism in America* (New York: Alfred A. Knopf, 1955). Russell Kirk, *The Conservative Mind* (Chicago: Regnery, 1953). Rossiter's volume was awarded the 1954 Charles Austin Beard Memorial Prize. Kirk's book was lavishly praised in *Time* magazine, largely at the behest of Whittaker Chambers. Nonetheless, the review is an important indicator of Kirk's early acceptance by outposts of middlebrow liberal culture. Max Ways, "Generation to Generation," *Time*, July 6, 1953, 88, 90–92.

4. Lionel Trilling, *The Liberal Imagination* (New York: Viking Press, 1950), x.

5. Arthur Schlesinger Jr., "The Need for an Intelligent Opposition," *New York Times*, April 2, 1950, 13, 56–58.

6. H. Malcolm Macdonald, "The Revival of Conservative Thought," *Journal of Politic* 19, no. 1 (February 1957): 80.

7. Arthur Schlesinger Jr., "Calhoun Restored," *Nation*, April 1, 1950, 302.

8. Gaylord C. Leroy, "The New Conservatism," *Bulletin of the American Association of University Professors* 41, no. 2 (Summer 1955): 276.

9. Schlesinger, "Need for an Intelligent Opposition," 164.

10. For characterizations of conservatism as a mood, see C. Wright Mills, "The Conservative Mood," *Dissent* 1, no. 1 (Winter 1954): 22–31; and Daniel Aaron, "Conservatism, Old and New," *American Quarterly* 6, no. 2 (Summer 1954): 99–110.

11. George H. Nash describes the process of conservative ideological fusion in *The Conservative Intellectual Movement in America Since 1945* (Wilmington, DE: Intercollegiate Studies Institute, 1996; 1976), especially chapter 5. Elsewhere I offer a critique of Nash and trace the changing definition of the word *conservative* in scholarly literature since the 1950s. See Jennifer Burns, "In Retrospect: George Nash's *The Conservative Intellectual Movement in America Since 1945,*" *Reviews in American History* 32 (September 2004): 447–62.

12. Schlesinger, "Need for an Intelligent Opposition," 58.

13. Gordon K. Lewis, "The Metaphysics of Conservatism," *Western Political Quarterly* 6, no. 4 (December 1953): 741.

14. Rossiter, *Conservatism in America*, 17, 229.

15. Gerhart Niemeyer, "Conservatism in America," *Journal of Public Law* 4, no. 2 (Fall 1955): 441, 445. Niemeyer was a fervent combatant within conservative circles, attacking Meyer for his advocacy of laissez-faire and defending Kirk against all comers. Despite his disagreements with Meyer and other libertarians, Niemeyer was generally not troubled by the alliance, for he remained a movement conservative. See "Interoffice Memos—1961," Box 14, William F. Buckley Papers, Yale University.

16. Dwight Macdonald, "Scrambled Eggheads on the Right," *Commentary* 21 (April 1956): 367–73. Other negative reviews of *National Review* include John Fischer, "Why Is the Conservative Voice So Hoarse?" *Harper's*, March

1956, 17–22; and Murray Kempton, "Buckley's National Bore," *Progressive,* July 1956, 13–16.

17. Not only the editors' fealty to business but their affection for Joseph Mc-Carthy placed *National Review* beyond the pale.

18. Wilmoore Kendall, "The Liberal Line," *National Review,* November 3, 1956, 17.

19. Arthur Schlesinger Jr., "Mr. Schlesinger: The Liberal Wants to Change Life and to Improve It," *New York Times,* March 4, 1956, SM6.

20. Gaylord C. Leroy, "The New Conservatism," *Bulletin of the American Association of University Professors* 41, no. 2 (Summer 1955): 276.

21. Arthur Schlesinger Jr., "The New Conservatism: The Politics of Nostalgia," *Reporter,* June 16, 1955, 10.

22. Ibid., 10.

23. August Heckscher, *A Pattern of Politics* (New York: Reynal and Hitchcock, 1947).

24. August Heckscher, "Where Are the American Conservatives?" *Confluence,* September 1953, 57, 62.

25. Ibid., 61.

26. Ibid., 63.

27. A sampling of this discourse includes Ludwig Freund, "The New American Conservatism and European Conservatism," *Ethics* 66, no. 1, Part 1 (October 1955): 10–17; Chadwick Hall, "America's Conservative Revolution," *Antioch Review* 15, no. 2 (June 1955): 204–16; Bernard Crick, "The Strange Quest for an American Conservatism," *Review of Politics* 17, no. 3 (July 1955): 359–76; Arnold A. Rogow, "Edmund Burke and the American Liberal Tradition," *Antioch Review* 17, no. 2 (June 1957): 255–65.

28. Daniel Bell, ed., *The New American Right* (New York: Criterion Books, 1955); and Bell, ed., *The Radical Right* (New York: Doubleday and Co., 1963).

29. Of all the articles discussing the New Conservatism, only a few commented on the role of religion in conservative thought, and these few did so only tangentially. See Crick, "Strange Quest for an American Conservatism." Leroy, "The New Conservatism," links conservatism to neo-orthodoxy but treats religion as unremarkable.

30. Clinton Rossiter, *Conservatism in America: The Thankless Persuasion,* 2nd ed. (New York: Knopf, 1962). Peter Viereck, *Conservatism Revisited,* 2nd ed. (New York: The Free Press, 1962), 17, 151. Significant portions of this new edition were also published in Bell, *The Radical Right.*

31. See Daniel Bell, "Afterword (2001): From Class to Culture," in *The Radical Right,* ed. Daniel Bell, 3rd ed. (New Brunswick, NJ: Transaction Publishers, 2002), 447–503.

32. David Plotke, "Introduction to the Transaction Edition (2001): The Success and Anger of the Modern American Right," in Bell, *The Radical Right,* 3rd ed., xiv.

4. LIBERALISM AND BELIEF

1. Christopher Lasch, *The True and Only Heaven: Progress and Its Critics* (New York: W. W. Norton, 1991), 530.

2. Michael Sandel, *Democracy's Discontents: America in Search of a Public Philosophy* (Cambridge, MA: Harvard University Press, 1996), 5–6.

3. Lionel Trilling, *The Liberal Imagination* (New York: Viking Press, 1950), ix.

4. Daniel Bell, *The End of Ideology: On the Exhaustion of Political Ideas in the Fifties* (Glencoe, IL: The Free Press, 1960), 21.

5. Reinhold Niebuhr, *The Children of Light and the Children of Darkness* (New York: Charles Scribner's Sons, 1945), 117; Niebuhr, "The Collectivist Bogy," *Nation*, October 21, 1944, 478–80.

6. Arthur M. Schlesinger Jr., *The Vital Center: The Politics of Freedom* (Boston: Houghton Mifflin, 1949), x, 36, 46.

7. Bell, *The End of Ideology*, 400–402.

8. John Rawls, "Kantian Constructivism in Moral Theory," *Journal of Philosophy* 77 (1980): 519.

9. Thomas Kuhn, *The Structure of Scientific Revolutions* (Chicago: University of Chicago Press, 1970).

10. Richard Rorty, *Achieving Our Country* (Cambridge, MA: Harvard University Press, 1997).

11. See Thomas L. Haskell, "The Curious Persistence of Rights Talk in the 'Age of Interpretation,'" *Journal of American History* 74 (1987): 984–1012.

5. LIBERAL TOLERANCE AT MIDDLE AGE

1. For a useful discussion of multicultural toleration, see Michael Walzer, *On Toleration* (New Haven, CT: Yale University Press, 1997), and David Hollinger, *Postethnic America* (New York: Basic Books, 1995). For a discussion of toleration's origin in the early history of classical liberalism and in individual freedom and religious toleration, see Harold J. Laski, *The Rise of European Liberalism* (1936; reprint, New Brunswick, NJ: Transaction, 1997), chs. 1–2.

2. Andrew R. Murphy, "Tolerance, Toleration and the Liberal Tradition," *Polity* 29 (Summer 1997): 594, 600–601. These quotations are examples of the opinions of others, not Murphy's own definitions of tolerance.

3. Darrick Lee, "Parental Advisory Warning Labels Steeped in Controversy," *Hushyourmouth* (student newspaper, Eastern Michigan University), Spring/Summer 2003, www.hushyourmouth.com/parental_advisory_labels.htm.

4. Bill Holland, "Revised Advisory Label Scrutinized," *Billboard*, September 16, 2000, 10; on Zappa's accusation, see *New York Times*, July 10, 1992, A17. The transcript of the 1985 Senate hearings is available at http://uweb.super link.net/~jdandrea/shrg99-529/index.html.

5. Lee, "Parental Advisory Warning Labels"; John Pareles, "Record Companies to Put Warnings on the Raw," *New York Times*, March 29, 1990, C17.

6. Philip Berroll, "Cultural Elites, Closet Values," *Tikkun* 8 (September–October, 1993): 41. The *Saturday Night Live* skit originally aired on March 24, 1990, and included Dana Carvey as Frank Zappa.

7. Despite several letters, e-mail messages, and phone calls, Ruthless Attack Musick declined to give me permission to quote the relevant lyrics. Thus, while staying within the protection of fair use, I've sought to quote enough of several

lines to give a sense of the material. To read the lyrics, visit one of many web-sites, such as www.lyricsdir.com/nwa-lyrics.html.

8. Bill Holland, "House Panel to Examine Rap," *Billboard,* February 19, 1994, 1–2.

9. bell hooks, "Sexism and Misogyny: Who Takes the Rap?" *Z Magazine,* February 1994, 12.

10. See the University of Virginia's American studies website at http://xroads.virginia.edu/~UG03/carter/rap/intro.html and http://xroads.virginia.edu/~UG03/carter/rap/rapup.html.

11. Laura Parker, "Rap Lyrics Likened to Literature," *Washington Post,* October 20, 1990, D1.

12. Leon E. Wynter, "NAACP Raps 2 Live Crew," *Wall Street Journal,* June 21, 1990, A16.

13. Pareles, "Record Companies," C17.

14. Ibid.

15. Danny Goldberg, "Less Noblesse Oblige, Please," *Tikkun* 8 (September–October 1993): 45–46. On Goldberg's creation of an anti-PMRC group, see Berroll, "Cultural Elites," 41.

16. Goldberg, "Less Noblesse Oblige," 47.

17. Berroll, "Cultural Elites," 40–41.

18. Ibid. For Wildmon, see also www.afa.net/about.asp.

19. For background on similar recent issues, see Edward T. Linenthal and Tom Engelhardt, eds., *History Wars: The Enola Gay and Other Battles for the American Past* (New York: Metropolitan Books, 1996).

20. Christopher Knight, "The Art That Dares Not Speak Its Name," *Los Angeles Times,* June 3, 1990, 90.

21. Ibid.

22. David Leavitt, "Fears That Haunt a Scrubbed America," *New York Times,* August 19, 1990, H1. See also Knight, "The Art That Dares Not Speak Its Name," 90.

23. Leavitt, "Fears," H1.

24. Luc Sante, "The Unexamined Life," *New York Review of Books,* November 16, 1995, 47.

25. Camille Paglia, "The Beautiful Decadence of Robert Mapplethorpe: A Response to Rochelle Gurstein," *Tikkun* 6 (November–December 1991): 77, 79–80.

26. Paglia, "Beautiful Decadence," 80.

27. Robert Storr, "Art, Censorship, and the First Amendment," *Art Journal* 50, no. 3 (Autumn 1991): 12.

28. Irving Howe, "This Age of Conformity," *Partisan Review* 21 (January–February 1954), 19–20; Granville Hicks, "Liberalism in the Fifties," *American Scholar* 25 (Summer 1956); Sidney Hook, "Our Country and Our Culture," *Partisan Review* 19 (September–October 1952), 573.

6. LIBERALISM AND DEMOCRACY

1. Hannah Arendt, "Reflections on Little Rock," in *Responsibility and Judgment,* ed. Jerome Kohn (New York: Schocken Books, 2003), 195.

2. Ibid., 203.

3. Ibid., 205, 206.

4. Ibid., 202.

5. Ibid., 209, 210.

6. David Chappell, *A Stone of Hope: Prophetic Religion and the Death of Jim Crow* (Chapel Hill: University of North Carolina Press, 2004), 155.

7. Sidney Hook, "Democracy and Desegregation," *New Leader,* April 13, 1958, 15. Arendt's article and Hook's response had gone through numerous gyrations before being printed. Arendt's article was originally commissioned by *Commentary* magazine in October 1957. The editors believed it controversial enough to warrant a counterargument, which they asked Hook to write. Then the editors got nervous and refused to print either article. Thus, Hook's response to Arendt (with a few revisions) actually reached print first, in the *New Leader,* and Arendt's went into print via *Dissent* after Hook's appeared. This story is told in Elisabeth Young-Bruehl, *Hannah Arendt: For Love of the World,* 2nd ed. (New Haven, CT: Yale University Press, 2004), 313–15. Hook was not the only critic who responded to Arendt. So too did Ralph Ellison, the author of *Invisible Man.* For an interesting assessment of Arendt and Ellison's debate, see Danielle S. Allen, *Talking to Strangers: Anxieties of Citizenship Since* Brown V. Board of Education (Chicago: University of Chicago Press, 2004), ch. 3. Allen comes to different conclusions from those I draw here, especially because she focuses on the young black women trying to enter the school and thereby on the ideals of citizenship and sacrifice. She also has a much more optimistic faith in the ability of "political friendship," as she calls it, to solve contemporary U.S. political problems.

8. Woodward quoted in Carol Polsgrove, *Divided Minds: Intellectuals and the Civil Rights Movement* (New York: Norton, 2001), 60.

9. Woodward quoted in Michael O'Brien, "C. Vann Woodward and the Burden of Southern Liberalism," *American Historical Review* 78 (1973): 590.

10. C. Vann Woodward, *The Strange Career of Jim Crow* (1955; reprint, New York: Oxford, 1974), 103.

11. See C. Vann Woodward, "Young Jim Crow," *Nation,* July 7, 1956, 9.

12. C. Vann Woodward, *The Burden of Southern History* (Baton Rouge: Louisiana State University Press, 1968), 12.

13. See Richard King, "American Dilemmas, European Experiences," *Arkansas Historical Quarterly* 56 (1997): 322.

14. Hook, "Democracy and Desegregation," 11.

15. David Spitz, "Politics and the Realms of Being," *Dissent* 6 (1959): 57.

16. Ibid., 58, 64.

17. Reinhold Niebuhr, *Moral Man and Immoral Society* (1932; reprint, New York: Scribner's, 1960), 240, 252, 254.

18. Reinhold Niebuhr, "The Supreme Court on Segregation in the Schools" (1954), in *Love and Justice,* ed. D. B. Robertson (Philadelphia: Westminster Press, 1957), 149.

19. Reinhold Niebuhr, "A Theologian's Comments on the Negro in America," *Reporter,* November 29, 1956, 25.

20. Reinhold Niebuhr, *The Children of Light and the Children of Darkness* (New York: Scribner's, 1944), 67.

21. Hook, "Democracy and Desegregation," 15

22. Isaac Kramnick, ed., *The Federalist Papers* (New York: Penguin, 1987), 126, 123, 319.

23. Reinhold Niebuhr, "A Faith to Live By: I. The Dilemma of Modern Man," *Nation*, February 22, 1947, 206; "Christianity and Humanism," a talk on January 14, 1952, Speeches section, Reinhold Niebuhr Papers, U.S. Library of Congress, Washington, DC.

24. Brett Gary, *The Nervous Liberals* (New York: Columbia University Press, 1999), 2.

25. Walter Lippmann, *Public Opinion* (1922; reprint, New York: Free Press, 1965), 18.

26. Arthur Schlesinger, "The Right to Loathsome Ideas," *Saturday Review of Literature*, May 14, 1949, 17.

27. "Hussein Link to 9/11 Lingers in Many Minds," *Washington Post*, September 6, 2003, A1.

28. Andrew Stephen, "America," *New Statesman*, October 4, 2004, 21.

29. See on this point Steven Kull, Clay Ramsay, and Evan Lewis, "Misperceptions, the Media, and the Iraq War," *Political Science Quarterly* 118 (2003–4): 569–98.

30. Richard Hofstadter, *Anti-Intellectualism in American Life* (New York: Vintage, 1963), 13.

31. "Bush's Next Target?" *Chronicle of Higher Education*, July 11, 2003, A19.

32. I borrow here from the political thinking found in Stephen Holmes, *Passions and Constraint: On the Theory of Liberal Democracy* (Chicago: University of Chicago Press, 1995).

7. WHAT LIBERALS OWE TO RADICALS

1. See, for example, Todd Gitlin, *Twilight of Common Dreams* (New York: Metropolitan, 1995); Richard Rorty, *Achieving Our Country: Leftist Thought in Twentieth-Century America* (Cambridge, MA: Harvard University Press, 1997), 73–107; Ronald Radosh, *Divided They Fell: The Demise of the Democratic Party, 1964–1996* (New York: Free Press, 1996).

2. David Horowitz, "Why Liberalism Has a Bad Name," March 7, 2005, www.discoverthenetwork.org/Articles.

3. See Steve Fraser, "The 'Labor Question,'" in *The Rise and Fall of the New Deal Order, 1930–1980*, ed. Steve Fraser and Gary Gerstle (Princeton, NJ: Princeton University Press, 1989), 55.

4. John H. M. Laslett, *Labor and the Left* (New York: Basic Books, 1970).

5. Martin J. Sklar, *The Corporate Reconstruction of American Capitalism, 1890–1916* (Cambridge: Cambridge University Press, 1988), 401–12. On the continuing influence of populism, see Elizabeth Sanders, *Roots of Reform: Farmers, Workers, and the American State* (Chicago: University of Chicago Press, 1999); and my *A Godly Hero: The Life of William Jennings Bryan* (New York: Knopf, 2006). The philosopher Richard Rorty has carelessly called for doing away with "the leftist-versus-liberal distinction" in U.S. history but

soundly observes that "the history of leftist politics is a story of how top-down initiatives and bottom-up initiatives have interlocked" (*Achieving Our Country,* 53).

6. Quoted in John Patrick Diggins, *The Rise and Fall of the American Left* (New York: Norton, 1992), 100.

7. The lines are from "The Internationale." On these figures and their movement, see Christine Stansell, *American Moderns: Bohemian New York and the Creation of a New Century* (New York: Metropolitan, 2000); Ann Douglas, *A Terrible Honesty: Mongrel Manhattan* (New York: Farrar, Straus and Giroux, 1995).

8. Irving Howe, "The Brilliant Masquerade: A Note on 'Browderism,'" in *Socialism and America* (San Diego: Harcourt Brace Jovanovich, 1985), 87–104.

9. For a succinct, if uncritical, summary of the Communist Party's work in the 1930s, see Eric Foner, *The Story of American Freedom* (New York: Norton, 1998), 210–16.

10. Michael Denning, *The Cultural Front: The Laboring of American Culture in the Twentieth Century* (London: Verso, 1996), 230–58.

11. The Communist Party—in a campaign led by Lester Rodney, a sportswriter for the *Daily Worker*—was the only white-led political body of any significance that demanded the integration of professional baseball. Jules Tygiel, *Baseball's Great Experiment: Jackie Robinson and His Legacy* (New York: Oxford, 1983), 36–37.

12. See Kevin Mattson's elegant, measured defense of cold-war liberalism, *When America Was Great: The Fighting Faith of Postwar Liberalism* (New York: Routledge, 2004).

13. Port Huron Statement, quoted in James Miller, *"Democracy Is in the Streets": From Port Huron to the Siege of Chicago* (New York: Simon and Schuster, 1987), 331–32.

14. Rorty, *Achieving Our Country,* 70.

15. Leszek Kolakowski, "The Concept of the Left," in *Essential Works of Socialism,* ed. Irving Howe (New Haven, CT: Yale University Press, 1976), 686.

16. Daniel Bell, *Marxian Socialism in the United States* (Ithaca, NY: Cornell University Press, 1996), 3. For an invigorating attempt to revive the tradition, see Russell Jacoby, *Picture Imperfect: Utopian Thought for an Anti-Utopian Age* (New York: Columbia University Press, 2005).

17. For a stark analysis of the situation in Central Africa, see Marc Lacey, "Beyond the Bullets and the Blades," *New York Times,* March 20, 2005, IV, 1, 14.

8. LIBERALISM, SCIENCE, AND THE FUTURE OF EVOLUTION

1. Charles Robert Darwin, *On the Origin of Species* (London: John Murray, 1859). I present an overview of Darwin and his achievements in *The Darwinian Revolution: Science Red in Tooth and Claw,* 2nd ed. (Chicago: University of Chicago Press, 1999).

2. I discuss the ideology of evolution in *Monad to Man: The Concept of Progress in Evolutionary Biology* (Cambridge, MA: Harvard University Press,

1996). I discuss the clash between evolution and creationism in *The Evolution-Creation Struggle* (Cambridge, MA: Harvard University Press, 2005). The definitive work on the history of creationism is Ronald Numbers, *The Creationists: The Evolution of Scientific Creationism* (New York: Knopf, 1992).

3. To understand the full significance of this event, see Edward J. Larson, *Summer for the Gods: The Scopes Trial and America's Continuing Debate over Science and Religion* (New York: Basic Books, 1997).

4. George Hunter, *A Civic Biology: Presented in Problems* (New York: American Book Company, 1914), 263.

5. An excellent work on these aspects of the sociology of science is David L. Hull, *Science as a Process* (Chicago: University of Chicago Press, 1987).

6. "President Voices Concern on U.S. Missiles Program, but Not on the Satellite," *New York Times,* October 10, 1957.

7. "Nation Is Warned to Stress Science," *New York Times,* October 8, 1957.

8. Note the underlying theme of progress in the title *Biological Science: Molecules to Men*. No one ever called a book *Biological Science: Worms to Warthogs* or *Biological Science: The Road to AIDS*.

9. Paul Boyer, *When Time Shall Be No More: Prophecy Belief in Modern American Culture* (Cambridge, MA: Belknap Press, 1992).

10. John C. Whitcomb and Henry M. Morris, *Genesis Flood* (Philadelphia: Presbyterian and Reformed Publishing Company, 1961).

11. This view reflects the theory that there are particular ages, dispensations, in earth history, all of them ending in disasters because of human failings.

12. I give a history of this event, together with many documents, in my edited volume, *But Is It Science? The Philosophical Question in the Creation/Evolution Controversy* (Buffalo, NY: Prometheus Books, 1988).

13. William R. Overton, "[1982] 1988. United States District Court Opinion: McLean versus Arkansas," in Ruse, *But Is It Science?* 307–31.

14. Phillip Johnson, *Darwin on Trial* (Washington, DC: Regnery Gateway, 1991). An excellent history of the intelligent-design movement is Barbara Forrest and Paul R. Gross, *Creationism's Trojan Horse: The Wedge of Intelligent Design* (Oxford: Oxford University Press, 2004).

15. See Phillip Johnson's *Reason in the Balance: The Case Against Naturalism in Science, Law and Education* (Downers Grove, IL: InterVarsity Press, 1995); and *Defeating Darwinism by Opening Minds* (Downers Grove, IL: InterVarsity Press, 1997).

16. Michael Behe, *Darwin's Black Box* (New York: Free Press, 1996); William Dempski, *The Design Inference* (Cambridge: Cambridge University Press, 1998).

17. For a full overview, see my *Darwinism and Its Discontents* (Cambridge: Cambridge University Press, 2006).

18. Jonathan Weiner, *The Beak of the Finch* (New York: Knopf, 1994); Edward O. Wilson, *The Diversity of Life* (Cambridge, MA: Harvard University Press, 1992), *Consilience* (New York: Vintage, 1998), and *The Future of Life* (New York: Vintage, 2002); Richard Dawkins, *Blind Watchmaker* (New York: Norton, 1986) and *The Ancestor's Tale* (New York: Houghton Mifflin, 2004); Stephen Jay Gould, *The Mismeasure of Man* (New York: Norton, 1981) and *Wonderful Life* (New York: Norton, 1989).

19. See also Neil Jumonville, "The Cultural Politics of the Sociobiology Debate," *Journal of the History of Biology* 35 (2002): 569–93.

20. I draw the information here and in the following paragraphs from the more extensive discussion in my *The Evolution-Creation Struggle.*

9. LIBERALISM AND FAMILY VALUES

Portions of this chapter previously appeared in Mona Harrington, *Care and Equality: Inventing a New Family Politics* (New York: Knopf, 1999); and "Women, the Values Debate, and a New Family Politics," *Dissent,* Winter 2005.

1. Joan C. Tronto, *Moral Boundaries: A Political Argument for an Ethic of Care* (New York: Routledge, 1993), 180.

2. Martha Minow and Mary Lyndon Shanley, "Relational Rights and Responsibilities: Revisioning the Family in Liberal Political Theory and Law," *Hypatia* 11, no. 1 (Winter 1996): 4.

3. Eva Feder Kittay, *Love's Labor: Essays on Women, Equality, and Dependency* (New York: Routledge, 1999).

4. Robin West, *Caring for Justice* (New York: New York University Press, 1997), 81–82, 111.

5. *Upton v. JWP Businessland,* 425 Mass.756 (Mass. 1997).

6. The MIT Workplace Center is an Alfred P. Sloan Foundation center.

7. The bill was passed by the Massachusetts legislature on December 28, 2006, pocket-vetoed by the outgoing governor, Mitt Romney, and refiled as a new bill in January 2007.

10. LIBERALISM AND RELIGION

1. www.ncccusa.org/news/04uighurchinese.html.

2. Perry Bacon Jr., "Trying Out a More Soulful Tone," *Time,* February 7, 2005, 32.

3. "Religion a Strength and a Weakness for Both Parties" (summary report), Pew Research Center for the People and the Press, August 30, 2005.

4. Charles Howard Hopkins, *The Rise of the Social Gospel in American Protestantism 1865–1915* (New Haven, CT: Yale University Press, 1940).

5. E. J. Dionne Jr., *Why Americans Hate Politics* (New York: Simon & Schuster, 1991), 209.

6. Nicholas Lemann, "Trying to Turn a Collective Sentiment into Government," *Washington Post,* February 24, 1981.

7. Amy Waldman, "Why We Need a Religious Left," *Washington Monthly,* December 1995, 37.

8. Interview, March 3, 2005.

9. Jim Wallis, *God's Politics* (San Francisco: Harper Collins, 2005), 4.

10. John F. Kennedy, Speech to the Greater Houston Ministerial Association, Houston, TX, September 12, 1960.

11. "Religion and Politics: The Ambivalent Majority," Pew Research Center for the People and the Press, September 2000.

12. Thomas Frank, *What's the Matter with Kansas?* (New York: Owl Books, 2004), 127.

13. Mike Gecan, "Taking Faith Seriously," *Boston Review*, April/May 2005.

14. "Religion a Strength and a Weakness."

11. LIBERALISM, ENVIRONMENTALISM, AND THE PROMISE OF NATIONAL GREATNESS

1. E. F. Schumacher, *Small Is Beautiful: Economics as if People Mattered* (New York: Harper and Row, 1975).

2. Bob Pepperman Taylor, *Our Limits Transgressed: Environmental Political Thought in America* (Lawrence: University Press of Kansas, 1992).

3. Ibid., 22.

4. Henry David Thoreau, "Walking," in *Civil Disobedience and Other Essays* (New York: Dover, 1997), 59.

5. Henry David Thoreau, "Civil Disobedience," in Thoreau, *Civil Disobedience*, 17.

6. Thoreau, "Walking," 62.

7. For the reference in this paragraph to Pinchot, I am indebted to Taylor, *Our Limits Transgressed*, 16–19.

8. Wendell Berry, *Citizenship Papers* (Washington, DC: Shoemaker and Hoard, 2003), 10, 159.

9. Bill McKibben, *The End of Nature* (New York: Random House, 1989), 175–76.

10. Bill McKibben, *Enough: Staying Human in an Engineered Age* (New York: Times Books, 2003), 196–97.

11. Taylor, *Our Limits Transgressed*, 137.

12. Ralph Nader, *Crashing the Party: How to Tell the Truth and Still Run for President* (New York: St. Martin's Press, 2002), 18, 314.

13. Senator Al Gore, *Earth in the Balance: Ecology and the Human Spirit* (Boston: Houghton Mifflin, 1992), 161, 220, 226.

14. Bjorn Lomborg, *The Skeptical Environmentalist: Measuring the Real State of the World* (Cambridge: Cambridge University Press, 2001).

15. David W. Noble, *Death of a Nation: American Culture and the End of Exceptionalism* (Minneapolis: University of Minnesota Press, 2002).

16. George Lipsitz, "Foreword," in Noble, *Death of a Nation*, x.

17. I elaborate on these points in Alan Wolfe, "Anti-American Studies: The Difference Between Criticism and Hatred," *New Republic*, February 10, 2003.

18. Jan Radway, "What's in a Name?" in *The Futures of American Studies*, ed. Donald E. Pease and Robyn Wiegman (Durham, NC: Duke University Press, 2002), 59.

19. Morton Keller, *Affairs of State: Public Life in Late Nineteenth Century America* (Cambridge, MA: Belknap Press of Harvard University Press, 1977), 252–53.

20. Ibid., 39.

21. Gary Gerstle, *American Crucible: Race and Nation in the Twentieth Century* (Princeton, NJ: Princeton University Press, 2001), 71.

22. Cited in David Hollinger, *Postethnic America: Beyond Multiculturalism* (New York: Basic Books, 1995), 158.

23. Carl Ogelsby, "Trapped in a System," in *"Takin' It to the Streets"*: A Sixties Reader, ed. Alexander Bloom and Wine Breines (New York: Oxford University Press, 1995), 221.

24. Howard Zinn, *The Twentieth Century: A People's History* (New York: Harper Perennial, 1998), 214.

25. Arthur Schlesinger Jr., *The Imperial Presidency* (Boston: Houghton Mifflin, 1973).

26. See John Micklethwait and Adrian Wooldridge, *The Right Nation: Conservative Power in America* (New York: Penguin, 2004).

27. Mark Crispin Miller, *Cruel and Unusual: Bush/Cheney's New World Order* (New York: Norton, 2004), vii.

28. T. D. Allman, *Rogue State: America at War with the World* (New York: Nation Books, 2004), 350–51.

29. Lewis H. Lapham, *Gag Rule: On the Suppression of Dissent and the Stifling of Democracy* (New York: Penguin Press, 2004), 133.

30. Miller, *Cruel and Unusual*, v.

31. Michael Klare, "John Kerry, the Enlightened Hawk," *Le Monde Diplomatique*, July 2004, at http://mondediplo.com/2004/07/02kerry.

12. LIBERALISM, INTERNATIONALISM, AND IRAN TODAY

1. Azar Nafisi, *Reading Lolita in Tehran: A Memoir in Books* (New York: Random House, 2003). Not surprisingly, some scholars have accused Nafisi's book of orientalism. For example, see Roksana Bahramitash, "The War on Terror, Feminist Orientalism and Orientalist Feminism: Case Studies of Two North American Bestsellers," *Critique: Critical Middle Eastern Studies* 14, no. 2 (Summer 2005): 221–35; Hamid Dabashi, "Native Informers and the Making of the American Empire," *Al-Ahram Weekly,* June 1–7, 2006, http://weekly.ahram.9rg.eg/2006/797/special.htm; and "Lolita and Beyond: Foaad Khosmood Interviews Hamid Dabashi," *ZNet,* August 4, 2006, www.zmag.org/content/showarticle.cfm?ItemID=10707. For a survey of the controversy, see Richard Byrne, "A Collision of Prose and Politics," *Chronicle of Higher Education,* October 13, 2006.

2. Andrei Codrescu, *The Disappearance of the Outside: A Manifesto for Escape* (Boston: Addison-Wesley, 1990).

3. Nafisi, *Reading Lolita in Tehran,* 338.

4. "The Fiction of Life," *Atlantic Unbound,* May 7, 2003, www.theatlantic.com/doc/200305u/int2003-05-07.

5. Public talk at the Harold Washington Library Center (Chicago Public Library), April 28, 2004. For an account of Popper's influence on Iran's leading dissident, Akbar Ganji, see Afshin Molavi, *The Soul of Iran: A Nation's Journey to Freedom* (New York: W. W. Norton, 2005), 157. (First published in 2002 as *Persian Pilgrimages: Journeys across Iran* by W. W. Norton.) Likewise, Abdollah Momeni, the leader of Iran's most prominent student-activist group (Daftar-e

Tahkim-e Vahdat), claims Habermas as his chief inspiration. See Laura Secor, "Fugitives: Young Iranians Confront the Collapse of the Reform Movement," *New Yorker,* November 21, 2005, www.newyorker.com/fact/content/?051 12 1fa_fact4.

6. On Kant's popularity in Iran today, see Claus Langbehn, "Kant Conference in Tehran: Understanding the Other to Understand Oneself," *Frankfurter Allgemeine Zeitung,* November 30, 2004 (in English on *Qantara.de,* www.qantara.de/webcom/show_article.php?wc_c = 478&wc_id=208). "There have been more translations of Kant into Persian in the past decade," Vali Nasr reports, "than into any other language, and these have gone into multiple printings." Vali Nasr, "Don't Hold Your Breath," *New Republic,* June 12, 2006, www.tnr.com /doc.mhtml?i=20060612&s=nasr061206. On the deep engagement with European thought in Iran, see Farzin Vahdat, *God and Juggernaut: Iran's Intellectual Encounter with Modernity* (Syracuse, NY: Syracuse University Press, 2002); and Mehrzad Boroujerdi, *Iranian Intellectuals and the West* (Syracuse, NY: Syracuse University Press, 1996).

7. Fred Dallmayr, "Critical Intellectuals in a Global Age: Toward a Global Public Sphere," in his *Small Wonder: Global Power and Its Discontents* (Lanham, MD: Rowman & Littlefield, 2005), 115.

8. Farideh Farhi, "The Democratic Turn: New Ways of Understanding Revolution," in *The Future of Revolutions: Rethinking Radical Change in the Age of Globalization,* ed. John Foran (London: Zed Books, 2003), 37.

9. Mehrdad Mashayekhi, "A New Era for Iran's Democracy," *openDemocracy,* June 16, 2005, www.opendemocracy.net/debates/article.jsp?id=3& debateId=128&articleId=2607.

10. Ramin Jahanbegloo, "Furughi and the Foundation of Liberalism in Iran" (paper presented at the Biennial Conference of the International Society for Iranian Studies, Bethesda, MD, May 28, 2004). Jahanbegloo's work embodies the intellectual conversation between Iran and the West. See, for example, his *Conversations with Isaiah Berlin* (New York: Scribner's, 1991). He has also written (in Persian) books on Hegel, Schopenhauer, Tagore, and Gandhi and published (in French) a book of interviews with George Steiner. Jahanbegloo has brought an endless stream of Western intellectuals to lecture in Iran in recent years, among them Fred Dallmayr, Richard Rorty, Antonio Negri, Michael Ignatieff, and Timothy Garton Ash.

11. For a useful overview of this landscape, see Ian Shapiro, *The State of Democratic Theory* (Princeton, NJ: Princeton University Press, 2003). See also John Gray, *Liberalisms* (New York: Routledge, 1989), and its sequel, *Post-Liberalism* (New York: Routledge, 1993). For a critical take on Gray, see Ira Katznelson, "A Properly Defined Liberalism: On John Gray and the Filling of Political Life," *Social Research* 61, no. 3 (Fall 1994): 611–30; Alan Ryan, "Live and Let Live," *New York Review of Books,* May 17, 2001; and Danny Postel, "Gray's Anatomy," *Nation,* December 22, 2003, www.thenation.com/doc/20031222/postel.

12. On the struggle for liberalism in Iran today, see Behzad Yaghmaian, *Social Change in Iran: An Eyewitness Account of Dissent, Defiance, and New Movements for Rights* (Albany, NY: SUNY Press, 2002).

13. See Reza Afshari, *Human Rights in Iran: The Abuse of Cultural Relativism* (Philadelphia: University of Pennsylvania Press, 2001).

14. Naghmeh Zarbafian, "Misreading Kundera in Tehran," in *My Sister, Guard Your Veil; My Brother, Guard Your Eyes,* ed. Lila Azam Zanganeh (Boston: Beacon Press, 2006), p. 63.

15. See the Human Rights Watch report "'Like the Dead in Their Coffins': Torture, Detention, and the Crushing of Dissent in Iran," released June 7, 2004, http://hrw.org/campaigns/torture/iran.

16. For an eloquent discussion of this point, see Alan Ryan, "Mill on Liberty and the Subjection of Women," introduction to *On Liberty and the Subjection of Women,* by John Mill, Penguin Classics ed. (London: Penguin, 2007).

17. "Beggars of the State: Iranian Journalist Akbar Ganji Talks with Katajun Amipur on the Possibilities for Democracy in His Country," *signandsight,* July 18, 2006, www.signandsight.com/features/851.html.

18. Pierre Manent, Marcel Gauchet, and Alain Finkielkraut, "The Perils of Identity Politics," *Journal of Democracy* 15, no. 3 (July 2004): 152–65. See also Manent, *A World Beyond Politics?* (Princeton, NJ: Princeton University Press, 2006).

19. Bonnie Honig, *Democracy and the Foreigner* (Princeton, NJ: Princeton University Press, 2001). See also my article on Honig, "Outsiders in America," *Chronicle of Higher Education,* December 7, 2001, http://chronicle.com/free/v48/i15/15a01201.htm.

20. Peter Osborne, introduction to *Socialism and the Limits of Liberalism,* ed. Peter Osborne (London: Verso, 1991), 2.

21. For an important, if flawed, discussion of the relationship between liberalism and neoliberalism, see Wendy Brown, "Neoliberalism and the End of Liberal Democracy," in her *Edgework: Critical Essays on Knowledge and Politics* (Princeton, NJ: Princeton University Press, 2005).

22. On liberalism's connection to racism and Eurocentrism, see Immanuel Wallerstein, *After Liberalism* (New York: The New Press, 1995), 2 (emphasis mine). On "the rhetoric of empire" and liberalism as a global virus, see David Peterson, "Beyond Neocolonialism: Human Rights and the Rhetoric of Empire," in *The Shadow of Kosovo: The War, the Left, and the Squandered Debate,* ed. Danny Postel (Christchurch: Cybereditions, forthcoming); Samir Amin, *The Liberal Virus: Permanent War and the Americanization of the World* (New York: Monthly Review Press, 2004). See also Slavoj Žižek, "Against Human Rights," *New Left Review* 34 (July/August 2005). Note the nonchalant vituperation many "radicals" employ when discussing liberalism, as in Eric Lott's drive-by reference to "liberal suckers" in "The Wages of Liberalism: An Interview with Eric Lott," *minnesota review,* nos. 63–64 (2005), www.theminnesotareview.org/journal/ns6364/iae_ns6364_wagesofliberalism.shtml. Lott's bombast can now be found in book form as *The Disappearing Liberal Intellectual* (New York: Basic Books, 2006). For a devastating takedown, see Russell Jacoby, "Brother from Another Planet," *Nation,* April 10, 2006, www.thenation.com/doc/20060410/jacoby. *The National Security Strategy of the United States of Amer-*

ica (Falls Village, CT: Winterhouse Editions, 2002) appears online at www.whitehouse.gov/nsc/ss.html.

23. Wallerstein, *After Liberalism,* 1.

24. Jürgen Habermas, *The Philosophical Discourse of Modernity* (Cambridge, MA: MIT Press, 1987).

25. Christiane Hoffmann, "The Unrest Is Growing: Habermas in Iran," *Frankfurter Allgemeine Zeitung,* June 18, 2002, online in English at www.pub theo.com/page.asp?pid=1073. For a vivid and more recent account of this process, see Morad Saghafi, "The New Landscape of Iranian Politics," *Middle East Report* 233(Winter 2004), www.merip.org/mer/mer233/saghafi.html.

26. The parallels to Eastern Europe under Communism are almost too obvious to mention. In political conditions and intellectual influences on opposition movements, the Eastern European and Iranian experiences share profound affinities, with Kolakowski serving as perhaps the most poignant bridge. On this subject, see Timothy Garton Ash, "Soldiers of the Hidden Imam," *New York Review of Books,* November 3, 2005.

27. Kolakowski interviewed on the *News Hour with Jim Lehrer,* November 5, 2003, www.pbs.org/newshour/bb/entertainment/july-deco3/kluge_11-05.html.

28. Javad Tabataba'i, quoted in Ali Mirsepassi, *Intellectual Discourse and the Politics of Modernization: Negotiating Modernity in Iran* (Cambridge: Cambridge University Press, 2000), 183.

29. Of course, the thinkers I discuss here don't fit neatly under the rubric of liberalism. Arendt's relationship to liberalism is a deeply fraught one, as is Kolakowski's. Although Habermas blends aspects of radicalism and liberalism, he clearly operates, broadly speaking, within a liberal framework. For all of their criticisms of the liberal tradition, Arendt, Kolakowski, and Habermas speak forcefully to Iranians today because of their emphasis on democracy and their critique of tyranny. On Arendt, see Craig Calhoun and John McGowan, eds., *Hannah Arendt and the Meaning of Politics* (Minneapolis: University of Minnesota Press, 1997).

30. Nadia Urbinati, introduction to Piero Gobetti, *On Liberal Revolution* (New Haven, CT: Yale University Press, 2000), xv. See also Bruce Ackerman, *The Future of Liberal Revolution* (New Haven, CT: Yale University Press, 1992).

31. Afshin Molavi, "In Iran, Daring to Dream of Democracy," *Washington Post,* March 7, 2004.

32. Faraj Sarkohi, "The Gulf between Population and Opposition," *Qantara.de,* March 1, 2005, www.qantara.de/webcom/show_article.php/_c-476 /_nr-331/i.html. For more on this theme, see Maziar Behrooz, *Rebels with a Cause: The Failure of the Left in Iran* (London: I. B. Tauris, 1999); and Stephanie Cronin, ed., *Reformers and Revolutionaries in Modern Iran: New Perspectives on the Iranian Left* (New York: Routledge, 2004). On the Western Left's debauched response(s) to the Iranian Revolution, see David Greason, "Embracing Death: The Western Left and the Iranian Revolution, 1978–83," *Economy and Society* 34, no. 1 (February 2005).

33. On this key point, see Danny Postel, "Ideas Whose Time Has Come: A Conversation with Iranian Philosopher Ramin Jahanbegloo," *Logos: A Journal*

of Modern Society and Culture 5.2 (Spring/Summer 2006), www.logosjour
nal.com/issue_5.2/jahanbegloo_interview.htm.

34. Nina Power, "Persian Empire," *Radical Philosophy*, March/April
2005, www.radicalphilosophy.com/default.asp?channel_id=2193&editorial
_id=17194.

35. On liberalism in the Middle East and in the Islamic world, see Saad Eddin
Ibrahim, "Reviving Middle Eastern Liberalism," *Journal of Democracy* 14, no.
4 (October 2003), www.journalofdemocracy.org/articles/gratis/Ibrahim-
14-4.pdf; and Danny Postel, "Islamic Studies' Young Turks," *Chronicle of
Higher Education,* September 13, 2002, http://chronicle.com/free/v49/i03/
03a01401.htm. On the relevance of Iran to the Islamic world as a whole, Ali
Gheissari and Vali Nasr have written, "Current debates on democracy in Iran are
critical not only to Iran but also to developments across the Muslim world. . . .
It is important to take note of changes in Iran, for they reveal the challenge of
building democracy in an avowedly Islamic state. These changes are also in-
structive for the larger issue of contending with Islam while democratizing," a
project whose scope extends "from Morocco to Malaysia." See Ali Gheissari and
Vali Nasr, "Iran's Democracy Debate," *Middle East Policy* 11, no. 2 (Summer
2004).

36. Notwithstanding the current radical bluster about human rights as an imperial discourse, socialists once made vital contributions to the development of
human rights thinking. See Micheline Ishay, "Human Rights and the Industrial
Age: The Development of a Socialist Perspective of Human Rights," in her *History of Human Rights: From Ancient Times to the Globalization Era* (Berkeley:
University of California Press, 2004); and Ishay, "The Socialist Contributions to
Human Rights: An Overlooked Legacy," *International Journal of Human Rights*
9, no. 2 (2005).

37. Leszek Kolakowski, *Main Currents of Marxism* (reissued as a single edition, New York: W. W. Norton, 2005), 1209. On the democratic deficit in Marxist thought, see Dick Howard, *The Specter of Democracy* (New York: Columbia
University Press, 2002).

38. Danny Postel, "Iran, Solidarity, and the Left: We Know What We're
Against, but What Are We *For?*" *Radical Society* 30, nos. 3–4 (October/Decem-
ber 2003).

39. Afshin Molavi, "Opinion: Sean Penn in Iran," Iran Scan, *openDemocracy,* June 10, 2005, www.iranscan.net/blog/iran/Afshin+Molavi/?permalink
=sean_penn_in_iran.html&smm=y.

40. For a devastating account, see Marko Attila Hoare, "Nothing Is Left,"
Bosnia Report, October–December 2003, www.bosnia.org.uk/bosrep/report
_format.cfm?articleid=1041&reportid=162; and Hoare, "Genocide in the For-
mer Yugoslavia: A Critique of Left Revisionism's Denial," *Journal of Genocide
Research* 5, no. 4 (December 2003).

41. See David Clark, "Iraq has wrecked our case for humanitarian wars: The
US neo-cons have broken the Kosovo liberal intervention consensus," *Guardian,*
August 12, 2003, www.guardian.co.uk/comment/story/0,3604,1016573,00.html;
and Mary Kaldor, "Iraq: A War Like No Other," *openDemocracy,* March 27,
2003, www.opendemocracy.net/conflict-iraqi_war/article_1106.jsp.

42. Gheissari and Nasr, "Iran's Democracy Debate." For a rich historical discussion of democracy's deep roots in Iran, see Janet Afary, *The Iranian Constitutional Revolution, 1906–1911: Grassroots Democracy, Social Democracy, and the Origins of Feminism* (New York: Columbia University Press, 1996).

43. Ervand Abrahamian, for example, has said in an interview that "these are internal issues for Iran, and they should be settled by Iranians." See David Glenn, "The Significance of Iran's Recent Elections," *Chronicle of Higher Education,* March 12, 2004.

44. "A Single Family: Shirin Ebadi Speaks," *openDemocracy,* June 17, 2004, www.opendemocracy.net/democracy-think_tank/article_1962.jsp.

45. "Beggars of the State."

46. Fred Halliday, "It's Time to Bin the Past," *Observer,* January 30, 2005, http://observer.guardian.co.uk/comment/story/0,6903,1401742,00.html. For an elaboration, see my "Who Is Responsible? An Interview with Fred Halliday," *Salmagundi,* nos. 150–151 (Spring–Summer 2006): 221–41, www.skidmore.edu/salmagundi/150–151/halliday.htm. The German sociologist Ulrick Beck uses the term *zombie categories* to describe this phenomenon, which he defines as categories that "are dead but somehow go on living, making us blind to the realities of our lives." See Ulrich Beck, "Goodbye to All That Wage Slavery," *New Statesman,* March 5, 1999, www.newstatesman.com/199903050020. See also Nicholas Gane's interview with Beck, "The Cosmopolitan Turn," in Nicholas Gane, *The Future of Social Theory* (New York: Continuum, 2004), 146.

47. For a critical response to Halliday, see Peter Waterman, "Fred Halliday, Come Down from Your Mountain!" *openDemocracy,* February 3, 2005, www.opendemocracy.net/globalization-world/article_2328.jsp.

48. On the historical links between liberalism and imperialism, see Anthony Pagden, "Empire, Liberalism and the Quest for Perpetual Peace," *Dædalus,* Spring 2005, www.amacad.org/publications/spring2005/pagden.pdf; Jennifer Pitts, *A Turn to Empire: The Rise of Imperial Liberalism in Britain and France* (Princeton, NJ: Princeton University Press, 2005); Jeanne Morefield, *Covenants Without Swords: Idealist Liberalism and the Spirit of Empire* (Princeton, NJ: Princeton University Press, 2005); Uday Singh Mehta, *Liberalism and Empire: A Study in Nineteenth-Century British Liberal Thought* (Chicago: University of Chicago Press, 1999); Bernard Semmel, *The Liberal Ideal and the Demons of Empire* (Baltimore: Johns Hopkins University Press, 1993); and Andrew Williams, *Liberalism and War: The Victors and the Vanquished* (New York: Routledge, 2005). See also David Glenn, "Liberalism: The Fuel of Empires?" *Chronicle of Higher Education,* September 2, 2005, http://chronicle.com/weekly/v52/i02/02a01901.htm.

49. For important examples of this perspective, see David Held, *Global Covenant: The Social Democratic Alternative to the Washington Consensus* (Cambridge, U.K.: Polity, 2004); Alison Brysk, ed., *Globalization and Human Rights* (Berkeley: University of California Press, 2002); Richard Falk, *Human Rights Horizons: The Pursuit of Justice in a Globalizing World* (New York: Routledge, 2000); and Amartya Sen, *Development as Freedom* (Oxford: Oxford University Press, 1999). Many others are also doing work along these lines. See Clifford Geertz's interesting "What Was the Third World Revolution?" *Dissent,* Winter 2005,

www.dissentmagazine.org/menutest/archives/2005/wio5/geertz.htm; and the symposium "Can Social Democracies Survive in the Global South?" with Richard Sandbrook, Marc Edelman, Patrick Heller, and Judith Teichman, *Dissent,* Spring 2006. For a stimulating theoretical meditation on the meanings of solidarity, see Iris Marion Young, "Responsibility and Global Justice: A Social Connection Model," *Social Philosophy & Policy* 23, no. 1 (Winter 2006): 102–30.

50. I sometimes do wonder if my friends in the green movement are right to argue that liberalism has no solution to the destruction of the earth. Of all the radical critiques of liberalism, this one seems to have the most force and gives me the most pause. I was therefore delighted to stumble upon Simon Hailwood's fascinating book *How to Be a Green Liberal: Nature, Value and Liberal Philosophy* (Montreal: McGill-Queen's University Press, 2004), which addresses this critique head-on. See also Piers H. G. Stephens, "Green Liberalisms: Nature, Agency and the Good," in *Contemporary Environmental Politics: From Margins to Mainstream,* ed. Piers H. G. Stephens with John Barry and Andrew Dobson (New York: Routledge, 2006), 32–51.

51. See Robert O'Brien, Anne Marie Goetz, Jan Aart Scholte, and Marc Williams, *Contesting Global Governance: Multilateral Economic Institutions and Global Social Movements* (Cambridge: Cambridge University Press, 2000); and Jackie Smith, Charles Chatfield, and Ron Pagnucco, eds., *Transnational Social Movements and Global Politics: Solidarity Beyond the State* (Syracuse, NY: Syracuse University Press, 1997). For a critique of the NGO/civil-society paradigm from the perspective of radical social movements, see Aziz Choudry, "All This 'Civil Society' Talk Takes Us Nowhere," *ZNet,* January 9, 2002, www .zmag.org/Sustainers/content/2002–01/09choudry.cfm. Although Choudry makes several valid points, I see social movements and NGOs as potentially complementary rather than as necessarily discordant.

52. Nafisi, *Reading Lolita in Tehran,* 6.

13. BEYOND IRAQ

1. The liberal hawks are thinking of realism in the darkest terms here. Henry Kissinger was certainly a realist, and the fate to which he helped consign, say, the East Timorese and Chile was a manifestation of his brand of realism. But an "ethical realism" school in the tradition of Reinhold Niebuhr has existed for a long time; its most effective proponent today, in my view, is Anatol Lieven of the New America Foundation. Ethical realism counsels prudence and limitations, rejects idealism, and has little use for good intentions. This strain of realism is different from Kissingerian realism. Whereas Kissinger supported the Vietnam War on the realist ground that preventing the spread of communism in Southeast Asia was in America's vital national interests, Niebuhr opposed the war, viewing it as an idealistic crusade. Ethical realists such as Lieven, then, are firm opponents of the Iraq War specifically and the general notion that the United States has an obligation to spread freedom and democracy.

2. See Thomas Cushman, ed., *A Matter of Principle: Humanitarian Arguments for War in Iraq* (Berkeley: University of California Press, 2005).

3. Jeffrey Goldberg, "Should the U.S. Invade Iraq?" *Slate,* October 3, 2002.

4. Some readers may question the omission of Christopher Hitchens. Whatever Hitchens is these days, he's not a liberal; in fact, he never has been. He would have called himself, and I suppose still would, a socialist. Goldberg may not exactly be a liberal in the Paul Wellstone sense of the term, but neither is he a conservative.

5. Thomas L. Friedman, "Iraq, Upside Down," *New York Times,* September 18, 2002, A31.

6. Paul Berman, "Thirteen Observations on a Very Unlucky Predicament," in *The Fight Is for Democracy,* ed. George Packer (Harper-Perennial, 2003), 280.

7. Paul Berman, "A Friendly Drink in a Time of War," *Dissent* 51, no. 1 (Winter 2004): 56.

8. In *The Fight Is for Democracy,* a collection of essays he edited and to which I contributed, George Packer titled his introductory essay "Living Up to It," the "it" being the historical moment, and he quoted from W. H. Auden's "September 1, 1939."

9. Howard Kurtz, "Under Peter Beinart, a New New Republic," *Washington Post,* February 24, 2003, C1.

10. Richard Just, "Liberal Realism or Liberal Idealism: The Iraq War and the Limits of Tolerance," in Cushman, *A Matter of Principle,* 210. Richard worked for me briefly, when I first arrived at the *American Prospect* as executive editor in the fall of 2003. He moved over to the *New Republic* toward the end of that year—because he felt more at home with the magazine's politics and not (he assured me at any rate) because of my proprietorship. And while I'm in full disclosure mode, I should note that Packer, Berman, and Goldberg are friends and that Berman and Goldberg are old colleagues.

11. Editorial, "The Limits of War," *Nation,* October 29, 2001, 3.

12. Brzezinski's full speech is available on the *American Prospect* website: www.prospect.org/webfeatures/2003/10/brzezinski-z-10-31.html.

Contributors

PETER BERKOWITZ teaches at George Mason University School of Law and is the Tad and Dianne Taube Senior Fellow at the Hoover Institution, Stanford University. He is cofounder and director of the Israel Program on Constitutional Government, is a member of the Policy Advisory Board at the Ethics and Public Policy Center, and served as a senior consultant to the President's Council on Bioethics. He is the author of *Virtue and the Making of Modern Liberalism* and *Nietzsche: The Ethics of an Immoralist*. He is the editor of *Varieties of Conservatism in America; Varieties of Progressivism in America; The Future of American Intelligence; Terrorism, the Laws of War, and the Constitution: Debating the Enemy Combatant Cases;* and *Never a Matter of Indifference: Sustaining Virtue in a Free Republic*. With coeditor Tod Lindberg, he has launched Hoover Studies in Politics, Economics, and Society, published in cooperation with Rowman & Littlefield. He has written articles, essays, and reviews on multiple subjects for a variety of publications, including the *American Political Science Review*, the *Atlantic Monthly*, the *Boston Globe*, the *Chronicle of Higher Education*, *Commentary*, *Critical Review*, *First Things*, *Haaretz*, the *Jerusalem Post*, the *London Review of Books*, *National Review*, the *New Republic*, the *New York Post*, the *New York Sun*, *Perspectives on Politics*, *Policy Review*, the *Public Interest*, the *Times Literary Supplement*, the *Wall Street Journal*, the *Washington Post,* the *Weekly Standard,* the *Wilson Quarterly,* and the *Yale Law Journal.*

ALAN BRINKLEY is Allan Nevins Professor of History and provost at Columbia University. Among his publications are *Voices of Protest: Huey Long, Father Coughlin, and the Great Depression; The End of Reform: New Deal Liberalism in Recession and War;* and *Liberalism and Its Discontents.*

JENNIFER BURNS received her AB from Harvard in 1998 and her PhD in history from the University of California, Berkeley, in 2005. She has published articles on the history of conservatism in *Modern Intellectual History* and *Reviews in American History* and is currently writing a book about Ayn Rand. She is a lecturer in the history department at the University of California, Berkeley.

JOHN PATRICK DIGGINS is Distinguished Professor of History at CUNY Graduate Center and the author of thirteen books, including *The Rise and Fall of the American Left* and the forthcoming *Ronald Reagan: Fate, Freedom, and the Making of History.* He frequently writes for the *New Republic* and other general-interest publications.

E. J. DIONNE JR. is a syndicated columnist with the *Washington Post,* a senior fellow in the Governance Studies Program at the Brookings Institution, and University Professor in the Foundations of Democracy and Culture at Georgetown University. He is the author of *Why Americans Hate Politics*—winner of the Los Angeles Times Book Prize and a National Book Award nominee—*They Only Look Dead: Why Progressives Will Dominate the Next Political Era; Stand Up Fight Back: Republican Toughs, Democratic Wimps and the Politics of Revenge.* He is the editor or coeditor of many books, including *Community Works, What's God Got to Do with the American Experiment?* and *United We Serve: National Service and the Future of Citizenship.*

MONA HARRINGTON, who holds degrees in political science and law from Harvard University, is program director at the MIT Workplace Center. At the center, which conducts action research on work-family-community connections, she chairs a project for the formation of a Massachusetts Work-Family Council. Her books include *The Dream of Deliverance in American Politics, Women Lawyers—Rewriting the Rules,* and *Care and Equality: Inventing a New Family Politics.*

NEIL JUMONVILLE is William Warren Rogers Professor of History at Florida State University. He has written *Critical Crossings: The New York In-*

tellectuals in Postwar America and Henry Steele Commager: Midcentury Liberalism and the History of the Present. His political and cultural writings have appeared in publications such as the New Leader, the New York Times, Atlanta Constitution, Miami Herald, Boston Review, and Die Zeit. His anthology The New York Intellectuals Reader is due in 2007 from Routledge.

MICHAEL KAZIN is a professor of history at Georgetown University. He is the author of A Godly Hero: The Life of William Jennings Bryan; The Populist Persuasion: An American History; and Barons of Labor: The San Francisco Building Trades and Union Power in the Progressive Era; coauthor of America Divided: The Civil War of the 1960s; and coeditor of Americanism: New Perspectives on the History of an Ideal. He writes frequently for the New York Times, the Nation, the American Prospect, Dissent, and other publications and is currently at work on a history of the American Left.

KEVIN MATTSON is Connor Study Professor of Contemporary History at Ohio University. He is author of Upton Sinclair and the Other American Century; When America Was Great: The Fighting Faith of Postwar Liberalism; Engaging Youth: Combating the Apathy of Young Americans towards Politics; Intellectuals in Action: The Origins of the New Left and Radical Liberalism, 1945–1970; and Creating a Democratic Public: The Struggle for Urban Participatory Democracy during the Progressive Era. In addition, he is coeditor of Steal This University! The Rise of the Corporate University and the Academic Labor Movement; and Democracy's Moment: Reforming the American Political System for the 21st Century. He has written essays on a variety of topics for the New York Times Book Review, the Washington Post Book World, the Nation, the American Prospect, Common Review, the Baffler, and Chronicle Review. He is presently an affiliated scholar at the Center for American Progress and is active in the American Association of University Professors. He serves on the editorial board of Dissent magazine.

DANNY POSTEL is senior editor of openDemocracy (www.opendemocracy .net), an online magazine of politics and culture, and the author of Reading Legitimation Crisis in Tehran (Chicago: Prickly Paradigm Press, 2006). He is a member of the Committee for Academic and Intellectual Freedom of the International Society for Iranian Studies; a contributing editor to Dædalus, the journal of the American Academy of Arts and Sciences; and a member of the editorial board of the Common Review. His work has appeared in *Logos, Salmagundi, Critical Inquiry,* the *Washington Post Book World,* the *Chronicle of Higher Education,* the *Nation,* the *Progressive, In These Times,* the *American Prospect, Radical Society, Left History, Philosophy & Social Criticism,* and *Exquisite Corpse,* among other publications.

MICHAEL RUSE is Lucyle T. Werkmeister Professor of Philosophy and director of the Program in the History and Philosophy of Science at Florida State University. He has edited or written more than two dozen books, most recently authoring *Darwinism and Its Discontents.*

AMY SULLIVAN is a contributing editor of the *Washington Monthly* and a writer who focuses on religion and politics. Her work has appeared in publications such as the *Los Angeles Times,* the *New Republic,* the *New York Times,* and the *Washington Post,* and she is a frequent commentator on MSNBC. Previously, Sullivan served as a legislative assistant to Senator Tom Daschle and as editorial director of the Pew Forum on Religion and Public Life. She holds degrees from the University of Michigan and Harvard Divinity School, and she is currently writing a book about religion and the Left, which will be published in the fall of 2007 by Scribner.

MICHAEL TOMASKY is the editor of the *American Prospect.* He is the author of *Hillary's Turn* and *Left for Dead: The Life, Death, and Possible Resurrection of Progressive Politics in America* and has contributed essays to several volumes. His work has also appeared in the *New York Review of Books,* the *New York Times Book Review,* the *Washington Post Book World, Harper's Magazine,* the *Nation, Dissent, GQ,* and numerous other publications.

ALAN WOLFE is professor of political science and director of the Boisi Center for Religion and American Public Life at Boston College. His most recent books are *Does American Democracy Still Work? Return to Greatness: How America Lost Its Sense of Purpose and What It Needs to Do to Recover It, The Transformation of American Religion: How We Actually Live Our Faith,* and *An Intellectual in Public.* He is the author or editor of more than ten other books. A contributing editor of the *New Republic,* the *Wilson Quarterly, Commonwealth Magazine,* and *In Character,* Professor Wolfe writes often for those publications as well as for *Commonweal,* the *New York Times, Harper's,* the *Atlantic Monthly,* the *Washington Post,* and other magazines and newspapers.

Index

Text: 10/13 Sabon
Display: Akzidenz Grotesk
Compositor: Binghamton Valley Composition, LLC
Printer and binder: Maple-Vail Manufacturing Group